FEELING THE UNTHINKABLE

This is a must-read collection for social justice activists. In these short essays and reviews, Gutierrez punctures America's wrongfully inflated sense of self. He sharply challenges our militarization, our repeated wars, and our promotion and acceptance of torture. He condemns our toleration of economic injustice and our blindness to our maintenance of the largest prison system in the world. But Gutierrez does not just critique, he promotes human rights as well as personal and communal solidarity. He calls us to respect human rights, to promote solidarity with others, and to change our world while we still have the chance.

—William P. Quigley, Professor of Law
Loyola University New Orleans School of Law
Director of the Law Clinic and Gillis Long Poverty Law Center

Dr. Gutierrez's work is Zinn-esque. His quality and style of writing is both accessible and engaging. Dr. Gutierrez has written a book that is compassionate, comprehensive, and thought provoking. His writing on social injustice at an individual, institutional, state, and global level is alarming. Dr. Gutierrez provides real-world examples that vividly illustrate his claims and strengthen his arguments about systematic terrorism, torture, cruelty, greed, racism and genocide. In the process, the United States is not given a pass. Dr. Gutierrez' work, across the board, is brutally honest and well documented. His claim that democracy is under attack is spot-on and his cry for activism is necessary and timely. Students of social science, political science, international relations, and media studies will greatly benefit from his book. I look forward to sharing his work with both my colleagues and students.

—Karen P. Burke, Ed.D, Associate Professor, Media Studies Department
Southern Connecticut State University, New Haven, Connecticut

What an incredibly powerful book! The oppressive atmosphere created by worldwide financial instability makes it difficult to face the inhumaneness presented by Professor Gutierrez. But, if we don't feel the pain of the unthinkable acts committed by our government and others, how can we reach into our reserves to find the fury necessary to stop the insatiable barbarism being committed in our name? Professor Gutierrez reminds us why public outrage is more necessary now than ever.

—Leslie Hall, Ph.D., Associate Clinical Professor
Washington State University, Spokane

Surely there is no more astute and sensitive observer of our political culture than Don Gutierrez. Whether eloquently decrying torture, our prison system or the failure of society to engage the humane wisdom of poets in matters of democracy and justice, Don is a prophet and also a historian and philosopher.

Whether he is resurrecting the shibboleth of Orwell's (could be Bush/Obama's) desecrations of hard-won democratic rights or assailing the class system in the U.S., Gutierrez' collection of essays and book reviews resonates with the literate indignation of time-honored heroes like Kant, Rousseau and Chomsky.

In the essay titled "The Great Military-Defense Industry Swindle of America," Don slices Pentagon rhetoric with a sword of pure scholarly research, a cutting edge he seems to have been born to swing. Most fascinating to me was his examination of the epithet, "fuck," in relation to (follow me): Hollywood excess, D.H. Lawrence, death metal lyrics, JFK saying, "I cut his (Khrushchev's) balls off," the A-10 Thuderbolt's ability to fire 4,000 cannon shells per minute, and the massive violence called forth by today's American Empire (whew).

Throughout all of Don's literacy and scholarship—his slash and burn attacks upon violence, racism, fascism, greed and political myopia—there lurks the compassion of the true liberal, a real liberal, i.e., someone who cares deeply about the flickering flame of liberty. He is a gentle man, but mightily pissed by the representatives of the Dark Side.

Don sees liberty's oxygen being squeezed by media-induced, corporate stupidity that is turning the scholar-citizens of Franklin, Postman and Socrates into the soma-guzzling robots of Huxley. This is definitely a treasure for the thoughtful.

—Bob McCannon, consultant <mccannon@flash.net>
President, The Action Coalition for Media Education
Media Literacy/Media Education: *Children, Adolescents and Media*,
3rd edition, college text, 2012

FEELING THE UNTHINKABLE

ESSAYS ON SOCIAL JUSTICE

Donald Gutierrez

edited by Zelda Leah Gatuskin

AMADOR PUBLISHERS, LLC
Albuquerque, New Mexico

Edited by Zelda Leah Gatuskin

Printed in the United States of America
First Printing, 2012
ISBN: 978-0-938513-44-5
Library of Congress Control Number: 2012947796

Cover Art: "Illuminating the Dark Side" by Marlene Zander Gutierrez.
Artwork and back cover photo courtesy the Gutierrez family.
Photo of Don Gutierrez in 1974 by Ed Brower.
Cover Design by Ashley N. Jordan.

Grateful acknowledgment is made to the periodicals which previously published, in slightly different forms, the essays and reviews collected herein:
ABQ Trial Balloon, Albuquerque Journal, Amnesty Now (Amnesty International USA), *Bloomsbury Review, The Catholic Worker, Chiron Review, Common Sense* (University of Notre Dame), *Desert Exposure* (Silver City, NM), *Eldorado Sun, El Tecolote* (San Francisco), *The Horsefly* (Taos, NM), *The Humanist* (Washington, D.C.), *Humanist Society of New Mexico* (Albuquerque, NM), *Justice Xpress, The Mustang* (Western New Mexico University), *North Coast Xpress, On the Bus* (Los Angeles), *The Peacebuilder, Progressive Populist, Rio Grande Tribune, Sun Monthly, Social Justice, Tikkun* (website), *War Crimes Times, Z Magazine.*

AMADOR PUBLISHERS, LLC
Albuquerque, New Mexico USA
www.amadorbooks.com

To my wife-artist Marlene
(April 1932–August 2011)

FEELING THE UNTHINKABLE

Contents

PART II. WAR AND DEMOCRACY –
WAR ON DEMOCRACY

PART III. BUSINESS AS USUAL –
GREED, RACISM AND GENOCIDE

PREFACE

The essays and reviews in this book were written during fifteen years of retirement beginning in 1994, a few of them before that year. All but one of them have been published in a variety of venues, and most of them in at least two or three different publications.

Feeling the Unthinkable is not a scholarly study or an organically structured work. It is a collection consisting of essays and reviews and one memoir. Nevertheless, the various pieces are, I feel, sufficiently interrelated in subject and polemical stance to lend *Feeling* a certain unity of voice, tone and social-political humanist outlook. That unity is based on the implication that a revolution in sensibility is essential to changing and repairing the world, and that that revolution could be brought about by coming alive in our feeling states and imagination to the social evil abounding in the modern era, no little of it created by governments (certainly ours) and the elites they serve.

We can think about the unthinkable, but feeling it is a challenge reaching to the depths of our being. Who knows what we become after that immersion into personal darkness. That is the ultimate challenge of *Feeling the Unthinkable*.

Donald Gutierrez
Albuquerque, New Mexico, 2012

...if way to the Better there be,
it exacts a full look at the Worst.

Thomas Hardy, "In Tenebris": II

INTRODUCTION

There is no such thing as "was";
if "was" existed, there would be no grief or sorrow.
William Faulkner

The title of this book, *Feeling the Unthinkable: Essays on Social Justice*, accents its cardinal stress: not just to think but *feel* about matters that too many people generally don't want to even think about—but should. Some of the horrors addressed and attacked in this collection of essays and book reviews include war, state terrorism and torture, human rights abuses, American imperialism, corporate and Wall Street avarice and domination, the American criminal justice system, Nazi concentration camps, brutalization of Muslim and Arab detainees in America and in the Middle and Far East, America's lurch towards fascism, and a woman named Helen Bamber who has worked for decades to heal torture victims. Reviews of books of virtual prosecution by Christopher Hitchens and Vincent Bugliosi put, respectively, Henry Kissinger and George W. Bush on trial for war crimes and/or mass murder. Essays and reviews less extreme in subject matter but certainly involving social-justice concerns include, among others, the perniciously high student costs of going to college, the relation of prep schools to America's ruling class, class structure and extreme privilege in America and, in virtual response to the two last topics, essays discussing the ethical, psychological and humane superiority of cooperation over competition and of community over business values.

Feeling may be briefer than thought but, sufficiently deep, can electrify what we think is important in life. Yet who wants to think about, let alone feel, the 1981 El Mozote Massacre in El Salvador: an entire village is slaughtered by the Salvadoran military, all the men tortured before being killed, and the larger number of the slain being children. Who wants to hear about such—and hundreds of other—horrors that have been perpetrated decade after decade in modern times? Yet Washington—*our government*—facilitated many of these atrocities through School of the Americas instruction as well as through funding, arms and intelligence delivery, and encouragement provided to demonic regimes, sometimes communicated by American embassies, as in the incredible Indonesian mass-murders during the 1960s. Supposedly, all this aid was designed to halt the spread of communism; instead, it actually undercut the activism of union organizers, peasants, students, religious and other groups trying to democratize the extremely concentrated wealth and power traditionally held in a vise-grip by the upper class and the military in so many Latin American countries. I feel, perhaps wrongly, that one would want to know that one's government is using his or her tax monies for despicable, brutal ends—especially a country like ours that brags so much about itself being the beacon on the hill, the shining example to the world of freedom and equality. The last hypocrisy touches on the major sub-theme of the collection and the second essay in *Feeling*: that the light on America's hill has too often become very dark indeed.

Millions of Americans either have no idea or any concern that their government has used their money and its immense power to assist—even direct—hellish activities abroad in their name. So one intention of the human rights essays in *Feeling the Unthinkable* such as "American Middle Eastern Detainees and You: The Extraordinary Cruelty of Extraordinary Rendition," "Where Is the Humanity? America's Use of Excessive Force Over There," and reviews of such books as Frederick H. Gareau's *State Terrorism and the United States*, is to exemplify some of the ruthless, exploitative behavior committed by the American state.

Other essays in the "State Terrorism" section deal with victimized individuals who symbolize Washington's egregious abuse of power domestically or abroad, whether it is the innocent American-Middle-Eastern detainees swept up shortly after 9/11 and violently treated in jail by guards or the long, graphically shocking memoir of the American Ursuline nun Dianna Ortiz who was tortured by Guatemalan military with the knowledge and tacit approval of American authorities.

xiv

Another section of *Feeling*, entitled "War and Democracy—War on Democracy" deals with problematic, even crucial, areas of America's democracy, including Chris Hedges' study of war, which indicates that there is nothing redeeming about any war; the application of George Orwell's definitive remarks on the corruption of political language to military conduct in America's more recent wars; the relation of the concept of universal jurisdiction to war crimes committed by the White House; the ominous threat to democracy and creeping fascistization of America outlined in ten steps in Naomi Wolf's *The End of America*; the sinister militarization and psychic regimentation of the country in the essay "American Global 'Democracy' and the Militarization of America," and two pieces dealing with the threat of nuclear war not only to democracy but to all life on earth, Dr. Helen Caldicott's *The New Nuclear Danger: George W. Bush's Military-Industrial Complex* and the book-title essay "Feeling the Unthinkable," in part a polemic against a rational approach to nuclear war conceptualized by Rand Corporation theorist Herman Kahn.

Part III of *Feeling* broaches issues of class, racism and greed in a variety of manifestations. It opens with an account of my experience of ethnic misidentification while traveling through the South in the 1950s. This journey underlined for me how racist perceptions can go the the root of one's—anyone's—being. Class is embodied in such essays as "Why Attending College Should be Free" and "Prep Schools and the Ruling Class"—two interrelated pieces. This section continues with the sense of class as genocidal racism in the far darker regions of a Nazi concentration camp. This is followed by an essay and a review of Christian Parenti's book, *Lockdown America*, on American prisons and penal injustice. Parenti's book in particular implies that society resolves superfluities and consequent frictions of class and race by putting "disposable" segments of the population—the lower and especially darker-skinned class for whom there is no or little work—in prison. Both pieces suggest in different ways that torture is a common feature of American prisons, whether in the form of solitary confinement stretching for years, the use of severely electrocuting devices on prisoners, prisoner rape of both sexes or sudden, incredibly savage beatings administered to key inmates by guard teams dressed in riot gear. Randall Robinson's book *Quitting America: The Departure from America of a Black Man from His Native Land* indicates one African-American's response to America's racist disposal of Blacks but, more effectively, projects a trenchant criticism of what the white race has done not only to Blacks but to all people of color.

The essay about the aboriginal people (the Chagossians) on Diego Garcia island continues the theme of gross white mistreatment of non-whites, but also ties in with the dominant themes in crack investigative journalist John Pilger's powerful book *The New Rulers of the World*: the violent presence of and financial domination by Western imperialism throughout the world. This imperialism, emblematic of ungovernable greed, is exhibited domestically in the case of Tyco International CEO Dennis Kozlowski who, along with an associate, cheated his company out of hundreds of millions of dollars. The essays "Leveling the Hierarchy" and, particularly, "American Presidents and Business Versus Community" and "Competition, Cooperation and 'Us' Versus 'Them,'" suggest resistance to the vectors of avarice and class privilege in the form of the libertarian, communitarian transformation of society.

Part IV offers a humanistic perspective against the preceding visible darknesses broached in *Feeling*. It poses the humanities and spirited iconoclasts and dissidents such as Howard Zinn, Edward Abbey, D. H. Lawrence, and the humane, empathic sensibility of poets, as significant forces against the massive social evil and the indifference to others besetting the contemporary world. Obviously, the humanities and the rebel icono-clasts hardly balance the scales against the enormous and pernicious state and corporate evil exposed in *Feeling*. Rather, humanist values centered in the human, the compassionate, the esthetic and psychologically liberating suggest an aperture in the darkness offering light, hope, creative energy, individual integrity and humane sociability from which community could bit by bit—or even suddenly—evolve.

Is this expecting too much? Dictatorships are suddenly resisted or dissolved with a fury of desire for freedom and democracy, as in the Middle East, at immense cost of life and agony. Wall Street seems indomitable today, yet even now perhaps some child has been born (another Brooksley Born or Ralph Nader!) who could have the organizing social genius or the moral, legal or political passion to restore financial sanity or a sense of limits and interdependence as basic to society. A grassroots movement, already existent, might grow into a potent force against the "Street's" egregious financial concentration. The 20th century French philosopher, anti-Nazi activist and concentration-camp survivor David Rousset, who created the phrase "L'Univers Concentrationnaire" ("The Concentrationary Universe") to describe his era, once said that "Normal men do not know that everything is possible" (epigraph to Hannah Arendt's *The Origins of Totalitarianism*). Buchenwald, Hiroshima, Vietnam, Pol Pot, the contemporary torture cells of the world come to mind.

But that 20th century prophecy, true enough then and today, bears its inescapable opposite: that anything beautiful, compassionate, noble, generous, humane, *empathetic* is also possible, and could provide a series of lattices upon which to lay new possibilities of the Good Life and the Beloved Community of the mystics and poets. Everything is possible, an expansion more open than Rousset might accept, but then he lived through the universe that a concentration camp surrounds with barbed wire, and that bears authority against over-valuing the potential of the benign.

If, as mentioned earlier, many of the essays and reviews deal with the "dark side"—no Dick Cheney's "sort of" about it—why would people even want to read them; there's more than enough terror and ugliness and misery in life and the world as it is. I feel (as well as think) that there are more than a few individuals who want to know about the terror being imposed on other human beings because they urgently want to extend their own humanity to others undergoing horrific brutality, pain and death. John Donne's "No man is an Iland [sic] intire [sic] of itselfe [sic]; every man is a peece [sic] of the Continent" (*Devotions* XVII, 1623) applies here. These individuals want to know about the malicious imposition of agony, suffering, injustice and death on anyone and everyone so as to *stop* it. They probably don't enjoy knowing that they might be living in reasonable comfort or safety while their government is savagely afflicting other nations and peoples directly or supporting and backing brutally repressive regimes or genocidal crackdowns—as Kissinger did Chile's General Pinochet or Ambassador Marshall Green did Indonesia's General Suharto.

Further, there are other individuals who, ignorant of their government's demonic behavior abroad, might find the pieces in the collection educational, even eye-opening. If some might feel that some of the essays and reviews are disturbing or even repulsive (and blame messenger Gutierrez), others might be spurred to further investigation or even to individual or organizational activism.

The range of the material offers at one extreme a review essay of an authoritatively researched study like *State Terrorism and the United States* that whitewashes absolutely nothing in the way of Washington's role in spreading hideous torture and mass murder abroad. At the other extreme are committed dissidents like historian/polemicist Howard Zinn and journalist/film-maker John Pilger, iconoclasts like Edward Abbey, D. H. Lawrence, B. Traven, Chris Hedges and others who fight for the humane, vigorously oppose the corporate state and annihilation of the environment or uphold the need for personal integrity and an inner life in a depersonalizing society. There are also essays in *Feeling* urging cooperation and community over competitive, commercial standards, the powerful libertarian implications of college free of costs for students or the dire need for a far more egalitarian society than exists at present in the United States.

And to further counter the essays or reviews that seem unrelievedly black in their subject matter, *Feeling* exhibits the individualistic, courageous voice of a Sister Dianna Ortiz, a Vincent Bugliosi, a Hersh, a Caldicott, a McCoy, a Wolf, an Orwell and others, many others, exposing, resisting, condemning the immensity of social evil and apathy in the modern era. In the hidden cells of "Black Ops personnel" torturing (sometimes to death) a Middle East detainnee of "high" or even "low" interest or some Guatemalan military electrocuting the genitals of a college student dissident is the action of a Kathy Kelly, a Noam Chomsky, a Chalmers Johnson, a Robert Fisk signifying, "Look what's happening!," "Stop!," "Enough!" An individual voice saying "Stop," though essential, is obviously not enough—but it is a crucial beginning.

Nevertheless, many of the essays and reviews in this book concern nihilistic policies and actions that appear to be insurmountable, inexpiable. Why, then, would someone want to write about them (let alone read them)? I have asked myself that more than once. Robert Duncan's poem *Groundwork: Before the War*—"The poet turns in his sleep, the cries of the tortured and of those whose pain / survives after the burning survives with him"—articulates a portion of my motivation. Are we wise, right or humane to hear and listen to those agonized cries or do we best tune them out, if we hear them at all?

Of course one doesn't have to be a poet to lose sleep thinking of the wrongly imprisoned, the tortured, the bombed and wounded, the starving people throughout the world. Still, as a good friend once told me, one can't take the suffering of the world on one's shoulders.

But surely there's plenty of room between, say, Christ and the Marquis de Sade for empathy towards, or even just sympathy for, gross suffering and agony imposed by institutional cruelty or greed. Yet, considering that the average person doesn't spend time worrying about the suffering or even the murder of Middle Eastern detainees by the CIA, American soldiers or NATO soldiers or, as Seymour Hersh observes, about many thousands of American soldiers poisoned (along with Iraqis) by depleted uranium shells, reminds me of the focus of my empathy: though far from exclusively, it is primarily on the suffering, torture, murder of victims imposed by American foreign policy. The thought that our own government, supposedly representing the American populace, has often behaved abroad with massive violence to defend the "interests" of major corporations and banks should strike even that insentient "average" American with disgust if not with horror and fury. One does well to contemplate the San Francisco poet Kenneth Rexroth's incisive point that if individuals committed the acts that their governments commit routinely, they would be imprisoned or even executed.

Some of my evolving detestation of Washington's conduct abroad was due to the larger amount of time allowed by my retirement in 1994. I had more time by then to educate myself about Washington's counter-insurgency wars in Central America, its despicable role around the world supporting dictator after dictator no matter how inhumane and vicious the regime, and the shocking (still unrepentant) violence of its own wars in Vietnam, Iraq and Afghanistan. George W. Bush's "foreign policy" (an egregious euphemism for his mass murder) indeed seemed to me so horrific that I had trouble understanding why masses of Americans weren't up in arms about it well beyond the minority closely observant of Washington's "realpolitik" abroad.

A substantial amount of material in *Feeling* is about the past. Some might say, then, that the past is past, no longer significantly with us. That of course is not true, as some of that past remains with everybody. For some categories of people, however, the past is all too unforgettable. Let us recall William Faulkner's "There is no such thing as 'was' if 'was' existed, there would be no grief or sorrow." For victims of torture, combat-experienced soldiers, war-stressed civilians, victims of family violence, misogyny, racial or ethnic prejudice and others, Faulkner's apothegm is overpoweringly true. For these types of individuals, the past and the present are virtually seamless. The past and its suffering and horror occasioned well up like an uncontrollable flood, re-animating terror, anxiety, helplessness, not to mention rage against tormenters. And if the torturers, for example, represent the state, the victimization might feel all the deeper, as one's antagonist(s) are shadow figures of a larger, dark, inaccessible authority. Franz Kafka's castle (in his novel *The Castle*) remains a looming symbol of inaccessible central power and authority.

Accordingly, the past maliciously imposed suffering and death and (endless) imprisonment and torture are not past for the victims and thus should not be a past that people fortunate enough to have escaped terrorization should dismiss. This dismissal should not occur for several reasons, first, out of deep concern for the *ongoing* pain and terror of the victims of state terrorism; second, for the inexpungible conviction and resolve that those responsible for state crimes (whether a former president or vice president like George W. Bush or Dick Cheney) should be brought to justice and, therefore, that one should do whatever one can to prevent major state evil from occurring again.

A final consideration glimmers here: that sympathetic awareness of the victims of state terrorism should make us realize that their fate could very possibly be ours some day, given the dynamics of concentration of power and wealth in our time, the sharply increasing class divides in the United States and globally, and the consequent need by rulers to preserve their ill-gotten estate. The last poignant lines of William Carlos Williams's poem "The Yachts" seems appropriate to our age of high-financed-induced mass destitution:

> ... the horror of the race dawns, staggering the mind;
> the whole sea becomes an entanglement of watery bodies
> lost to the world bearing what they cannot hold. Broken
> beaten, desolate reaching from the dead to be taken up
> they cry out, failing, failing! their cries rising
> in waves still as the skillful yachts pass over.

As remarked earlier, some might question peering into the Abyss when, as the common retort has it, "there's already so much unhappiness and misery in the world." People who say that often don't realize how far worse off others have been than themselves, and, tightly connected, how the grief and agony of others is firmly connected to the United States, their country. If nothing else, Americans have a profound moral responsibility to know what their government and the military and commercial forces it represents are up to at home and, especially, abroad. If they don't accept that responsibility, they are missing out on what might further empower their own humanity: confronting their own interdependence with all other people everywhere.

PART I

STATE TERRORISM

MY COUNTRY MUST NOT TORTURE IN MY NAME

1
My Country Must Not Torture in My Name

Spiritual contemplation, state political torture and the individual either vulnerable to or secure from the latter—what do or can these matters have to do with each other—and with us today? The individual safe—at least, for the time being—from political intimidation and terror inhabits a different world from the person vulnerable to, say, the Salvadoran para-military, the Shah of Iran's SAVAK (taught by the CIA how to torture women) or our Special-Access-Program Elite Forces working over some Iraqi or Afghan detainee picked up in a sweep. These two individuals might as well be in different universes, as the experience of being savaged by state personnel administering intentional pain and agony can only be understood either by someone who has undergone torture or by those capable of considerable empathy.

Individuals tortured lie in the inconceivable clutches of the demonic. The tortured inhabit a world of extreme psychic and physical torment that separates them ineffably from ordinary life experience; they undergo experiences of extremity that people in the "safe" world don't want to even *think* of. Though the argument for empathy for the tortured rooted in our common humanity should be persuasive and even obvious, we allow barriers of space, culture, race, gender, ideology and an excessive trust in the ideal of the democratic state to desensitize us to the diabolic world of maliciously devised pain. Pain is bad enough in a politically neutral environment, such as pain following surgery, but when it results from omnipotent, deliberate intent, such as the remarkable Argentinian Jewish journalist, publisher and author Jacobo Timerman experienced at the hands and electrodes of his overtly anti-Semitic Argentinean tormenteers, it is likely to be overwhelming.

Any affirmative conception of community and of the sanctity of vulnerability of the human body and mind urges that people should be outraged about states—especially their own government—torturing individuals, let alone being responsible directly or even indirectly (as ours is) for such massacres as occurred in Indonesia in the 1960s, Vietnam, Central America in the 1980s, Fallujah in 2004 or Gaza in December 2008.

It is one thing to be struggling with a $20,000 income for a family of four, but quite another to be in the murderous vise-hold of, say, Guatemalan General Efrain Rios Montt's paramilitary thugs or the torture practices of Pretoria from 1960 to the late 1980s when 83 percent of Black-African detainees experienced torture from the White Afrikaner government that "included hitting, kicking, slapping sometimes with the help of implements" (Frederick H. Gareau, *State Terrorism and the United States*). In our era, many people have vanished into the extra-judicial mazes of tyrannical political regimes. We occasionally read or hear about these disappearances, then go about our business, secure in the faith that we won't be arrested—or tortured. Yet these terrifying abductions have happened all too frequently to those who have held such a faith, let alone to tens of thousands who didn't.

Part of the terror of illegal arrest (often by the state's soldiers, paramilitary or police with a heavy right wing tilt) is that one cannot identify one's place of captivity. Often the captors are unidentifiable, their vehicles unmarked. Why this plight is so terrible is obvious: Anything can happen to you. All too often in these arrests, ghastly things do happen—solitary confinement, incarceration without explanation, hideous torture and death and/or threats thereof against ourself or our loved ones.

Torture is a daily occurrence in 20th and 21st century societies, and its horror and outrage all the deeper and wider, considering that two-thirds of the world's governments practice illegal detention, incarceration and torture—one government, Israel, overtly. According to Amnesty International (*Amnesty Now*, Nov.–Dec. 1991), almost any person arrested in Mexico is likely to endure torture in police custody. Further, the penal treatment of political protesters or social prisoners in the United States is far worse than is usually realized. For example, consider Norman Mailer's *The*

Armies of the Night (particularly the horrific beatings given female demonstrators by war-seasoned paratroopers—Ch. 8, "An Aesthetic Tested"), or the grisly prison section of Christian Parenti's *Lockdown America*. Other compelling examples of savage American penology can be found in Anne-Marie Cusac's shocking study *Cruel and Unusual: the Culture of Punishment in America* or Darius Rejali's authoritative, more than 800-page *Torture and Democracy*—not to mention the vicious "in-house" treatment of peaceful protesters in Seattle and Washington D. C. during the demonstrations against the IMF and the WTO in 1999 (or the 2011 virtually military attacks by Oakland and Manhattan police against the Occupy Wall Street groups).

Some governments, following Washington's lead, have externalized terrorism from themselves by pinning that label on Palestinians, Chechens, al-Qaeda and other groups. These people are the only ones who explode bombs or decapitate individuals, driven by ruthless ideological extremity. But memory is short and denial deep. No "insurgents" or "anarchists" or suicide bombers have dropped or exploded anywhere near as many bombs as the United States unloaded on Vietnam or as its "Shock and Awe" fury unleashed on Iraq. And in regard to torture, the evidence is indisputable that the United States, through torture training schools like the former School of the Americas or the funding of the IMET programs (International Military Education and Training) of some of the most repressive regimes of our time, has caused an immeasurable amount of torture and vast terror among victimized populations in client states around the world, from Latin American nations to Indonesia and the Philippines.

The purpose of such instruction of course was (and is) to terrorize large, disadvantaged classes of people into silence and conformity about the disastrous impact on their lives of commercial deals American corporations were making with the elite of these third world nations—Naomi Klein's "shock doctrine" in action. Put more baldly, there has been, and continues to be, an electronically direct connection between the low-ranking personnel who torture dissidents and the international economic policies set primarily by Washington that further savage the lives of masses of people. If this is so, it means that we taxpayers in "first world" nations, and certainly in the United States, are indirectly but definitely supporting state terrorism in the insidious form of state torture. America's state terrorism has also been direct in the form of American international violations (including war crimes, torture, crimes against humanity) committed in, say, Baghdad, Bagram (Afghanistan) or Vietnam.

What can be done about global state torturing? One can certainly join or support organizations like Amnesty International, Human Rights Watch or the San Francisco based Survivor's International (an organization that helps in the healing of torture victims *and* in restoring them to stable social-economic conditions). Or one can even go further, as Helen Bamber's organization Medical Foundation for the Care of Victims of Torture has done, to try to change the *source* of political torturing in a repressive foreign regime as various American NGOs did in boycott campaigns against racist South Africa. This is obviously more far-reaching and challenging than the very worthwhile enterprise of dealing with resultant victims of repressive police states through techniques of healing, itself a formidable enterprise.

The more immediate need here, however, is to create a revolution in sensibility in the average person towards the worldwide phenomena of political torture—including rape. That our own government has massively helped support repressive governments around the world, from Somoza's Nicaragua or Pinochet's Chile to the Shah's Iran, Suharto's Indonesia, and Saddam Hussein's Iraq and thus has contributed sizably to the impoverishment, physical and mental agony and murder of millions of people in the past half-century suggests several things. The obvious one is that Americans concerned with global political incarceration and torture should compel changes through, or, better, *in* their own government. (Obama would appear to be superior to Bush in this respect, yet his considering illegal combatants as beyond constitutional provision and deciding to pardon CIA torturers and especially the Bush administrators who ordered torture constitute a grave setback to imposing juridical accountability on Bush, Cheney, Rumsfeld and others and to restoring America's legal integrity. Nor has his record in the lethal use of drones in the Mid- and Far East, much worse than Bush's, as well as targeted assassinations such as that of Bin Laden, exhibited evidence of legal respect for sovereignty by Obama.)

Further, state political torture is often internationally interrelated through a very powerful government defending the interests of its major corporations and Wall Street by supporting dictatorships in other countries. Thus, exposing state terrorism must in turn be international in scope, a complex goal in itself. A third point, and surely the one that should be—but often is not—most powerfully persuasive in empathizing with torture victims, is that of intensifying our realization of our common humanity with the tortured. An Afghanistan female in the unrelenting grip of the Taliban or a Palestinian male undergoing what Palestinians call the Shabeeh torture in an Israeli prison will feel pain and terror as much as one's own spouse, parent or child in a context of terror, and that reality is as overwhelmingly horrible to their kin as ours would be to us—a fundamental truth that all too many barriers, including our daily just-making-ends-meet routines, tend to diminish.

To deal seriously then with state torture and particularly with state torture perpetrated by Washington, one needs to come alive to the essence, the *being* of torture. This could involve the daunting prospect of imagining, even re-living the present of those tortured in the past, at least, to what extent one can bear. This might strike some as morbid; what is truly morbid, however, is dismissing the plight of the tortured as beneath one's concern. Many of the examples—a mere selection cited in this chapter—of the people tortured by the state occurred in the past half-century or so. Nevertheless, something timeless and eternal exudes from the experience of the radically violated body and mind of tortured individuals. Most might never fully transcend their terror and agony, and we who have been so fortunate as to have lived free of such horror should consider the moral obligation of bearing witness contemplatively and responsively to their terror and to the radical government evil that brought it about.

We must attempt to sense the cast of mind of politicians, military brass, free-market lobbyists, mega-corporation, and defense-industry moguls who forge and enact the policies that result in the oppression and torture of populations in nations vulnerable to Washington's power; *that* contemplation might help us realize more deeply what we are up against, the better to oppose and overcome it. We need to realize that the person writhing in agony from electrodes applied by the state's military or police to one's gums or genitals, or gasping for crucial air from having one's head forced under water or face covered by a drenched tight-fitting cloth is often as "innocent" as we are, and that his/her pain and terror constitute a reality as immediate, substantive and "human" as one's own daily experience of breathing, salivating and drinking. Olga Talavante, a torture victim in Argentina in 1974 (a powerful anti-torture activist since), strapped to a bed naked, her hands and legs tied to the bed posts, said that when her tormentors pushed a pillow down on her face every time they would re-commence electrocuting her, she survived suffocation by turning her head to the side after the pillow was put on her face but just before it was pressed down, not only allowing her to breathe, but implementing a strategy that helped Olga sustain her sanity (*Social Justice*, v. 33, no.2, 112-13). Developing a keener sense of shared human reality can occur through an imagining of the violated body and mind of the tortured with a force and clarity sufficient to prevent that body, though not one's own, from ever being disowned or entirely forgotten.

Though past torture may never be fully redeemed by any kind of contemplation or imagining leading to political action, the experience of torture in Guatemala related by Sister Dianna Ortiz in her extraordinarily moving book *The Blindfold's Eyes: My Journey from Torture to Truth* suggests an exception to this surmise. Ortiz's subsequent activism against high-placed state individuals in Guatemala and Washington responsible for her torture and that of many other victims may help protect future potential victims of state terror. The average person might not easily or readily achieve that level of communal empathy and selfless activism against state terrorism, nor would anyone want to undergo Ortiz's or Talamante's torture. Nevertheless, attempting that identification constitutes as valid and fulfilling a spiritual path as any. And, again, terrorism as political torture imposed by *our* government means that we as tax-paying citizens are supporting this illegal and ineffably brutal foreign "policy." Who wants their tax money used to torture other human beings?

According to *The New York Times* (Jan. 11, 1982), one Salvadoran General, advising Army recruits *in the presence of eight American military advisers*, claimed that watching individuals (in this instance, teenage prisoners) being tortured "will make you feel more like a man." I suggest that an immeasurably superior definition of manhood or womanhood is to confront the brutal reality of torture in all its human and inhuman dimensions of radical violation, evil and horror, and vow to do whatever one can to end it. The torture victim, after all, is not a stranger; conceived by the moral imagination he, by virtue of being human, is ourself.

"My Country Must Not Torture in My Name" by Donald Gutierrez—*Amnesty Now*, Winter, 2001–02; *Common Sense*, November 2007; *Justice Xpress*, November 2007; *Humanist Society of New Mexico*, March 2008; *Tikkun* online, January 2007.

2

The Black Light On The Hill:
United States Foreign Policy Hypocrisy

He may be an SOB and a dictator, but he is our SOB...
Robert Simmons, former CIA officer
(quoted in *Inside the CIA*, by Ronald Kessler)

For years the American public had been told by their political leaders how horrible a monster Saddam Hussein was as a motivation to remove him from power. Yet, horrific as Saddam was to political opposition or to Iraqi suspects, Saddam's Iraq was in some respects an advanced if not a politically liberal society. It had the sophisticated, complex infrastructure before the Gulf War of a G-8 nation, including an internationally admired medical system, more freedom for women than some other Arab countries, and important universities, museums and other cultural institutions. True, political prisoners were tortured in Iraq; political prisoners called "terrorist suspects" are also tortured by the CIA and Special-Forces units in Black Cells around the world. The Baath Party under Saddam ruled Iraq savagely; corporations have pretty much ruled the United States since the Civil War. What's curious about the Iraq-Better-Without-S.H. outlook is that it appeared to be the last gasp of American pro-war polemicists running out of valid reasons for Washington's illegal and unprovoked invasion of Iraq. When all the arguments for removing Saddam were proven to be false, wrong, dishonest, the myth-making machine in the White House/Pentagon inner sanctum produced its final argument: bringing Democracy to Iraq (and to the "unstable" and undemocratic Mid-East) and thus the need to remove The Tyrant.

As the neo-con position always seemed to circle back to Saddam Hussein and to the murderousness of his regime, it is crucial to judge whether his wickedness was truly immeasurable or whether there have in the past half century or so been other leaders, rulers, dictators just as bad as, if not considerably worse than, Saddam that Washington has not just tolerated but supported, encouraged, financed and even created. If we can come up with a significant number of such consummate monsters and demonstrate as well that these fiends and their regimes in power *were* both worse than Saddam *and* fully supported by American presidents through the CIA and other agencies covertly and illegally, then the staggering hypocrisy of our government would be fully exposed and its moral arguments for attacking a sovereign nation like Iraq (and next Iran?) shown up for the massive international crime it really is.

"Hideous torture," claim Noam Chomsky and Edward S. Herman, "has become standard practice in the U.S. client fascist states....Many people [in Chile] were tortured to death [after the military coup of 1973] by means of endless whippings as well as beating with fists, feet and rifle butts. Prisoners were beaten in all parts of the body, including the head and sexual organs. The bodies of prisoners were found in the Rio Mapocho, sometimes disfigured beyond recognition..." The authors continue, "Such horrendous details could be repeated for many thousands of human beings in Argentina, Brazil, Chile, Uruguay, Paraguay, Guatemala, Nicaragua, Indonesia, U.S.-Occupied South Vietnam up to 1975, Iran, and in quite a few other U.S. client states," and then remind us that "much of the electronic and other torture gear is U.S. supplied, and great numbers of client state police and military interrogators are U.S. trained" (*The Washington Connection and Third World Fascism*, 9-10).

The United States School of the Americas (now euphemistically titled the Western Hemisphere Institute for Security Cooperation) provides vivid examples of the deliberateness of Washington's foreign policy being oriented towards proxy methods of terror carried out by Third World governments obligated to Washington and American corporate power. The SOA (first located in Panama, then later at Ft. Benning, Georgia) was a school for torturers. Latin American military and police officers were taught, among other things, how to torture by American military instructors. Torture consequently became the quintessence of state terrorism policy in a number of Latin American countries. Innumerable dictators and despots, as well as military and civilian personnel, ordered or carried out acts of torture that would be unthinkable to the average American as something his own government would permit, let alone finance, encourage and administer—and often observe or occasionally even participate in.

If it is thought that high-level American foreign-service represen-tatives might represent a more humane outlook than SOA pedagogues, as, for example, in Indonesia during the Sukarno ouster and Suharto takeover, one should think again. One American ambassador was worried that "their" Indonesian faction would not be "tough" enough to, in the infernal Washington euphemism, "do the job." But they were, and they did, with the result that possibly up to ten million Indonesians, many of them apolitical peasants, were slaughtered by the faction fully supported and virtually directed by the White House. So, there's General Suharto, *"our* SOB" from 1965 on for several decades, until he overdoes the war crimes in East Timor in the 1990s and had to be restrained by the Clinton Administration and finally replaced. The list of "He's an SOB but he's *our* SOB" seems almost endless, but would certainly include Cuba's Batista, Mobutu Sese Sesu, Efrain Rios Montt, Thieu and Diem, the Shah, Somoza, Idi Amin, Pinochet, and former Vice President Cheney's recent ally, the President of Uzbekistan, whose regime Chalmers Johnson describes in *The Sorrows of Empire* as one of the worst violators of human rights in the contemporary world (dissenters, for example, being boiled alive).

Starting with human rights abuses in Central America, in El Salvador alone, according to a United-Nations-selected Truth Commission, more than 22,000 complaints of serious human rights abuses that occurred between 1980 and 1991 were reported. The United States had close ties with the Salvadoran institutional torturers. According to William Blum in *Rogue State*, Salvadoran military personnel involved in torturing Salvadorans claimed to have learned their ABCs of "depth questioning" from the SOA in Panama. Salvadoran security forces worked closely with the CIA and the U.S. military in the deceptively termed "counter-insurgency operations." In Guatemala, a School of the Americas graduate, General Manuel Antonio Callejas y Callejas, was responsible for the death of thousands of Guatemalans, according to Frederick H. Gareau, author of *State Terrorism and the United States.* Another Guatemalan jefe, Hector Gramajo Morales, Guatemala's Defense Minister in the 1980s, expressed a "humanitarian" policy that would have embarrassed even Saddam Hussein: "We instituted civil affairs [in 1982] which provides development for 70 percent of the population while we kill 30 percent" (Blum, 81). "Before," Blum states, "the strategy was to kill 100 percent," a public-policy perspective that pretty much resembled that of America's "anti-terrorist" ally Russia in its outlook towards and treatment of the Chechnyans. From 1953 to 1990 over 200,000 Guatemalans were murdered by the country's repressive regimes. This genocide was supported by Washington because these regimes were accommodating to corporations like United Fruit whose monopolistic interests were threatened by Guatemalan political leaders like Jacobo Arbenz and dissidents striving to free the country's economy from Washington's control.

President Nixon, who wanted to make the Chilean economy under President Allende "scream," did more than that. Nixon and Henry Kissinger destroyed democratic Chile (and its democratically elected President). They brought terror and horror to the country by undermining the economy and supporting its military foes with money and weapons and by helping General Augusto Pinochet take over the country. Further, the White House ordered CIA involvement in overturning the Allende government. According to Gareau, "Our estimate is that the military and the security force 'tortured tens of thousands of Chileans'" (73), and that at least 20,000 Chileans fled the country. Washington, far from disapproving of this criminal conduct, affirmed and supported it. Kissinger, in an 1976 "Memo of Conversation," said that the United States was sympathetic to Pinochet's government and thus to its usurpation of Allende's legal government.

Washington's support for Argentinean state terrorism under Generals Viola and Galtieri was also substantial and, as so often has been the case, crucial, as its disapproval would have possibly discouraged or even halted such brutal takeovers and repressive regimes, opening countless numbers of people to agonies of state terrorism. Again, one witnesses the White House pattern—not only various kinds of support and affirmation of violently suppressive right wing forces by Washington but sizable increases of American funding and, often, arming and training of the military and police of the illegally imposed dictatorial regimes.

What's being described in the case of Argentina is a regime that, among other atrocities, brutalized Argentinean Jews (who comprised ten percent of its victims) and dropped its tortured victims into the Atlantic Ocean from planes as well as introducing rats into victims' orifices through a "rectoscope." Such diabolic treatment did not prevent President Reagan at the time from receiving one of the generals in Washington who had helped implement Argentinean state terrorism—General Roberto Viola—with high honor. Argentinean Admiral Jorge Enrico was, according to John Pilger, "associated with the infamous 'Dirty War' of torture and 'disappearances' in the 1970s…" (*The New Rulers of the World*, 139). That Enrico now lives in Hawaii, a free man, suggests that Washington tolerates terrorists after all, as long as they are *state* terrorists and hospitable when in power to Washington's predilections. (Further exemplification of the White House's double standard on terrorism is its allowing the notorious anti-Castro Venezuelan, Luis Posado Carrilles, widely regarded as the key person responsible for the bombing of a Cuban airliner in 1976, to go free in an El Paso court—and not of terrorist charges but for violating immigration.)

In view of Washington's policy of supporting such anti-Communist regimes friendly to American corporate investments, this treatment as observed by numerous independent analysts from Chomsky to Stephen Kinzer was consistent with traditional American foreign policy going back to the early 20th century.

Washington's foreign policy hypocrisy was also flagrantly criminal in South Africa. Prime Minister Tik Botha and F.W. de Klerk represented virulently racist administrations. Just two aspects of white South African government, of many, exemplify ethnic cleansing, genocide and war crimes. In 1986 in Angola and Mozambique, 140,000 children under five died because of South Africa's "total strategy," a war campaign designed to destabilize Black African populations adjoining South Africa. Almost nine million people from these two nations were displaced by that "strategy." Washington knew that Apartheid South Africa was developing chemical and bacteriological warfare materials. Moreover, South Africa's "weapons of mass destruction" program would not have been possible without foreign aid from four nations, including the United States. Those materials included cholera, anthrax, chemical poisoning, and other deadly germs. Apparently, it was all right then (and remains so now) if an *ally* such as Israel developed WMDs but if a nation less receptive to American corporation needs abroad and Pentagon global strategy also might have WMDs, then they are automatically transformed into a terrorist-rogue state by a wave of the Washington wand.

Looking at Washington's policy in Indonesia further illustrates how globally illegal and criminal it has at times been and remains. The White House and State Department were involved in the 1965 massacre by supplying arms, money, detailed "enemies" lists, communications technology and training and even air support and the Seventh Fleet to the anti-Sukharno rebels—that's immense involvement. Secretary of State Dean Rusk approved the massacres. American Ambassador to Indonesia Marshall Green brutally referred to it as a "cleanup" and Rusk insisted the massacres be continued. A legal expert and historian named Gabriel Kalko states that Washington "was an accessory to the state terrorism in Indonesia" and called it "one of the most barbaric acts of humanity in a century... and ranks as a war crime of the same types as those the Nazis perpetrated" (Gareau, 149). "The same types as those the Nazis perpetrated"—those are extremely strong words; if taken as true, and as that seems unavoidable, they suggest a terrifying darkness at the core of America's political soul.

America is the "city on the hill," the light to a benighted world, a country whose statesmen proclaim that America abominates torture, that it has always stood for freedom, liberty, decency and so on. One all too frequently hears these self-admiring nationalistic cliches uttered by politicians, media commentators, editorialists and historians, and can conclude only three things: either these publicly conspicuous individuals are ignorant of America's foreign policy and history; aren't, and therefore are lying to win popularity, office and its retention or acceptance by the powers that be; or have been deluded by the myths about the uniqueness and excellence that most societies and their ruling class manufacture about themselves to maintain social coherence and domination.

Yet, if one looks at the record of our government's behavior abroad, as I have referenced in selective (hardly all-inclusive) examples, it should be painfully clear that our government representatives—particularly our presidents and their cabinets—have often behaved criminally in policies pursued abroad. As writers and analysts like Robert Fisk, Noam Chomsky, John Pilger, William Blum, Howard Zinn, Chalmers Johnson, Tom Engelhardt and others as well as numerous international and national Truth Commisssions and organizations like Amnesty International and Human Rights Watch have detailedly and cogently shown, Washington has committed war crimes, crimes against humanity, genocide, assassinations, massacres and torture in other countries. They have done so either directly (Vietnam, Iraq, Afghanistan, Panama, Nicaragua, Grenada, Pakistan) and/or indirectly (Nicaragua, Guatemala, El Salvador, Chile, Argentina, Indonesia, Lebanon, South Africa, East Timor, Cambodia) but "indirectly" with such astounding force of money, ordnance, intelligence, communications equipment and technology and overt and covert encouragement of "our SOB" that the line between direct and indirect involvement verges on being, as they say, academic.

The extent and depth of misery, grief, agony and excruciating, lingering dying and violent death the White House has brought about is colossal. Could powerful American statesmen like Secretary of State Rusk and Ambassador Green have actually encouraged Indonesian soldiers and hooligans to continue their rampage of indiscriminate slaughter (including innumerable decapitations)—*and for years*? Did Presidents like Johnson and Nixon actually plan out huge bombing campaigns of civilian-centered towns and cities while having lunch with associates? Did Reagan and his cabinet realize or care that not only were Nicaraguan harbors mined, but hospitals, schools and agricultural centers were bombed by American-supported Contras? Or, going back to the 1950s, did John Foster Dulles imagine that depriving Guatemala and Iran of their democratically elected Presidents would lead to decades of genocide (and, for Iran, hideous SAVAK torture) and suffering for innumerable Guatemalans and Iranians? If so, these men are either extremely cruel or totally abstracted from the concrete human, bodily consequences of their atrociously violent plans. Perhaps, however, it's the same thing: lack of compassion towards, and fear of, the alienated other or the unknown represent the failure of the mind to imagine or feel what should be the inalienable flesh-and-blood reality of other human beings, what the San Francisco poet Kenneth Rexroth called the holiness of the real, by which he also meant the holiness of the other's individuated being.

Soft thinking, this? Bleeding-hearts liberalism? Our Presidents, their cabinet members, unelected but powerful advisors and our innumerable highly secretive intelligence agencies, including Presidential secret armies like the CIA, might want the public to think so. To "get the job done," one has to be tough, hard, *hard*. You can't make an omelet without breaking eggs—the inexcusable excuse given by Soviet apologists for the massive horrors perpetrated by Stalin and Mao. Are our own Presidents in *that* league? Surely not. And yet one tolerated the slaughter of possibly over ten million Indonesians because some of them were—*or were said to be*—Communists or Communist suspects. Even one of our most humane and humanitarian presidents, Jimmy Carter, was kowtowing to the Shah of Iran after almost three decades of Pahlavi crushing of Iranian dissenters because of Cold War politics. And our military invaded Panama to nab Washington's own "SOB" Manual Noriega for trying to become his own "SOB," unnecessarily, according to Martha Gellhorn's *The View from the Ground*, killing and wounding around 8,000 Panamanians and deliberately destroying a Panama barrio during this very violent, illegal incursion.

The Washington pretense of liberating Panama from Noriega (or Iraq from Hussein) is hardly worth serious attention as an ethical rationale. Indonesia, however, is far more atrocious because of the astounding scale of violence and Washington's deep involvement in that violence. The "liberation" of Indonesia from the democratically elected and independent Sukarno to the despotic General Suharto meant, as analysts like Pilger, Chomsky, Blum and others have persuasively shown, the opening of a country of vast natural resources and population to Western corporate exploitation. *That* story of freedom for Capitalist exploitation is not well known by or honestly presented to the American public. Less familiar generally is the sheer hypocritical brutality involved, for if that realization dawned on enough Americans, one would think it would—or, at least, should—have led to huge street demonstrations of protest. But what mainstream journalist is going to bring that dawn to the American public?

What is behind all this proxy—and direct—violence committed by Washington abroad? Why has it supported dictator-monsters worse than Saddam Hussein, then set up Saddam as, in effect, one of the worst political villains of modern times, ridiculously compared by some hysterical pundits even to Hitler? The numerous right wing regimes supported by Washington before the Gulf Wars were of course seen as noble bulwarks against the alleged global threat of global communism. While Soviet Communism could be considered a threat to global Capitalist interests and investments and unquestionably embodied a totalitarian social order, transforming it into a threat to American democracy or Western values is easily seen as mostly a sham in view of Washington's full-scale support of anti-democratic values embodied in the extremely bloody regimes of the Pinochets, Amins, Suhartos, Rios Montts and the rest. It is still not understood by the general public that many nationalistic movements of liberation in "Third World" countries were deliberately misidentified as Communist in order to undercut the drive to reconfigure severely impoverished societies run by elites friendly to and supported by Washington. What is shocking is the global breadth and extremes of violence to which the White House would go to preserve commercial, corporate demands virtually anywhere assets that can be possessed exist.

Certainly there must have been American officials who regretted or were even horrified by "excesses" created by *their* SOBs in Third World nations, a protest or even resignation here or there. But two of the main defenses of high-placed political officials against the mass murder and horrific misery caused by their policies abroad were either ideology or plausible deniability or both combined. They either believed or pretended to believe their own myths of the Free World versus Reagan's Evil Empire, or perhaps, conceivably, half believed and half didn't believe this ideological polarization in which their own ruthlessly domineering energies, greed and fear were imposed on the Other (the Other also captured by the same opportunistic projection and fear).

As for plausible deniability, modern political executive institutions are so complex and multi-layered that a president could pretend he didn't know what was going on in regard to criminal behavior abroad by, say, the CIA. Did Eisenhower really know that Secretary of State Dulles had engineered the overthrow of the democratic government of Iran? Researchers like Stephen Kinzer in his book *All the Shah's Men* have stated that he did. However, whether Eisenhower did or didn't know, the overriding consideration regarding an event such as the overthrow of another nation's government in a country the United States is not at war with, is whether the president or his close advisors *should* have known. It is also easy and cheap for presidents either to urge the myth of the Free World or to urge ignorance of egregious misconduct by one of a president's countless agencies. In view, however, of the crucial importance to American presidents since Truman of knowing what its chief intelligence agency concerned with government destabilization or assassinations abroad is doing, it would seem that presidents obviously must take responsibility for the results and consequences of their foreign policies. If those policy consequences involve war crimes, genocide, torture or an illegal war, they must be held fully accountable legally, including not only impeachment but *imprisonment*.

Chomsky and Herman have stated that "If the facts were faced, and international law and elementary morality were operative, thousands of U.S. politicians and military planners would be regarded as candidates for Nuremburg-type trials" (*The Washington Connection and Third-World Fascism,* 30). Some might demur at this shocking conclusion as Chomskyan radicalism and extravagance. However, General Telford Taylor, U.S. Chief Prosecutor at the Nuremburg Tribunal for World War II, urged much the same thing for General William Westmoreland in regard to war crimes perpetrated in the Vietnam War. Leaders of victorious nations who commit war crimes are not likely to be thrown into prison or executed, although their condemnation by representative world legal institutions might bear significant symbolic and thus repercussive value, even within the criminal leader's own nation. It is easy to see how grossly violative Bush-Cheney-Rumsfeld and, now, President Obama (with his drone attacks killing hundreds of civilians, including children) have been of the moral norms of political leadership. When, however, a whole string of American presidents from Eisenhower on are viewed as in one way or another condoning or covertly encouraging war crimes abroad, it gives the character of American political leadership an entirely different moral appearance, one that, hidden behind the successful cover of plausible deniability, is shocking in its realpolitik ruthlessness. Instead of naming statues and airports and freeways and public buildings after these men, we should label them felons and at least imprison them in print and in memory if we can't bodily.

"The Black Light on the Hill: United States Foreign Policy Hypocrisy" by Donald Gutierrez—*War Crimes Times*, January 2009; *Common Sense*, February 2010.

3
Review: Stephen Kinzer
All the Shah's Men: An American Coup and the
Roots of Middle East Terror

One of the major ironies and tragedies of twentieth century American foreign policy is that nations like the United States and Great Britain proclaim their support of democracy throughout the world but deliberately bring about or support despotic regimes. Such installation and support, usually originating in the White House, lead to the torture and murder of a foreign nation's population.

A crucial example of this policy is dramatically elaborated in *All the Shah's Men: An American Coup and the Roots of Middle East Terror* by *New York Times* journalist Stephen Kinzer. *Shah* deals with the overthrow of the Mohammed Mossadegh government by the CIA with the tacit approval of President Eisenhower and the fanatical complicity of John Foster Dulles, secretary of state, and his brother Allen, CIA director.

A key actor in Washington's subversion was Kermit Roosevelt, grandson of President Teddy Roosevelt and a CIA agent, who, with the help of the British intelligence agencies and key Iranians, engineered the overthrow of the democratically elected Mossadegh.

Though the CIA coup against Mossadegh is central to *Shah*, Kinzer effectively lays out the coup's broader context. He devotes a chapter to the entire history of Iran, indicating not only its high culture as an ancient civilization but its experience of oppressive Persian and foreign rulers. Among the latter, it was the impact of the British that did the most to determine the fate of Iran during the first half of the twentieth century. The British got a firm foothold in Iranian oil late in the nineteenth century, and used their position to exploit these vast reserves, turning Iran into a British colony in the process. This resulted in enormous wealth and industrial and military empowerment for England and increasing destitution for the large majority of Iranians.

Enter Mohammad Mossadegh, a statesman passionately dedicated to the liberation and democratization of Iran, and utterly unyielding to British imperial might. He was soon recognized by London as a menace to their elaborate oil interests in Iran. When he finally moved to nationalize Iranian oil, England prepared to attack Iran with sea power and troops but backed off after encountering U.S. President Harry S. Truman's total disapproval. However, when Dwight D. Eisenhower became president, the United States came on board.

According to Kinzer, the British played on Washington's fear of Soviet Union expansion into Iran. Washington was also worried about a Soviet Communist domino effect in the oil-rich Middle East. What followed can aptly be called Washington's opportunistic paranoia. Not only did the United States "secure" Iran through its real life "007" Kermit Roosevelt (with the covert help of millions of tax payers' dollars distributed to influential Iranians), it also profited handsomely as part of an international consortium controlling Iranian oil.

This development required the "stabilization" of Iran, which Washington and Roosevelt achieved through illegal actions leading to Mossadegh's ouster and the Shah's installation, the latter becoming America's man in Iran. As, however, the Shah imposed a tyrannical regime and Iranians came to realize Washington's major role in their suffering and repression, their attitude changed from admiration of the United States to hatred. According to Kinzer, "it is not far-fetched to draw a line from Operation Ajax [the CIA coup] through the Shah's repressive regime and the Islamic Revolution to the fireballs that engulfed the World Trade Center in New York" (203-04). According to Kinzer, what resulted was "blowback," the CIA term for foreign policy producing unexpected and terrible consequences.

Kinzer near the end of *Shah* quotes six historians on the 1953 coup, who, while they differ in some respects, agree that the subverting of Mossadegh's democratic government and nationalistic independence from the Western powers has both profoundly reshaped Iran ever since and released enormous Muslimic extremist forces throughout the Middle East and beyond.

Mohammed Mossadegh, claims Kinzer, was a titanic figure in the twentieth century struggle of colonialized countries for independence and freedom. As it looks from the twenty-first century, the political destruction of Mossadegh by England and the United States, besides belying their claims to represent the Free World, appears today to bear major responsibility for destabilizing the world ever since. Such, at least, is the ultimate implication of *Shah,* a book everyone should read to understand the blowback that often results from a secretive, illegal foreign policy by a nation's leaders.

"Review: Stephen Kinzer, *All the Shah's Men; An American Coup and the Roots of Middle East Terror*" by Donald Gutierrez—*Eldorado Sun*, March 2003.

4
Review: Frederick H. Gareau,
State Terrorism and the United States:
From Counterinsurgency to the War on Terrorism

> Washington publishes an annual list of governments that it
> alleges aid terrorists. Typically, this list contains a majority of
> governments of Arab states plus Iran, Cuba and North Korea.
> This highlights the importance of how terrorism is defined. If
> state terrorism were included in the definition, Washington
> would have to include itself in the list. (Gareau, 15)

The main thrust of Frederick H. Gareau's *State Terrorism and the United
States* is to demonstrate that the United States, in carrying out state terrorism
to win the Cold War, backed to the hilt savagely repressive right wing
regimes and dictatorships resulting in the horrendous suffering, brutalizing
and murder of millions of human beings.

This is an extraordinarily damning indictment of the nation that has
prided itself as being the exemplar of liberty, freedom and societal decency
in the modern world. The indictment is also stunningly ironic in view of how,
especially under the last Bush Administration, the United States has been
foremost in identifying itself as the citadel of democratic anti-terrorism. The
evidence assembled by Gareau and other researchers indicates that the very
opposite is the case—that the United States has inflicted a degree and scope
of terrorism throughout some third world countries that make anti-state
guerrilla terrorism seem minor by comparison. More important, Gareau
demonstrates with evidence from eye witnesses, truth commissions, other

observers and terror victims that most individuals, groups and organizations stigmatized as terrorists or insurgents were actually either nonpartisan or people attempting to peacefully implement essential social reform in extremely corrupt societies ruled by elites.

Gareau defines terrorism as consisting of "deliberate acts of a physical and/or psychological nature perpetrated on a select group of victims....the overall purpose of terrorism is to intimidate and coerce" (14-15). He then poses several questions structuring his study:

> Did the government being studied actually commit state terrorism? To what extent was the terror committed by states, and to what extent was it private terror committed by the guerrillas? Was the country that perpetrated the terror upon its own citizens actually supported by Washington? In what ways was this support provided? (19)

The chapters that follow deal with state terrorism and American counter-insurgency training in El Salvador and Guatemala, as well as terrorism in Chile exercised by the Pinochet regime. Then come discussions of Argentinean state terrorism and torture, apartheid and terrorism in South Africa and three massacres in Indonesia. The final section of *State Terrorism* presents what Gareau terms the Root Doctrine as it applied to Nicaragua, the Congo and the Khmer Rouge, Washington's Middle East policy (which focuses on Iran and on Israel's state terrorist treatment of the Palestinians) and President George W. Bush's "War on Terrorism," dealing with the Afghanistan and Persian Gulf Wars.

Much of what happens in the four Latin American countries dealt with early in the book can be traced to the training in counter-insurgency methods learned at 150 "schools" in the U.S. The most notorious of these is the School of the Americas. The SOA "has trained upward of 59,000 Latin American military personnel, policemen and civilians" (23). Some of these students were hardly inconsequential. Ten became presidents/dictators; twenty-three, defense ministers; and fifteen, ministers of other departments.

Counterinsurgency is a broad, euphemistic term disguising what basically results in extreme intimidation and repression of the poor in third world societies. Not only had the enormous wealth of the elite of these nations been amassed at the expense of the huge majority of the populations in nations like El Salvador. In addition, the military and police institutions there have been closely related to the powerful land, banking and business interests. The consequences were inevitable—extreme measures implemented to "adjust" the masses to their miserable lot. Anyone or any group that resisted or embodied disapproval of this iron-fisted control would be terrorized—he or she would be submitted to torture, maiming or even savage death to exemplify a regime's absolute authority.

Latin American military officers and police chiefs as well as individuals later to become politically significant would attend the School to learn these terrorizing "counter-insurgency" operations. Supposedly the School was intended to train state leaders to import order and security so as to stabilize their countries and transmit American democratic values south of the border. What the School really was about was indoctrinating law-enforcement personnel with the means of crowd control to "stabilize" their societies for economic investment and control by American corporations. This goal could not be achieved if labor leaders, students, organized peasants, teachers, religious organizations and others tried to introduce social reform into societies top-heavy with wealth and power. To prevent such reformism, Washington, through the SOA (among other channels), stigmatized reformers and liberating forces as either being communist or communist-inspired; as such, they needed to be exterminated.

The commercial interests of the American elite were thus allied to those of some Latin American nations through the terrorizing muscle of politicized armies and police, paramilitary units and death squads. SOA military instructors hardly taught respect for due process, habeus corpus and other civil liberties to mass killers like Guatemalan General Hector Gramajo Morales (himself stung to death on his farm by African bees before he could commit more genocide), or to Guatemalan general Manuel Antonio Callejas y Callejas, who was responsible for the deaths and disappearances of thousands of Guatemalans. Bolivian general Hugo Banzar Suarez, another SOA grad, had from 1971 to 1976 "murdered 468 Bolivians, imprisoned ...4,318 for their political beliefs and activities, deported 663, and tortured 100 who had survived their ordeal" (23). Suarez's portrait hangs in the SOA's Hall of Fame. Father Roy Bourgeois, long the chief activist trying to close the SOA, put the real purpose and effect of the School concisely: "This [SOA] is where the killing starts" (23).

What is Washington's role in the government terrorism being imposed in El Salvador and other Latin American countries? In 1962 the American Joint Chiefs of Staff defined insurgency in terms sufficiently broad to range from passive resistance to guerrilla activities, and branded all of it as communistic. No middle ground existed. One was either for us or against us, and "against us" included peasants ground down by the dominant interests or accused of sympathy with the guerrillas, liberation Catholic religious and lay people trying peacefully to alleviate the unrelenting poverty, or anyone critical of the regime. A brutally repressive policy was facilitated by an American Special Forces Manual entitled "Counter-insurgency Operations" that "eschewed ethical limits on counter-guerrilla warfare and reserved the use of terror as a legitimate tactical tool of unconventional warfare" (30). The CIA had around 150 agents in El Salvador; by 1984 it came out that top Salvadoran officers had been trained by the United States, and that many top members of the army, police and paramilitary were being funded by the CIA. Combining those facts with the 75,000 Salvadorans murdered and one-fourth of the population displaced by the Salvadoran authorities makes Gareau conclude that "Washington trained the army in El Salvador for the repression it committed and subsidized the government while it was engaged in the repression" (31).

The trouble with terms like "repression," "human rights abuses" or even "excessive violence" is their abstractness. They conceal such actions of government military as "impaling victims, amputating their limbs, burning them alive; extracting their viscera while still alive and in the presence of others [and] opening the wombs of pregnant women" (46). This is merely a selective list of atrocities that occurred in Guatemala during the 1980s.

We know about the atrocities and *matanzas* (massacres) in El Salvador or Guatemala, Argentina, Chile because of Truth Commissions, sometimes established slowly for a very sensible fear of retaliation (an ongoing dread to this day). In El Salvador the Commission received more than 22,000 complaints of major acts of violence that had taken place between 1980 and 1991. This violence included the now well-known El Mozote massacre in 1981 in which over 900 individuals were systematically tortured and murdered, the majority of them children. Ten of the twelve officers responsible for this incredible butchery were SOA grads.

An extremely important "fact" pervading these Truth Commission Reports was the extent of institutional responsibility for the "abuses" of the population. The percentage of involvement and responsibility are revealing and typical of all the countries analyzed in *State Terrorism*. The Salvadoran government, for example, was responsible for ninety-five percent of the atrocities, torture, massacres, while the guerrillas were responsible for *five* percent. Washington provided these lethal government institutions with six billion dollars in aid from 1979 to 1992. Gareau consequently deems Washington guilty as an accessory before and during the fact by financing state security-forces terrorism and training these forces. He holds Washington responsible as an accessory *after* the fact by concealing Salvadoran abuses through providing its government—and thus its financial and land elite—with diplomatic support. With minor variations, this proportional pattern of state versus guerrilla responsibility for terrorism characterizes all the nations analyzed in Gareau's book.

Though El Salvador elicited an immense number of complaints about violence for their Truth Commission, Guatemalans had twice as many— 42,275. A United Nations Commission, which recorded the human rights violations in Guatemala, estimated 200,000 victims either killed outright or "disappeared." Most of the victims, Gareau indicates, were civilians: "One fourth were women, who were often raped before they were tortured or killed, and many were children, who were also sometimes raped before they were tortured or killed" (45). Over 80 percent of the victims were Mayans.

Some consideration should be given about how these military institutions and auxiliaries (paramilitaries, death squads and the like) could even perform the atrocities carried out in the Third World nations surveyed in *State Terrorism*. First, Gareau mentions the counter-insurgency training transmitted to the armies of Guatemala, Nicaragua (the Contras) and the rest by Washington. Accompanying this education is a brutalizing of sensibility in males frequently from the same class and ethnicity as their victims. This included a rigorous training in de-individualization along lines of severe punishment (including death) for disobedience. These new soldiers literally had their hands stained with the blood of victims to desensitize them.

The trainees were also forced to kill animals, eat them raw and drink their blood. In addition, they were subjected to three days of instruction in torture techniques, pedagogic methods acquired by their instructors from their SOA-educated superiors. Rules of engagement in war and in the handling of POWs have often been violated even in traditional wars between states. And when a state is in effect declaring ideological war on its own population with instruction, funding, arms and technical assistance and diplomatic approval coming from an outside superpower like the United States, there is little to restrict military and law-enforcement institutions from doing anything they want to a given sector of the population. This is especially true if it is one like the Mayans whom high-placed civilian and military officials have traditionally held in contempt.

According to the Commission in Guatemala, the majority of the atrocities occurred with the knowledge or even at the bidding of the Guatemalan state. The only higher authority during this period was Washington, which was intimately connected with the Guatemalan communications and intelligence institutions that, according to the Commission, perpetrated the mass savagery. Approximately $777,000,000 of aid to Guatemala from Washington from 1981 to 1990 as well as President Reagan's virtual approval of the Guatemalan army's carnage underline Washington's support of Guatemalan state terrorism.

The scenario of state violence in Chile is in many respects similar to that in the Central American nations. Under General Pinochet's regime, "the military and the security forces tortured tens of thousands of Chileans" (73). Chile's intelligence organization, DINA, did much more than amass information. It was responsible for much of the worst state terrorization from 1975 to 1977. And, once again, the United States was complicit, 1,437 Chilean military officers having attended the SOA. "[DINA's] specialty," claims Gareau, "was forced disappearances" (77). The major roles played by President Nixon and Secretary of State Kissinger in destroying President Allende's government are well known, as is their sympathy with Pinochet's *putsch*.

One significant aspect of Chile's state terrorizing is the general apathy of the Chilean public to the savage human rights violations being executed under Pinochet. According to Gareau, a key reason for this was the media. Shortly following Pinochet's violent takeover, the government clamped down on the media, transforming it into a publicity and propaganda channel of the military.

Much of the state violence in Chile and elsewhere in Latin America was based on a crusade against communism intensely encouraged by Washington. A crucial aspect of this crusade was to identify all forms of civil reform movements as Communist, no matter how pacific and even anticommunist they actually were. This very effective and malicious mislabeling enabled right wing regimes from Chile and Guatemala to South Africa and Indonesia to stigmatize *any* resistance to or criticism of government rule and repression as insurgency and, worse, terrorism. So, when left wing guerrilla movements did commit violence (including atrocities), it was termed "terrorism" whereas, according to Gareau, the far more widespread and ferocious terrorism of right wing governments was provided the gentler label of "human rights abuses" which doesn't convey the Guatemalan army-training practice of decapitating village boys to toughen recruits.

Thus, to stop any kind of reform movement, communist or otherwise, Washington and its proxy governments in Latin America and elsewhere embarked on a campaign of terrorization by and large shielded from the American public. Even the *New York Times* all too often misrepresented state terrorism as liberating a society into free enterprise and thus democracy.

Washington funded not only Chilean but Argentina's state terrorism, between 1960 and 1975 offering Argentina's government $810 million for military aid. That counter-insurgency was the main purpose of the bountiful donation is made clear in statements made by Argentine General Ramon Camps, Chief of the notorious Buenos Aires province police force, who claims that Washington "organized centres for teaching counter-insurgency techniques (especially in the United States) and sent out instructors, observers and an enormous amount of literature" (103). From 1950 to 1979, over 4,000 Argentine military received training by the United States, including two generals who were SOA graduates and later became Argentine dictators.

Though many of these Latin American terrorist states "disappeared" their victims, Argentina was unique in facilitating the disappearance by throwing still live victims from airplanes into the ocean, having slit their bellies so they would sink to the ocean floor. Argentina state terrorism surely reached its most diabolical level in its overtly anti-Semitic treatment of Argentine Jews:

> All kinds of torture would be applied to Jews, including "the rectoscope". Israel was one of the main suppliers of arms to Argentina during the overtly anti-Semitic character of what was called Argentina's Dirty War. And Washington's Kissinger gave the green light to the "forthcoming 'dirty war.'" (Gareau, 108) [See Ch. 2, "The Black Light on the Hill," for related material.]

South Africa serves as a glaring example of Washington's support of state terrorism going to the extreme of assisting an anti-Communist ally in the development *and use* of weapons of mass destruction. The development included chemical and bacteriological elements of warfare, and received the assistance of Belgium, Israel, England and the United States. Pretoria's chemical agents were used against Mozambique guerrillas. That 83 percent of the opponents of the South African government were tortured apparently did not concern the White House. Neither did Pretoria's extremely brutal policy of Apartheid (initiated in 1949), which is savagely ironic considering Washington's proclaimed ideal of globalizing Democracy going back at least to Woodrow Wilson's presidency.

While beatings were the most common form of torture exercised by the government of South Africa, forced standing was also frequently used not only there but elsewhere. In a 2008 *Democracy Now* radio interview, a British male working contractually in Saudi Arabia was falsely accused by the government of involvement in a bomb explosion. Kidnapped by Saudi security forces and incarcerated, he was tortured (including rape) by his captors. One of the torments was sleep deprivation caused by chaining him upright to the cell bars. Donald Rumsfeld has opined that coercive techniques such as sleep deprivation and stress positions do not constitute torture, a judgment based on a White House legal counsel's determination that torture is constituted only by acts that lead to loss of limbs or threaten life. This British captive claims, however, that after the third bout of sleep deprivation (which lasted eleven days or so), he had two heart attacks, surely a life-threatening symptom.

The last nation's state terrorism examined at length by Gareau is Indonesia (148). The Indonesian government's killing was massive, estimated at anywhere from one million to one and a half million between 1965 and 1970. Among the slaughtered were not only Communist suspects, but "peasants who had alienated their landlords, apolitical persons denounced by their neighbors, [and] religious elements the Muslims did not like..." Washington supported the widespread slaughter that its approval would let loose. America's Ambassador to Indonesia, Marshall Green, worried whether the Indonesian government would have "the courage to go forward against the PKI [Communist Party of Indonesia]."

> Experts at the State Department knew that the PKI had neither the arms nor the will to resist.... Bluntly put, the Secretary of State under President Johnson [Dean Rusk] expressed his approval of the practice of state terrorism by the Indonesian army. (148)

After the defenseless "enemy" was wiped out by weaponry, intelligence and communications apparatus supplied by the Pentagon, the United States and other Western powers recreated the financial and economic base of Indonesian society. Once a democratically elected President Sukarno had been dislodged and then replaced by the genocidal General Suharto, "order" thus re-established, huge investments from American and European corporations flooded Indonesian markets. Indonesia, through free trade, was now part of the Free World. During this period of genocide in Indonesia, the United States provided arms to the country amounting to $40 million annually. Under President Ford, financial military aid to Suharto's Indonesia was raised to $140 million and, under President Jimmy Carter, remained above $100 million. Gareau quotes Gabriel Kolko's unforgettable summary of the White House's proxy financing and administrating of genocide, torture and massacre in Indonesia from the mid 1970s well into the Reagan era:

> No single American action in the period after 1945 was as bloodthirsty as its role in Indonesia, for it tried to initiate the massacre, and it did everything in its power to encourage Suharto, including equipping his killers, to see that the physical liquidation of the PKI was carried through to its culmination. (149)

A rationale for America's state terrorism and for its proxy terrorism through right wing regimes was set forth by State Secretary Elihu Root in 1922. Root felt that a state, specifically, the United States, had the right to protect its interests abroad. That these were basically economic, corporate intererests is the essential point, but it is a point traditionally camouflaged by various expressions of idealism centered on spreading democracy, freedom and equality throughout the world. As, according to Root, certain countries could not fend democratically for themselves, they required the order and stability that right wing dictatorships supposedly could provide, which in turn would win Washington's full backing. Latin American nations lacking such tyrannical stabilizing found themselves being invaded by the colossus in the North: "Prior to the Spanish American War, the United States carried out 103 interventions; between the end of that war and the Great Depression, it sent troops to Latin America 32 times" (163).

Gareau's next chapter deals with Washington's more recent policies in the Middle East, focusing on America's highly supportive relationship with Saddam Hussein from the early 1960s up to the first Gulf War. Gareau also reveals Washington's role in usurping the democratically elected, popular Muhammad Mosaddegh and installing the Shah and thus decades of repression and torture of Iranians under the SAVAK. The CIA coup against Mosaddegh was approved by President Eisenhower and maintained through support of the tyrannical Shah by Presidents Kennedy, Johnson, Nixon, Ford and Carter. Washington's support of Israel is also laid out by Gareau, including its non-objection to Israel's building of nuclear weapons, its ethnic cleansing of Palestinian populations in 1967 and its involvement in 1982 in the Lebanese Sabra and Shatilla refugee-camp massacre of over 2000 Palestinians. Moreover, Washington provided Israel $53 billion from 1948 to 1991, and from 1988 on $3 billion annually in military and economic assistance.

The chapter "The War on Terrorism" offers insightful discussions of the American war against Afghanistan and its second war against Iraq. But especially worth highlighting is the chapter's sub-topic on Guantanamo. That section emphasizes how counter-insurgency is transformed into counter-terrorism in the sinister confines of a high-security prison full of terrorist "suspects" randomly picked up in street sweeps. Discussing Pentagon photographs, Gareau insists that Guantanamo detainees are clearly being psychologically tortured:

> The photographs "showed some of the prisoners kneeling before their captors, their legs in shackles, bound in manacles, their mouths covered by surgical masks and their eyes blinded by large goggles with black tape." (198)

Former President George W. Bush and Secretary of State Donald Rumsfeld described Muslim terrorists as being the most dangerous people in the world in broad enough terms to include Guantanamo detainees, most of whom would probably be proven to be innocent in a court of law. Their status of illegal enemy combatant is, according to Gareau, more aptly applied to the Pentagon for illegally and savagely attacking a sovereign nation without cause. Aside from the 350 suicide attempts in the first year and a half at Guantanamo, the level of daily psychological sadism that the Pentagon photos describe is so apparent that statements by Rumsfeld that these men are being treated humanely are utterly and viciously dishonest.

The final chapter, "Conclusions and Recommendations," intimates that Washington's aid to the nations that Gareau describes as state terrorist was of such proportions that their governments might not have been able to unleash terrorism without it. Washington's proxy state terrorism also took the form of selling and even giving away sizable amounts of ordnance. Further, it exported "thumb cuffs, thumb screws, leg irons and shackles" (220) to nations with pronounced human rights violations records such as Bahrain, Bolivia, Colombia, Egypt, Israel, Mexico, Pakistan, Saudi Arabia and Turkey. It also offered "electro-shock batons, cattle prods, shot guns and shot-gun shells" to over 105 nations. Worst, Washington has trained more than 100,000 military personnel from over 100 nations as part of its sinister IMET (International Military and Training Education program), thereby making more *matanzas* (massacres) anywhere from Guatemala to Indonesia possible or even likely.

Near the end of his book, Gareau climactically exposes the hypocrisy of Bush's "War on Terrorism":

> President Bush's resolve to capture the terrorists and bring them to justice is compartmentalized and exclusive. It does not include the members of the death squads in Guatemala, nor General Pinochet and Suharto and the other military officers, former state terrorists, who are enjoying their retirement with their families in their own countries or in the sunshine of southern Florida. (230)

This certainly sounds like the United States is harboring terrorists. Thus, by the logic used by Washington to justify attacking both Afghanistan and Iraq for either harboring terrorists or embodying terrorism, Guatemala, Nicaragua, Chile (among other nations) could feel justified in initiating a preemptive strike against the U.S.

The principal thrust of *State Terrorism* is posed at the end of the book: the crucial need for a Truth Commission for the United States (i.e., Washington). "The public should be educated as to what its government has done" (22). Were Americans to discover, for example, that Washington ignited the mass slaughter of possibly over a million Indonesians to clear the ground for transnational corporate investment, their brainwashed notion that America is only a force for good in the world might be jolted. Much has been made by the media of the frightening savagery of the El Salvadoran gangs rampaging throughout the United States; they are inordinately cruel, murderous and greedy. It might shock many Americans to know that Washington and Wall Street elite wearing starched white shirts, conservative blue ties and $1,000 three-piece suits have activated an international policy far more widespread in its murderous brutality than these Central American gang thugs could ever pull off. The Three-Piece-Suits keep blood off their hands by outsourcing some of their terrorism.

The implementation of Gareau's Truth Commission on atrocities committed in their safe command centers by Nixon, Johnson, Reagan, Clinton, both Bushes and Obama, their various Cabinet members and their mega-corporation allies is an essential first step towards some form of redemption in the psyche of America. Without full disclosure, the American state will become even more violent, corrupt and arrogant, fatally ripe for a drift either into radical dysfunction or into a totalitarianism that Americans have not imagined in their worst dreams.

"Review: Frederick H. Gareau, *State Terrorism and the United States*" by Donald Gutierrez—*Social Justice*, v. 33, no. 1.

5
"Where is the Humanity?"
America's Use of Excessive Force Over There

Air bombardment is state terrorism, the terrorism of
the rich. It has burned up and blasted apart more
innocents in the past six decades than have all
the anti-state terrorists who ever lived.
C. Douglas Loomis, THE NATION (Sept. 26, 1994)

That is really not a matter I am terribly interested in.
Colin Powell on being questioned in 1991 about
Iraqi casualties, THE NATION (Feb. 2, 2002)

Though this essay was originally written in 2004 in response to the George
W. Bush Administration's assaults on Afghanistan and Iraq and the earlier
Gulf War attack during the administration of his father, George H. W. Bush,
the piece seems tragically relevant to what is now being called President
Barack Obama's "War on Terrorism" in Afghanistan and Pakistan. It is high
time then to present a side of America's wars in the Middle East that
receives brief mention in the mass media and scarcely any ethical
evaluation: Washington's "collateral-damage" bombing in the Middle East.

All Americans know that on September 11, 2001, thousands of
Americans were killed by Middle Eastern suicide-terrorists. Further, the
death of any American serviceman killed in action in Afghanistan is fully
and prominently publicized in our media. This publicity is understandable
and deserved. What is not asked, though, is why Afghan civilian casualties

committed by American forces are given scant attention in our media. Any reports of Afghan or Pakistani civilian deaths are either deemed "mistakes" or justified by assertions that Taliban fighters were in the bombed location. The murders are seen as somber occasion for American generals like Stanley McChrystal to urge avoiding such killings, though such advice appears designed more for diplomatic than moral ends (especially true in General McChystal's case, given his reputation for running a secret detention camp near Baghdad called Camp Nana where, according to Tom Engelhardt, "bad things happened regularly" (*The American Way of War*). Yet, not only does the massacre of civilians by American drones continue in the Obama administration, but the rate of bombings and civilian deaths is greater than under Bush's sponsorship.

Perhaps our leaders can "regret" the deaths of the enemy's civilians, but then such "collateral damage" is, we are informed, inevitable in war. The Pentagon claims it does all it can to avoid collateral damage and that it mainly practices surgical bombing. There is evidence, however, that the United States has dropped cluster bombs in Iraq (Ramsey Clark, *The Fire This Time*) and Yugoslavia, as well as in Afghanistan, a practice condemned by human rights groups as "indiscriminate weapons of mass destruction" (William Blum, *Rogue State*, Noam Chomsky, *The New Military Humanism*).

Further, one American general admitted that American planes intentionally bombed civilian infrastructure in Kosovo in order to motivate civilians to rise against their rulers. It is now common knowledge that more bombs were dropped by the U.S. on Vietnam than all the bombs dropped by the Allies in World War II—indeed, three times as many, according to Howard Zinn (*The Zinn Reader*). Zinn also claims that four Vietnamese civilians were killed by American bombing for every one Vietnamese soldier.

It is commonly accepted that a nation at war, especially its military, is not humanely concerned about the fate of the enemy, either military or civilian. That perspective, apparent in warring nations, nevertheless overlooks another one usually ignored, and of which more people should be aware: that international covenants exist which state that the commanders of opposing warring forces are responsible for achieving their military goals with as little harm to the enemy forces as possible, that the captured enemy should be treated humanely, and that the military leaders of the victorious side should be concerned about casualties on both sides. This last position contrasts sharply with Colin Powell's statement in the epigraph above. It suggests as well a standard of warfare which, if it strikes us as quixotic, thus also measures our own alienation from humane standards of war conduct.

Public attitudes towards war ethics are generally shaped by a nation's leaders and the mass media. If these two agencies can whip up enough fear and hatred in the country towards the foe, such conditioning will make it fairly easy for the government to effect such war crimes as Ramsey Clark and others indicate occurred in the Gulf War: "[the] killing [of] tens of thousands of essentially defenseless soldiers, soldiers withdrawing without weapons; burying soldiers alive; using illegal weapons; disrespect for the dead and many others. The combat death toll alone—125,000 Iraqis to 148 Americans—reveals the defenselessness of the Iraqis and the dimension of the war crime. This was certainly a violation of the Hague Convention requiring that force used be proportional to a legitimate military objective" (*The Fire This Time*).

Clark asserts that these crimes violate not only the Hague Convention but also the Nuremberg Charter and the Geneva Conventions and Protocols. International treaties restricting military behavior in war are designated by the Geneva Conventions of 1864 and 1901 which, Clark states, "provided protection for soldiers wounded in action. The Hague Convention of 1869, revised in 1907, was the first international codification of the laws of armed conflict." This convention also prohibits the employment of excessive force.

The United States is obviously not the only major violator of those ethical international agreements concerning humane treatment of the other side in wartime. Many nations have brutally treated enemy forces and civilian populations. But the United States in recent decades has been extraordinarily destructive and imperious towards both. A 1998 headline in the *Albuquerque Journal* read, COHEN: "WE'LL POUND IRAQ!" One assumes that the defense secretary didn't mean every square foot of that country, but the ubiquitousness of that threat suggests as much. Indeed, the United States might as well have bombed the entire nation as, according to Clark, it violated both the Hague Convention and the 1977 addition to the Geneva Convention of 1949 by devastating the civilian infrastructure of Iraq. The United States, according to the Pentagon, flew 109,876 sorties, and up to 40,000 pounds of bombs were dropped during each carpet-bombing sortie by B-52s on military installations.

Michael Parenti claims that earlier, during the Vietnam War, the massive bombing included "schools, hospitals, bridges, cement plants, TV and radio stations, and railway depots, shops, restaurants and homes"

(*Against Empire*, 126). The twelve-year sanction by the United States against Iraq clearly constitutes violations of civilian protection guaranteed by war-ethics conventions. More recently, Senator Hillary Clinton, while running for the presidency in 2008, threatened to "nuke" Iran if it dared attack Israel. Nuclear bombing, of course, would exterminate entire civilian populations.

Further, the American use of weaponry like cluster bombs, and the carpet bombing and depleted-uranium shelling of Iraq, Yugoslavia and Afghanistan constitute even more evidence of such violation. According to William Blum, President Clinton bombed the people of Yugoslavia for 78 days and nights, "taking the lives of many hundreds of civilians and producing one of the greatest ecological catastrophes in history" (*Rogue State*). Blum also mentions President Clinton's "illegal and lethal bombings of Somalia, Bosnia, Sudan and Afghanistan," all attacks obviously including civilians.

Citing remarks about, and excessive action against, the enemy made by key American military and civilian leaders is apropos here. Directing the NATO aerial attack on Yugoslavia, General Wesley Clark, banging his fist on a table, shouted, "I've got to get the maximum violence out of this campaign—now!" (Blum). General Norman Schwarzkopf, commander in chief of the Central Command during the Gulf War, besides continuing to slaughter Iraqis two days after the cease fire, is reputed to have said, "I want every Iraqi soldier bleeding from every orifice" (Clark, *The Fire This Time*).

Secretary of State Henry ("Power is the ultimate aphrodisiac") Kissinger was centrally, if sometimes covertly, involved in the misery and murder of millions of civilians through America's interventions in Cambodia, Vietnam, Chile, Angola, East Timor, Iraq and Bangladesh. And, of course, American presidents like Lyndon Johnson, Richard Nixon, Ronald Reagan, Bush Sr., Clinton and Bush Jr. have been centrally responsible for catastrophic actions of often undeclared war against sovereign states, involving the deaths and maiming of millions and the devastation of their military and civilian infrastructure.

Journalist Martha Gellhorn once said, "I thought it would be fine if the ones who ordered the bombing and the ones who did the bombing would walk on the ground sometime and see what it is like" (*The Face of War*, 1986). Indeed, one would love to take the Pentagon brass, the President and Congress for a compulsory walk to look close up at what American bombing has actually been doing to Afghan and innumerable other civilians. Howard

Zinn in a *Nation* article entitled "The Others" (February 2, 2002), provides that closer look at the "collateral damage" caused by American bombing in Afghanistan. First, he gives us various examples of excuses offered by the Pentagon for bombing "mistakes" (observing that such events get little attention on national television): "incorrect coordinates had been entered"; "the village was a legitimate military target" (Zinn's accounts derive from sources like *The New York Times*, *The Times of London*, Reuters and *The Washington Post*).

In Zinn's article, a family in the village of Madoo states that fifteen houses were bombed. He quotes a young man named Paira Gul, deeply embittered that his sisters and their families were killed, as saying, "Most of the dead are children." The village of Charyhari was bombed by an American B-52, and the villagers claimed that thirty people died. One man, Muhibullah, had his daughter killed and son injured by cluster bombs, not to mention six of his cows and the loss through burning of all his rice and wheat, all this representing a catastrophic loss. Bombs began dropping around 7 p.m. near Torai village, killing twenty villagers: "'I saw the body of one of my brothers-in-law being pulled from the debris,' Maroof said. 'The lower part of his body had been blown away. Some of the other bodies were unrecognizable. There were heads missing and arms blown off.'" In the town of Kabul, a bomb hit a "flimsy mud-brick house, blowing apart seven children as they ate breakfast with their father" (18). According to journalist Alexander Cockburn, "the U.S. bombardment of Bala Baluk [in 2009] yielded 140 dead villagers torn apart by high explosives including 93 children." The Pentagon's argument that these villages harbored Taliban, whether true or false, implicitly assumes the right in attacking the enemy to murder a lot of civilians, including children.

Perhaps the most chilling event that Zinn cites occurred in Quetta, Parkistan. A man, awakened by bombs exploding, watches with his daughter as "[civilians] who survived the bombing run, including his niece and a woman holding her five-year-old son, were gunned down by a *slow-moving* [emphasis added] aircraft circling overhead," leaving twenty-five civilians dead. Regarding the civilian casualties, one American official stated, "We don't know. We're not on the ground." Finally, in one village (Kama Ado) that no longer exists, B-52s dropped dozens of bombs, killing 115 men, women and children. The Defense Department insists: "It just didn't happen." This cavalier dismissal looks all too much like the arrogance and contempt of the super-strong towards the super-weak. Even trees are not spared. "Our trees," says Muhammed Tahir, "are our only shelter from the cold and wind. The trees have been bombed. Our waterfall, our only source of water—they bombed it. Where is the humanity?"

By being poorly informed by our leaders about the casualties on the "other" side, Americans are denied a sense of the graphic reality of the experience of Afghan, Iraqi, Yugoslavian victims of Washington's enormous violence. This, of course, is what the American leadership wants. It may, if pressed, insist it wants to protect the public from the concrete horrors of war. Its real motivation, however, is surely to soothe and still public protest about the White House and Pentagon war mode of extreme force, which can be summarized in Colin Powell's incredibly brutal phrase "Shock and Awe." The media in turn helps the state to minimize coverage of military and civilian wounded and dead on the other side. Walter Isaacson, CEO of CNN, for example, issued a memo to his staff to downplay Afghan suffering, or to qualify any data on it.

Further, one is reminded, they did it to us. Moreover, al-Quaida terrorists have shown themselves brutally indifferent to American civilian casualties. Still, these charges clearly do not apply to these Afghan civilian "casualties." Washington, according to Noam Chomsky, has likely used countries like Iraq, Yugoslavia, Afghanistan and Pakistan as testing grounds for its high-tech ordnance. If that sinister tendency continues, accelerated by our munitions industry and Pentagon war zealots, the crucial ethic of humane treatment of enemy civilians and military will go on being misrepresented or ignored.

What will it take to make the average American realize that in modern wars, it is mainly civilians who get blown to bits by bombs, and that the civilian (usually non-White) "foe" obliterated are as human and as vulnerable to pain, terror and grief as she or he is? And what can be done to evolve social institutions that better inform its citizens of, and empower them against, massively evil violence perpetrated by Washington abroad? It is a strong possibility that more 9/11s can be avoided if America truly joined the comity of nations by *not* placing its geopolitical national "Interests" abroad above everything else.

"Where Is the Humanity?: America's Use of Excessive Force Over There" by Donald Gutierrez—*Eldorado Sun*, September 2002; *Albuquerque Journal*, 2002; *Humanist Society of New Mexico*, June 2009; *ABQ Trial Balloon*, September 2009.

6
Review: William Blum
Rogue State: *A Guide to the World's Only Superpower*

> *A survey showed that six times as many South Koreans*
> *feared the United States as feared North Korea.*
> THE ECONOMIST (June 1994)

As the title of William Blum's book *Rogue State: A Guide to the World's Only Superpower* suggests, its formidable and, to some, audacious, thesis is that Blum's rogue state is the United States. The argumentation and evidence generally support this idea, that the nation most dangerous and oppressive to other nations in the past fifty years has been the United States.

A guide book inclines towards a skimpy treatment of ideas, opinions and facts, and that is occasionally a flaw in *Rogue State*. In Chapter 20, for example, Blum presents almost 150 examples of the United States taking extremely unsupported and immoral positions on such resolutions as, "Cessation of all nuclear test explosions." Some of these resolutions could have profited by discussion. He also often fails, despite thirty-one pages of footnotes, to provide sources to substantiate serious charges such as claims that the Immigration and Naturalization Service (INS) and U.S. Border Patrol are grossly mistreating "detained" illegal immigrants (pushing heads into toilets, for example).

Nevertheless, *Rogue State* is invaluable. Ignited by a powerful introduction, Blum's book provides striking data and discussion arguing that the United States is hardly the beacon of democracy, freedom and justice it proffers itself to the world and to itself as being. Blum presents this point forcefully:

> From 1945 to the end of the century, the United States attempted to overthrow more than forty foreign governments, and to crush more than thirty populist-nationalist movements struggling against intolerable regimes. In the process, the U.S. caused the end of life for several million people, and condemned millions more to a life of agony and despair. (2)

Why America did all this soon follows: "1) making the world open and hospitable for globalization, particularly American-based transnational corporations, 2) enhancing the financial statements of defense contractors at home ..., 4) extending political, economic and military hegemony [over the world] to prevent the rise of any regional power that might challenge American supremacy" (13-14).

To elaborate these grave indictments, Blum divides his book into three crucial themes: Washington's ambivalent relationship with terrorists and human rights violators; America's use of weapons of mass destruction (WMD), and "Rogue State" America versus the world. A chapter on assassinations running from 1949 to 1999 lists thirty-five foreign leaders our government either tried to or did assassinate, including Nehru, Sihanouk, de Gaulle, Lumumba, Allende, Che Guevara, Zhou Enlai.

Another chapter dealing with the U.S. Army and CIA training manuals indicates that the conduct of American intelligence services abroad is often savagely criminal. Particularly disturbing in these manuals is the total lack of any moral restraint in what they instruct the military or police of client nations to impose on political dissidents. Techniques range from psychological traumatization to electrocuting victims' genitals.

Blum lists eleven countries in which the CIA taught (and, occasionally, participated in) the torturing of a regime's critics. In Uruguay, an American associated with the U.S. Office of Public Safety named Dan Mitrione would play in an adjoining room tapes which purported to be the screams of a prisoner's family just then undergoing torture. Blum also offers evidence of torture in America such as routine terrorization of Black and Hispanic prisoners by the Chicago police from 1973 to 1986. Methods included, among other things, electric shocks to testicles and suffocation with plastic bags. Chapter 8 argues convincingly, if briefly, that presidents

Ronald Reagan, George W. Bush and Bill Clinton, generals like Colin Powell, Norman Schwarzkopf and William Westmoreland, and civilian statesmen like Henry Kissinger are all war criminals for a variety of specific offenses against civilian populations and nations that never attacked America.

The second section of *Rogue State* deals with weapons of mass destruction employed for decades by the United States both abroad and *at home*. Particularly shocking in this segment are chapters 11 through 13, entitled, respectively, "Bombings," "Depleted Uranium" and "Cluster Bombs," which detail America's use of chemical and biological weapons. Blum acutely observes that bombs are weapons of mass destruction and that depleted uranium Tomahawk Cruise missile warheads certainly qualify as chemical WMDs. His discussion of the millions of American bombs dropped on other nations in the second half of the 20th century from China in 1945-46 to Yugoslavia in 1999 further corroborates the book's title and thesis.

According to the Chinese, the United States dropped quantities of bacteria on North Korea early in 1952, including plague, anthrax and encephalitis, as well as napalm. Agent Orange was widely used in Vietnam during 1968-69. "Tens of thousands of tons of herbicides [were sprayed] over three million acres of South Vietnam (as well as parts of Laos and Cambodia)" (105).

Panama, Cuba, the Bahamas and even Canada (Winnipeg in 1953) were, according to Blum, also intentionally contaminated. Other sites poisoned by the United States include Guam, the Philippines *and the United States*.

The contaminating of the United States might constitute the biggest shock to the average American in view of Washington's endless moralistic hype about foreign anti-American terrorism. Yet, Blum states, "for two decades those two institutions [Department of Defense and the CIA] conducted tests in the open air, exposing millions of Americans to large clouds of possibly dangerous bacteria and chemical particle without informing the potentially affected populations" (113).

Further, the army admitted that between 1949 and 1969, "239 populated areas from coast to coast were blanketed with various organisms" (114). Blum specifies nine sites affected, including the San Francisco Bay area, Chicago and New York City. His sources for these allegations are mainstream American newspapers, professionally researched studies and Senate investigatory committees. If only a tenth of these charges were true, they still would comprise a major instance of felonious hypocrisy on the part of the American government.

The final segment of *Rogue State* includes three particularly significant chapters. Chapter 17 lists 69 global interventions by the U.S. from 1945 to the present. One of the most genocidal was the now well known American-supported Suharto takeover in Indonesia that led to the murder of perhaps over a million political "suspects." Lists of "Communists" were supplied to Suharto's forces by the American Embassy. The roster of criminal intrusions by the American state seems endless—Bolivia, Brazil, Ghana, Iraq (1972-75), Australia (1972-74), Mexico and the Zapatistas. A Washington directive to Uruguayan Intelligence that captured Tupamoros were first to be pressured for information (i.e., tortured) and then killed, further exemplifies America's realpolitik abroad.

The final chapter, "How Does the U.S. Get Away with It?" cites once unfamiliar charges which, more recently, have indeed become well known and of grave concern to civil libertarians. Examples include the CIA and FBI opening citizens' mail; private corporations bugging their employees' offices and restrooms; law enforcement and intelligence agencies harassing activists; passengers on public transport having belongings searched by Drug Enforcement Administration agents; and police cameras being set up with increasing frequency to scrutinize people on public streets, and banks, telephone companies, utility companies, hotels and other businesses supplying various government authorities with requested information about their customers.

Unfortunately, Blum does not summarize his book. Also, he might have said something about the massive social terrorism imposed on their own populations by Stalin and Mao (not to mention, respectively, Eastern Europe and Tibet). Nevertheless, as a catalog of our government's transgressions, *Rogue State* makes a convincing argument that the United States, citadel of global democratic idealism, has for over fifty years been—and remains—the most terrifying military force in the world to many nations. When will the American state's terrorism reach the *average* American? "They," Blum concludes, "only have to wait" (273).

Note: One of the major disappointments concerning the Obama administration has been its failure to hold the Bush administration responsible for its various forms of criminal behavior, including the torture of detainees. "Moving ahead" without addressing the enormous evil committed by the preceding administration gives subsequent administrations a green light to continue such grossly illegal and radically immoral policies in the future.

"Review: William Blum, *Rogue State: A Guide to the World's Only Superpower*" by Donald Gutierrez—*North Coast Xpress*, November 2000; *Common Sense*, November 2000; *Bloomsbury Review*, v.20, Issue 5, November 2000.

7

American Middle Eastern Detainees and You

Americans should realize that the terrible experience of America's Middle East detainees affects their own lives and view of themselves as Americans. After 9/11, hundreds of males were treated by our Justice Department as if already guilty, a crucial violation of the Constitution and due process. Further, they were subjected to physical and extreme psychological roughing-up. According to the detainees, they were slammed against jail walls, deliberately tripped in their ankle chains by guards at the Brooklyn Metropolitan Detention Center, in some instances beaten and kicked, told they were going to die and placed in cells with violent criminals. Further, they had their afternoon prayers intentionally disrupted by guards and their cell lights kept on 24 hours a day. Labeled "Bin Laden Junior" by guards further exemplified these detainees being convicted before being tried.

Aside from this treatment, somewhat reminiscent of Stalin's gulags or the conduct of police in repressive regimes like Mynamar, Egypt, Iran, Syria, China and North Korea, these detainees were picked up suddenly off the street, on their jobs, in their homes and not allowed contact with their families, lawyers—anyone. Their destination or location was not disclosed to anyone, including family. One suspects that the enormous psychic stress and terror of such treatment did not register much, if at all, on the consciousness or conscience of the average American, still under the illusion that America is the land of the free. These "bad guys" were getting what they probably deserved, never mind the Bill of Rights or the fact that they were Americans.

This very American indifference has several causes. First, these detainees are Middle Easterners, Arabs, Muslims, surely a suspect group in our media-drugged minds before and especially after 9/11. Further, they are dark-skinned, which might incite a racist reaction among some lighter skinned individuals. Then, the White House had been pushing the panic button about this type continually, despite the Bush family's intimate financial connections with the Bin Laden family up to September 11, 2001 and President George W. Bush's avowal of respect for Middle Eastern Americans and Islam. Finally, these "foreigners" were convenient scapegoats for the brutish guards at the Brooklyn Metropolitan Detention Center and elsewhere.

Despite the fact that all of the detainees have since been cleared of serious violations or crimes, their "suspect" status beforehand rendered them vulnerable to the gross legal abuse of their person. They were also kept in the dark about when their incarceration would end and their future location or destination determined, what their legal rights were and when their physical and psychological torment by undisciplined, sadistic guards would end. In addition, some remained incarcerated for months *after* being found innocent.

The plight of these detainees, then, was aggravated by being suspect in the United States, despite its being their own country. In law, to be suspect does not mean one is guilty of some crime—that remains to be proven. Yet, as indicated above, some Americans have acted as if being regarded as suspect is tantamount to being guilty. This egregiously inappropriate judgment in its most violent, extreme form can be understood in historical context: In conducting foreign policy in the last half century, the United States government has either directly or indirectly been responsible for the death of enormous numbers of individuals in other countries regarded as "suspects"—not to mention innumerable people who were not even "suspect"—Indonesians, Congolese, Central and South Americans, Vietnamese, Cambodians, among many others. In one instance, people riding in a car in another country—a sovereign state—had their car bombed and all of its occupants killed by an American war plane. The car had been occupied by terrorist "suspects"—and nonsuspects.

Most alarming here is the extreme vulnerability of terms like "suspect" and "terrorist" to definition by the type of American political leadership prone to use these terms to win the nation's support for waging war abroad, and for waging it against American citizens. One such victimized American was John Walker Lindh who joined the Taliban before 9/11 to fight against the Northern Alliance, not against the United States. But victimization could apply as well to *any* American critical of Washington or engaged in activism to oppose and defeat the government's onslaught on the poor, the unemployed, the elderly, the environment.

The American philosopher Sidney Hook clearly differentiated dissent from treason in *Heresy, Yes, Conspiracy, No*, but the Bush Administration, abetted by the right wing media, had been transforming dissent by Americans into treason. "Traitor" in this process becomes a synonym for "terrorist." If one doesn't think this process can be effective and intimidating, he or she should recall the paralyzing impact of Attorney General John Ashcroft upon Congress when, late in 2001, he stated in an uncontested speech to that body that anyone critical of the president's policies towards designated terrorists would be aiding terrorists.

In the late 1940s and the 1950s, anyone "too" liberal could be labeled a Communist and have his or her job, family, reputation, freedom and health threatened. More recently, the same pressures have been applied to people designated "terrorists" or suspected of being such by criteria that are themselves dangerously broad, flexible and inclusive. Thus, even someone supporting Amnesty International or the Sierra Club—not to mention Kathy Kelly's organization Voices For Creative Non-Violence—could conceivably be labeled as supporting terrorist organizations and therefore a terrorist. And why not? Amnesty has aided dissenters detained and often tortured by Washington-backed repressive regimes that conveniently stigmatize dissenters as terrorists. And, as far as former President Bush and his friends in the extractive and energy industries were concerned, any environmentalist group or critic of those industries threatening their profits were surely terrorists.

The fact that America's energy corporations are undermining the nation's health and wealth with their depredations of the earth should of course mark *them* as terrorists. Such a blatant truth is, however, ignored by the media. This ravaging of American's natural resources—air, water, land—should convey the obvious: that the most deadly terrorists around have been the White House and its corporation intimates. Abroad, this state terrorism exhibits itself in an imperial United States invading much weaker, unthreatening nations and dropping quantities and types of bombs (such as cluster bombs) declared illegal by various conventions of war conduct.

So, who is the worst terrorist? That could be debated one way or another. What is less controversial is the domestic terrorism inflicted by former President Bush's "Military Order" established on November 13, 2001. According to Barbara Olshansky, assistant legal director at the Center for Constitutional Rights, "This new system radically abandons the core constitutional guarantees at the heart of American democracy: the right to an independent judiciary, trial by jury, public proceedings, due process and appeals to higher courts....all of these safeguards against injustice are gone" (*Secret Trials and Executions: Military Tribunals and the Threat to Democracy*, 7-8). Under the "Military Order," Olshansky observes, Bush and Ashcroft became "rule-maker, investigator, accuser, prosecutor, judge and jury, sentencing court, reviewing court, and executioner [without any] provision for accountability to any other branch of government or to the people" (59-60).

Some might say that this extreme power by the executive branch of government only applies to Taliban prisoners of war, that American citizens have nothing to worry about. That outlook is questionable. The Lawyers Committee for Legal Rights, a New York based professional organization, observed, "The government can hold United States citizens as enemy combatants during war time without the constitutional protections guaranteed to Americans in criminal prosecutions, according to a fourth United States Circuit Court of Appeals" (LCLR website, Media Room, 1). This ruling applied to an American named Yasser Hamdi captured in Afghanistan in 2001. Holding Hamdi indefinitely suggested to the LCLR that this treatment could also be applied to other Americans. Further, the revelations that surfaced about a possible Patriot Act II, not long after the first Patriot Act became law, were grave. In the Patriot Act II proposal, citizen rights protected by the Constitution would be eliminated in the case of *alleged* supporters of *alleged* terrorist organizations.

Would American political and legal authorities treat American citizens with such authoritarian ruthlessness? They well might. American citizens who spoke up against World War I were fired from their jobs, beaten up and even tortured by patriot vigilante mobs. The Socialist labor leader Eugene V. Debs was imprisoned for years. In the 1950s, Senator Joe McCarthy and the House Un-American Activities Committee caused widespread terror by accusing American progressives of being Communists. During the 1970s, anti-Vietnam War demonstrators at the University of California, Berkeley were tear gassed from helicopters by then Governor Ronald Reagan's orders, and concentration camps near Berkeley were being planned for these "rioters." Perhaps most egregious, during World War II, Japanese Americans were carted off to camps in the desert, their property confiscated by the government.

Totalitarian government sometimes proceeds step by step in consolidating full power and abolishing fundamental civil rights. One recalls the famous 1946 statement by Pastor Martin Niemoller, which begins, "First they came for the socialists and I did not speak out because I was not a socialist." Then they come for trade unionists and then for Jews, he goes on, and "I did not speak out because I was not a Jew. And then they came for me and there was no one left to speak for me." The treatment of the Taliban fighters as "Enemy Combatants" instead of as prisoners of war, of innocent Middle Eastern aliens and Middle Eastern American citizens, and, more recently, of progressive activist Americans is following this pattern.

Even if the fate of innocent resident aliens means little personally to the average American—and that of Taliban imprisoned in Guantanamo, Cuba, even less so—linking the dots should make us realize that anyone's civil liberties being potentially dissoluble could thus very possibly include ours. Not only should we American citizens be outraged by the brutal, illegal treatment being accorded Middle Eastern American citizens and non-citizens in jails like the Brooklyn Metropolitan Detention Center, we should also realize that in a society flinging more than 700 Americans a month into prison for social offenses, "detaining" Americans with names like Mary Smith and Bob Jones for political dissidence could be increasingly possible.[1] Washington's paranoia about terrorism roots itself deeper and deeper in the psyche of America.

Debs's great cry of empathy quoted from Upton Sinclair's *The Cry for Justice* rings as true today as ever: "While there is a lower class I am in it, while there is a criminal element, I am of it; while there is a soul in prison, I am not free."

---

1. The latest egregious step towards a fascist police-state America has emerged in the form of the NDAA (National Defense Authorization Act). Signed by President Obama (with reservations that don't seem to amount to much and that can be discounted by future presidents), the Senators Levin and McCain sponsored law denies *all* Americans of due process and habeus corpus and thus of the right to defend themselves in a civil court. Instead, it imposes indefinite rendition on anyone that the President deems either a terrorist or a person supporting terrorism. Considering the enormous flexibility of the terms "terrorism" and "supporting

terrorism," virtually anyone openly critical of the government can be charged as a terrorist or terrorist supporter and swept off any time to Guantanamo, Bagram or those terrifying black sites in unknown parts of the world run by U.S. Special-Forces types.

"American Middle Eastern Detainees and You" by Donald Gutierrez—*Justice Xpress*, Winter 2003.

8

The Extraordinary Cruelty of Extraordinary Rendition

*For some time now I have thought it possible to believe
that America was going insane. In her own way.*
Martin Amis, *London Fields*

Rendition comes from the verb "render" that means to deliver, hand over, provide. The word describes a process or action which can be pleasant or unpleasant depending on what is being delivered. A pizza or loan car can be "rendered." So can justice—or injustice.

Rendition as defined and implemented by the administration of George W. Bush was an example of language sugarcoating an action that is savagely unjust and terrifying.[1] The adjective "extraordinary" in the phrase "extraordinary rendition" contains a certain accuracy though, for what the White House's secretive and menacing agents were doing to terrorist "suspects" like the Canadian-Syrian Maher Arar certainly was extraordinary—extraordinarily illegal, terrifying and savagely unjust. These "suspects," picked up off streets, at airports, at their homes, were physically overwhelmed and drugged by their hooded captors. They were then sedated by a suppository forced up their rectum and their clothes cut off their body with scissors, handcuffed and their mouth covered with duct tape. These rendered "detainees" were hustled with violent and terrifyingly covert dispatch to the extreme punishment of torture in a foreign country without having been proven guilty. They didn't even know what their alleged or possible offense was, exactly who was arresting—or kidnaping—them, and, worse, where they were being taken. Nor did their families and friends know. Thus, they are being deprived of basic legal and human rights supported by all advanced nations—including the United States. These are rights affirmed by the 1948 Universal Declaration of Human Rights which, among other things, were designed to *universally* prevent such invasive and illegal actions as improper detention, abuse and even torture being used against anyone.

Who can blame Arar for weeping when, after being forced onto the white Gulf Stream jet, used mainly for transporting rendered suspects, he overheard that he was being flown to Syria. He knew—as George W. Bush and Defense Secretary Donald Rumsfeld certainly knew—that Syria was a synonym for torture. Torture there would take the forms of continual beatings with thick electrical cables; blows on the soles of the feet; hours-long suspension from a post by one's wrists with arms pulled behind one's back; near drownings; electrical shocks to the ears and genitals; threats of dog attack; and, worst of all, weeks, even many months in solitary confinement, in dark, underground cellars or vaults, not knowing how long one would be buried there, when the next round of torture would begin, what it would include and whether the torment would thrust one over the edge into insanity or even death. And at the center of all this would be the searing question "Why? Why is this happening? What have I done? Will somebody or some authority get me out of this unending horror?" But the horror surely intensifies as one realizes that some authority flung one *into* this hell.

Arar was relatively fortunate, being released in a year without charges. Without charges! In other words, he was innocent. Yet, he had been treated illegally and with incredible brutality for many months, and not only by the Syrian government but by the American government. What he was "guilty" of was *knowing* a suspected terrorist. When picked up by American officials, he was questioned in the United States for thirteen days. Even after that length—and, surely, intensity—of questioning, the American authorities were not satisfied about his innocence. They decided to send him to Syria, being either ignorant or crass enough to think that torture wrings the truth from the guilty. (The truth is that torture usually makes even the innocent confess to anything the tormenters want to hear just to stop the horrific pain.)

United States officials have claimed that they have sent terrorist suspects to countries like Egypt, Morocco and Syria with the understanding that torture would not be used. But if that were the case, why did they bother to send them to these nations known to practice torture? The grim truth comes from an American intelligence agent quoted in the *Washington Post*,

(December 26, 2002): "We don't kick the shit out of them [terrorist suspects]. We send them to other countries so they can kick the shit out of them." Another *Washington Post* report indicates that "a number of officials essentially admitted that, despite assurances, suspects are sent to places [where the officials know] they'll be treated harshly." And one FBI agent states in Jane Mayer's *New Yorker* essay of February 14, 2005 "Outsourcing Torture" (to which this essay is indebted) that the CIA, rather than regretting the extreme abuse administered by Egypt and other nations, "liked rendition from the start. They loved that these guys would just disappear off the books."

It seems clear then that the CIA, the Pentagon and the special forces not only knew that these suspects were going to be tortured but fully approved it. Indeed, they would likely have tortured these suspects themselves here in the United States if they could get away with it. From authoritative information now emerging in such media as the radio and television program *Democracy Now*, it appears that the CIA and Special Forces *are* abusing and torturing suspects abroad in secret cells around the world.

Former Secretary of Defense Rumsfeld even allowed suspects "of interest" to be kept off lists of detainees ordinarily accessible to investigative organizations like the International Red Cross. This means these suspects were totally removed from the illumined world of legal propriety, control and justice. Thus, they were completely at the mercy of institutional jailers, sadists and tormenters dedicated to the Bush administration's fiat that it could do anything it wanted to other people and nations, an attitude usually associated with dictators, tyrants and serial killers. (More recent information reveals that both Rumsfeld and former Vice President Dick Cheney administered and closely followed the torturous interrogation of "high interest" detainees like Ibn al-Sheikh al-Libi (al-Libi had headed an al-Qaeda training camp). And former president George W. Bush admitted in his best-seller book *Decision Points* to approving the water-boarding of al-Libi.

Indeed, one of the crucial evils that resulted from the Bush administration's megalomaniacal attitude was just such a sinister and pernicious activity as rendition. This practice led to the torture and even murder of detainees by the American military in sites like Abu Ghraib in Iraq, Bagram Air Base in Afghanistan and Camp Justice in Diego Garcia Island. As a consequence of the former president's savage policy towards

Arab detainees, many innocent people were picked up as terrorist suspects and horribly treated. Arar's ordeal of ten months, for example, occurred in an underground cell that was three feet wide and seven feet high, and had no light—conditions that might have driven most people insane.

Often these individuals were let go without a charge after months, even years, of abuse and torture, not even offered an apology—let alone compensation—for extreme damages. Sometimes they were just dumped on a rural road in a country adjacent to their own. None have had legal protection, due process, habeas corpus or communication with their terrified family and friends during their detention. Extraordinary rendition is a clear violation of the United Nations Convention Against Torture and Other Cruel, Degrading and Inhuman Treatment, an international pact to which the United States is formally committed.

Prominent Americans like Harvard law Professor Alan Dershowitz and former Attorney General Alberto Gonzalez have attempted to make a case for torture. They claim torture can be justified by certain exigent circumstances, particularly a looming terrorist attack that might be averted through intelligence "extracted" in the nick of time from a high-profile terrorist suspect. What if Mohamed Atta, the mastermind of the 9/11 attack on the World Trade Center, had been caught before 9/11? Would it have been all right for him to have been "rendered"?

An equally appropriate question, though, is not only whether crisis-averting torture would have been acceptable morally but also whether it would have been effective as a way of achieving valid intelligence. The crucial case of al-Libi suggests the opposite. Rendered by the CIA to Egypt (i.e., to beatings with thick metal rods, electrocuted genitals, and other tortures), al-Libi supplied bad information about the use of chemical weapons in Iraq. This coerced disinformation, conveyed to the United States by the helpful Egyptians of the former Mubarak dictatorship, was exploited by Secretary of State Colin Powell to justify the invasion of Iraq. How likely is it that either the Army Special Forces in, say, Jordan or Uzbekistan or Indonesia or Bagram Air Base or the Egyptians or Syrians would have squeezed, punched, kicked or near-drowned the truth out of an Islamic extremist like Atta? It seems probable that Atta would have told his tormenters anything they wanted to hear as long as it didn't reveal the real 9/11 plans.

However willing the United States government is to, as Cheney once memorably put it, "work through, sort of, the dark side," one can only go so far towards securing truth through brutalizing and dehumanizing captive individuals, especially fanatics. And as should be obvious, innocent suspects will likely be deeply embittered by torture if not pushed into extreme retaliatory feelings especially towards the United States. Further, according to Mayer and unembedded journalists like the British Robert Fisk, a very high percentage of terrorist suspects have proven to be innocent. Furthermore, many others who indeed might be engaged Islamic foes of the West really are said to know so little about terrorists threats as to be persons of virtually no "interest." Thus, the American intelligence community and their White House commander-in-chief could be doing our country serious harm throughout the world by their contemptuous violation and dismissing of the basic legal and human rights that all people deserve.

One of the major justifications of rendition the Bush administration resorted to was that terrorists recognize no difference between military and civilian targets. Thus, it argued, new rules of engagement are essential. President Bush always talked about protecting the American people every time he wanted to implement some new repression of Americans such as renewing the Patriot Act and enlarging its provisions or arbitrarily dismissing international consensus or treaties.

It is certainly true that Islamic extremists deliberately make no distinction between civilian and military targets. Yet it is savagely ironic and dishonest for the American government to trumpet that fact to justify rendition in view of its own far more extensive annihilation—directly, deliberately and by proxy—of civilian populations in the Vietnam War, the counterinsurgency wars in Central America in the 1980s, and the more recent wars in Iraq and Afghanistan.

A consequence of this cruelly nondiscriminative practice of the Pentagon annihilating innocent Iraqis and of the rationale the White House pursues of depriving what they deem terrorist suspects of their basic civil rights could be some dangerous vulnerability for American citizens. Rendition could more and more be the fate of Americans abroad if the United States continues to flout both international principles of justice—to which it has formally agreed—and its own tradition of democratic ideals. Powerful empires in the past have overreached themselves through imperialist expansion and put their own citizens at risk of foreign captivity and, often, into serious jeopardy. This is vividly illustrated in Linda Colley's *Captives: Britain, Empire and the World, 1600-1850*.

Barbara Olshansky of the New York Center for Constitutional Rights makes the point about Bush's Military Order (which in November 2001 set up military tribunals to try non-citizen terrorist suspects) that it "would be creating a system of secret proceedings in which the charges, the evidence, the verdicts and the punishments would never have to be revealed to the public" (*Secret Trials and Executions: Military Tribunals and the Threat to Democracy*). Olshanksy continues, "We will have advertised and exported to the world a model that gives license to the most repressive regimes to implement actions that will violate the human and civil rights of their citizens." An Associated Press release in July 2003 mentioned by Mayer indicated that the American authorities at the Guantanamo Naval Base were not only constructing trial facilities but an execution chamber as well. (A very large percentage of the prisoners at the base are now generally regarded as being innocent.)

The American concentration camp at Guantanamo that Olshansky is describing has a certain official aura about it. The public knows that detainees are put there even if it has no official knowledge of the reports by investigators of serious abuses at the base. Wretched as the conditions at Guantanamo are for detainees, those for victims of extraordinary rendition are worse in being even more secretive and sinister.

Rendition is based on a particularly sinister and pernicious form of secrecy. As the American ethicist Sisela Bok observes, "While all secrecy can thwart reasoning, invite abuse and spread, military secrecy therefore carries special risks. The need for the security it offers seems so self-evident, and the forces that deflect criticism and efforts to limit it are so strong, that what it conceals and the methods used to ensure it are often taken for granted; yet the combination of these methods with the power that military secrecy now shields can transform individuals and institutions in ways that threaten society more than all other forms of secrecy" (*Secrets: On the Ethics of Concealment and Revelation*).

What is most alarming is that this radical threat emanated ultimately from our civilian heads of state. Thus, in the process of rendering—and rending—mostly innocent individuals, the Bush government was also tearing apart America's tradition of legal democracy. The day might be not far off when solid American citizens could be jarred by a loud knock on their door, or get picked up off the street by masked government agents and whisked off to some unidentified location. A paranoid concern? Fascism and authoritarianism can develop in practically any society over a period of years, even months, given the misinforming of modern mass society populations induced by governments and the pervasive media. The enlarging habit by some sectors of our government to cast dissent as disloyalty if not treason lends some credence to this scenario as does the intensifying concentration of power in increasingly unregulated American political, business and military institutions.

It is also alarming that the average American doesn't appear to respond much to the profound moral darkness of extraordinary rendition. He or she is not involved, too busy these days trying to make ends meet in America's melt-down economy or obsessed by sports or sensational celebrity trials. There is little empathy for Muslims and Middle Easterners who seem too foreign, too dissimilar to American standards of acceptable ethnicity. Consequently, they aren't as human as we are.[2]

Americans need to understand when jolted by a gross violation of their rights that saying, "This is AMERICA!" does not necessarily possess the magical force of freedom and respect for the individual that they have been conditioned into assuming. It is indeed AMERICA where Blacks, Hispanics, Asians and even Whites have been lynched, Native Americans swindled and massacred by the government, Japanese American citizens put in concentration camps and workers in mines and mills treated not significantly better than workers under Stalin or Mao. Many dissident American citizens were threatened or jailed during America's numerous wars; they were certainly beaten, sometimes savagely, by patriotic mobs during World War I.

Societies harbor varying degrees of flexibility, resourcefulness and regenerative libertarianism as well as subtle and brutal repressiveness and abuse of concentrated institutional power. Extraordinary rendition is a very serious symptom of a society autocratic and malignant at the top. Those Americans who think this governmental evil concerns only despised foreigners—"suspects"—are at best naive; they are also more vulnerable than they realize to their own freedom and liberty being rendered and rended.

---

1. *The New York Times* assumed that the Obama administration would continue extraordinary rendition but would closely monitor the treatment given the detainee by the foreign nation chosen by Washington for rendition (August 4, 2009). *The Huffington Post* claims that extraordinary rendition is continued by the Obama White House "but rarely, and only if U.S. officials are confident the prisoners will not be tortured" (January 5, 2011). This position on the matter merely repeats the unconvincing rationalization of the Bush administration that detainees would only

be sent to foreign interrogation sites that did not torture detainees. This outlook, however, raises again the obvious question of why they are sent to such places at all. Among other sources and news releases, OMB Watch states that the practice of rendition is being sustained by the Obama Administration.

2. As of December 2011, Maher Arar had not received an apology from Washington for his rendition; he also remained on America's No-Fly List. Canada, on the other hand, offered Arar a formal apology and a sizable sum of money, although taking an unconscionable amount of time to do either.

"The Extraordinary Cruelty of Extraordinary Rendition" by Donald Gutierrez—*Sun Monthly*, December 2005; *Common Sense*, December 2005; *The Humanist*, January-February 2006.

9
Review: Alfred W. McCoy, *A Question of Torture:*
CIA Interrogation from the Cold War to the War on Terror

"The United States does not torture." "Torture is against America's democratic principles." "Abu Ghraib was caused by a few bad apples." *A Question of Torture: CIA Interrogation from the Cold War to the War on Terrorism* by Alfred W. McCoy gives the lie to such Bush administration hypocritical platitudes. *Question* concerns the history of the development of psychological torture by the CIA from the 1950s to Abu Ghraib in Iraq in the early 2000s. It attempts to establish several key points: that the agency investigated, experimented with and applied methods of psychological torture for decades; that indispensable aspects of this enterprise were performed with the assistance of psychologists, psychiatrists, universities and hospitals; and that it led to the widespread practice of torture around the world. Earlier instances occurred in Latin America and Southeast Asia, later in Vietnam, then Central America, and, more recently, at Abu Ghraib and elsewhere.

Central to Professor McCoy's thesis is that psychological torture is indeed not only a reality, but, according to victims, is far more harrowing than physical torture. Furthermore, the CIA has spent decades and many millions of taxpayers' dollars refining its techniques of psychological torture, which is described, with implicit irony, as "no-touch torture" and "self-inflicted pain."

Early in *Question* McCoy asserts that his account of CIA research into and use of psychological torture hardly depicts a marginal undertaking or responsibility:

> [A] search for the roots of Abu Ghraib in the development and
> propagation of a distinctive American form of torture will
> implicate almost all of our society—the brilliant scholars who
> did the psychological research, the great universities who
> housed them, the august legislators who voted funds, and the
> good Americans who by their silence allow[ed] the process to
> continue. (6)

This quotation reveals that *Question* is not a catalog of tortures. Rather, it elaborates on the development and application of devastatingly cruel modes of torture that particularly indict the Bush administration.

The CIA was formed in 1947 under President Harry S. Truman's National Security Act. Being attached to the executive branch gave the CIA cover from Congressional oversight. This was the beginning of a covert character for CIA conduct that allowed the agency to hide enormous unethical, criminal conduct for decades. Examples include its extremely secretive MKUltra program involving research into mind control, its work within the deceptively innocuous contours of the USAID and Office of Public Safety programs in South America, the mass-murdering Phoenix program in Vietnam and the proxy genocide campaigns in Central America in the 1980s.

The well-financed MKUltra operation involved the research of eminent psychologists and psychiatrists at major universities from 1953 to 1963. The CIA paid out "$25 million for human experiments by one hundred and eighty five non-governmental researchers at eighty institutions" (25), these funds often conveyed through private foundations. This potentially unholy alliance between the CIA and behavioral science academics seemed especially ominous in view of results of the Milgram experiments at Yale. By revealing the willingness of average people to electrocute a subject on command, these experiments exhibited to the CIA how willing policemen in Third World countries could be to torturing civilian dissidents.

Academic research on the psychological effects of isolation fascinated the CIA, revealing a formidable way of devastating prisoners. McGill University psychologists found that just four hours of isolation under special conditions of sensory deprivation could seriously disorient a subject, even leading to psychosis. Thus, "no-touch" changes of a subject's environment, involving heat, sound, sight and touch, could result in shocking dehumanization.

The CIA's MKUltra program was published in 1963 in its *Kubark Counterintelligence Interrogation* handbook. This handbook was used to transmit the agency's questioning and training programs in Third World nations for the next forty years. *Kubark*, amplifying the power of psychological torture, observes that, unlike pain exerted from the outside, self-inflicted pain appears to sap resistance, as does the threat of imposing pain.

After exhibiting psychological torture in the "laboratory," McCoy depicts its application in the field, indicating twenty-four of forty-nine countries utilized in the torture technique made possible by Kubark. Polygraph and electroshock machines were transported to public safety offices in nations like Brazil and Uruguay. In the Provincial Interrogation Centers in Vietnam, each directed by CIA personnel, physical and psychological torture was applied to countless Viet Cong suspects. This culminated in the Phoenix program's massive extra-judicial executions. By 1972, almost 26,000 Viet Cong suspects had been killed in a "pump and dump" practice that would pose legal problems for practitioners of this murderous approach in the Middle East decades later.

Washington's resistance to what it claimed was the spread of communism in Central America initiated a Project X. This secret program transferred counterinsurgency torture methods learned in Vietnam to Latin American nations from the 1960s to the 1990s, sending torture manuals and army trainers south. Congress cut funds for front institutions like the OPS (Office of Public Safety), but did nothing to halt the agency's dissemination of psychological torture, which by this time had turned its torture training over to the army's Military Adviser Program.

Two other major regions of CIA plotting were Iran and the Philippines. Up to one-half million Iranians were beaten or psychologically tortured by the Shah's secret police. This led to a result that McCoy links as well to President Ferdinand Marcos's dictatorship in the Philippines: the rise of an opposition that would overwhelm the ruling regime. An estimated 35,000 Filipinos were tortured, possibly, according to McCoy, with CIA training.

Materials instructing Latin American police and military officers in psychological torture were distributed from 1966 to 1996. Available knowledge about actual techniques used then and more recently in Guantanamo, Iraq and elsewhere were compiled in the CIA's 1983 *Human Resources Exploitation Training Manual* used in Honduras. Among listed

CIA techniques are the persistent manipulation of time and the disruption of sleep schedules. A comparison of the *Kubark* and Honduras manuals reveals almost identical language in regard to "a disorienting arrest, isolation, manipulation of time, threats of physical pain or drug injection" (91).

These "no-touch" methods seem rather general and abstract until one observes them applied and perceives their impact on the sanity of the subjects. Two examples (of many) will suffice: South or Central American civilian dissidents made to stand for many hours without permission to urinate or sleep; or Middle Eastern detainees of low as well as "high interest" beaten and kicked savagely every time they collapsed from forced standing. Despite psychological stress being primary, physical coercion, according to the *Manual*, remains in force.

Although Congress attempted to inquire into CIA torture programs, both the Reagan and Bush II administrations found ways around such investigations. The Reagan White House, for example, identified only physical torture as torture. Media exposure in 1997 of CIA torture training through its one-thousand-page Honduran *Handbook* elicited no citizen or civic responses nor calls from the media for investigation. That and Congress's silence suggest a shocking motif of acquiescence supporting the pernicious phenomenon of impunity for state torturers.

According to McCoy, the Bush administration's secret foreign policy was torture. A few days after 9/11, Bush enlarged the CIA's capacity for dealing with terrorists, including sending them to nations notorious for practicing torture. The White House buttressed this decision through various legal maneuvers carried out by "house" lawyers like John Yoo and Attorney General Alberto Gonzales. This gave free rein to Defense Secretary Donald Rumsfeld to develop Special Access Programs that gave elite troops like Delta Force prior permission for kidnapping, assassination and torture as well as to develop secret CIA prisons globally. According to one source, up to three thousand terrorist suspects were being incarcerated in CIA locations around the world. (Special Forces have continued this illegal practice in Pakistan under the Obama Administration, according to Jeremy Scahill in a December 2010 interview on *Democracy Now.*)

However, McCoy argues that Rumsfeld's CIA plan was extremely ill-advised. Unlike the FBI, the CIA "had little legal training and less experience in taking custody of suspects with procedures that would allow their later prosecution" (119). McCoy stresses repeatedly that the FBI's traditional practice of humane interrogation was far more successful in eliciting intelligence than the CIA's terrorizing interrogations.

The Justice Department's inhumanely narrow definition of torture ("pain must be equivalent in intensity to the pain accompanying serious physical injury, such as organ failure, impairment of bodily function or even death") exempted the CIA's "sensory deprivation" techniques. It thereby increased the torture that could be applied to terrorist suspects and endangered the criminal liability of military personnel from top to (especially) bottom. This definition shielded the CIA's "sensory deprivation" techniques from being considered torture. Although this position violated the *Army Field Manual* and the UCMJ (Uniform Code of Military Justice), to White House lawyers this complication carried less weight than the supposed right of the president to do what he wished in time of war.

The Justice Department's definition of torture resulted in 14,000 Iraqi detainees being very harshly treated, occasionally tortured, and 1,100 "high value" suspects systematically tortured at the Guantanamo base in Cuba and the Bagram air base in Afghanistan, plus 36 tortured for years "and twenty-six detainees murdered under questioning, at least four of them by by the CIA" (124-25). Many of the techniques employed at Guantanamo, for example, had a pronounced CIA stamp in combining sensory dislocation with self-inflicted pain. The latter included extremely painful stress positions, long-term isolation (thirty days), hooding, and the use of wet towels and dripping water to approximate drowning. General Geoffrey Miller, through Rumsfeld's urging, added more methods of psychological torture, including naked isolation in dark cells in excess of thirty days.

A colossal miscarriage of justice behind all this brutal increase of psychological and physical torture emerged when it became clear that, according to military intelligence from allied nations, 70 to 90 percent of Iraqi detainees had been arrested by mistake. What comes across in this massive injustice is the culpability of a chain of command from the White House lawyers to Rumsfeld to senior military officers like Generals Geoffrey D. Miller and Ricardo Sanchez to the ordinary soldiers who followed their orders. Who takes the blame if all this torture came to be proven illegal leads McCoy to the crucial issue of impunity.

The events of 9/11 provided the Bush administration with a powerful rationalization for justifying "depth questioning," amplified by the concept of a unitary executive who could do anything necessary to protect the country. One tactic employed by the White House and Rumsfeld to continue torturing detainees was arguing that psychological methods of interrogation were not torture. Another Defense Department mode of justifying torture (while claiming America does not torture) is to insist that detainees are really "bad guys," and thus don't deserve legal rights.

Alberto Gonzales, escalated from White House counsel to attorney general, provided Bush with another bulwark from liability, as Gonzales was able to use his office to temporarily block congressional and independent inquiries into detainee abuse. As for holding senior military officials responsible, all were exempted except, ironically, General Janis Karpinski who was kept ignorant of "Gitmoizing" Abu Ghraib. (Karpinski was demoted to the rank of Colonel.)

While the White House has pinned the blame for detention "abuses" on the CIA, part of the academic community has supported torture in terms of the "ticking bomb" argument. Harvard professor Alan Dershowitz's scenario has a key terrorist being captured with knowledge of a WMD (weapon of mass destruction) ready to go off, imperiling many thousands. McCoy claims that his scenario is unrealistic. How likely, he asks, is it that such a crucial terrorist would allow himself to be caught and at that climactic moment?

If we agree to torture one supposedly crucial suspect, McCoy continues, why not torture hundreds of thousands who might be knowledgeable about a "ticking bomb"? (This path led, for example, to the extra-judicial murder of over 20,000 through the CIA's Phoenix program during the Vietnam War.) McCoy argues, further, that torture is not effective against terrorism, citing the very high number of innocent detainees from whom meager intelligence was coerced at Guantanamo. Moreover, the torture at Guantanamo and Abu Ghraib did the United States enormous damage internationally.

The racism implicit in the CIA's torture programs is one significant area *Question* doesn't address. The majority of the victims of CIA and American military torture have been non-White, Third World peoples. Judging by the history of racism and genocide in America, our government's treating Asians, Middle Easterners and Hispanics as less than human apparently comes naturally. Nevertheless, *Question* is a richly documented and absorbing study of the pernicious "black cell" dimension of American government. It makes us realize that our country, in radically dehumanizing other (and mostly innocent) human beings through extreme and prolonged psychic and thus physical torment, is committing a diabolical crime against humanity in our name.

Torture is a radical invasion of the privacy and unending vulnerability of human beings. Ultimately, CIA torture is terrorism, state terrorism. The United States bombing Iraq in 2003 exemplified state terrorism. And having a prime intelligence service of the White House like the CIA directly and indirectly kidnapping, imprisoning, torturing, or even murdering hundreds of thousands of suspects over decades is an act of institutional terrorism far more pervasive and massive than the terrorism of guerrilla terrorist cells. McCoy has performed a noble service in convincingly informing us of this grave corruption in our government and society.

"Review: Alfred W. McCoy, *A Question of Torture: CIA Interrogation from the Cold War to the War on Terror*" by Donald Gutierrez—*Common Sense*, December 2006; *Progressive Populist*, March 2007.

10
Diliwar's Thigh: Deep Inside the Dark Side

In the documentary film, *Taxi to the Dark Side*, the audience beholds an American soldier weighing well over 200 pounds time after time savagely kneeing the thigh of a small adult Afghan male named Dilawar. The kneeing assault had occurred off and on for five days. Dilawar, his arms strung to an overhead beam by handcuffs, was totally vulnerable. He died the next day. Officially listed as a homicide, his death was ascribed to a blood clot in his brain that apparently resulted from the continuous battering of his femoral artery.

Dilawar's fate embodied extreme punishment *preceding* judgment, an act all too typical in the justice accorded Arab and Muslim terrorist suspects. According to Colonel Lawrence Wilkerson, (who appears in *Taxi*), of 98 deaths in detention, 25 were homicides. As it turned out, Dilawar was later declared innocent of the charge that he had been involved in a rocket attack on an American air base. But it was too late—he had been gradually beaten *towards* death over a period of five days. The several low-level soldiers immediately involved in Diliwar's brutalization either received dishonorable discharges, prison sentences or other punishments.

What was obvious in the film is that these American soldiers were themselves low level functionaries of a policy and climate of extreme mistreatment of detainees going up the ranks to, and emanating from, generals and ultimately from Secretary of Defense Rumsfeld and Vice President Cheney and backed by the Justice Department's Office of Legal Counsel. Virtually all of these higher-ups, generals like Geoffrey D. Miller (the "Gitmoizer" of Abu Ghraib) and Ricardo S. Sanchez, got off scot-free.

So of course did Donald Rumsfeld, Dick Cheney and George W. Bush.

Rumsfeld was finally removed from office, but not for imposing a regime of detainee torture. As for Cheney, he of course remained in office, doing his utmost to prevent any light from illuminating what his and Rumsfeld's directions had been perpetrating inside the darkness. Dilawar's thighs were so pulverized by the repeated heavy knee slams that, according to a medical evaluator, had Dilawar lived, amputation of both legs would have been necessary.

But what kind of treatment should a detainee suspect of "high interest" receive? A case in point was Ibn al-Sheik al-Libi. As one FBI agent put it (according to McCoy's *A Question of Torture*; see review, Ch. 9), they didn't beat the truth out of him; they beat out of him what they wanted to hear. The crucial consideration that the false information tortured out of al-Libi was used by Secretary of State Colin Powell to formally justify starting the 2003 Iraq War harbored a felonious dishonesty that should have exposed not only Powell but other top Bush administrators to impeachment if not legal indictment.

Beneath the vast horror of the war against Iraq and the radical evil of the Bush administration in starting it resides the dreadful image of a powerful American military knee slamming into a man's totally vulnerable thigh. The film narrates screams that this and other forms of beating wrenched from Dilawar and the sadistic, crazed fury of the military guards who continued to beat Dilawar to silence his screams. I focus on Dilawar because epitomizing his atrocious end might aid in particularizing and dramatizing the plight of thousands like him in American detention globally. There are many thousands of Middle and Far East people in American military incarceration, and, according to reliable authorities, most of them are innocent. Nevertheless, those caught adjacent to the violent death of American soldiers, even if innocent, are likely to become convenient targets either of savage American military vindictiveness and retaliation or of local warlords selling captive "terrorists" to American authorities. And the result of such vindictiveness and greed, as a Marine Sergeant A. at Forwarding Base Mercury said in 2005, is that "... half of these guys get released because they didn't do nothing. But if he's a good guy, now he's a bad guy because of the way we treated him" (*New York Review of Books*, Nov. 3, 2005). According to this whistle blower Sergeant, such treatment resulted in detainees' broken bones from baseball bats wielded by FBM Marines. The unconscious implication of this attitude of course is that turning "good guys" into "bad guys" through extreme abuse turns the abusers into "bad guys" and the civilian authorities at the top into super "bad guys."

Meanwhile, many innocent Iraqis, Afghans and others languish in Abu Ghraib, Bagram, Guantanamo, Diego-Garcia's "Camp Justice" and elsewhere in undisclosed locations in the hands of black-masked Elite Forces and contract agents. All too many of the thousands of detainees, either being knee-whacked, chained naked and handcuffed for hours to floors or window-bars above their head or caged like animals, are also being psychologically tortured. Indeed, detainees claim that psychological torture is worse than physical torture. According to the lawyer Clive Stafford Smith cited in Jane Mayer's *New Yorker* article "The Black Sites" (April 30, 2007), his detainee-client, Binyam Mohamed, said that speakers "blared music into his cell while he was handcuffed," which included "ear-splitting rap anthems" (54). As reported in Stephen Gray's *Ghost Plane: The CIA's Torture Program Plan*, Mohamed found this incessant horrible noise more intolerable than experiencing several ordeals of razor cuts to his penis when later held in a Moroccan detention center. Psychological torture had driven some detainees insane, as it can most people, and sometimes within 48 hours, which would explain why, again according to Mohamed and other witnesses, some detainees have endlessly banged their heads against walls or have attempted suicide at Guantanamo and other sites.

And, as if all of this accumulative physical and psychological pain is not sufficiently formidable, these detainees are victims of what McCoy has meticulously shown to be CIA modes of the "clean" torture of sensory deprivation—their bodies and minds cut off from sound, sight and touch by ear pads, heavy goggles and thick gloves, further inhibited by being shackled at waist and ankles when taken out of cages or windowless isolation cells. Even if the "Gitmo" prisoners were, in Rumsfeld's maliciously inappropriate phrase, the "worst of the worst," this crazy-making treatment, according to American and international legal sanctions, itself constitutes an extreme violation of the treatment any imprisoned person should receive. But then who told Bush's Washington what it could or couldn't do to detainees even if not yet proven guilty, even if not tried for years—or ever? The Military Commissions Act of 2006 allowed Commander-in-Chief Bush to do anything he wanted to anyone, including any American.

Dilawar is only one extreme example of the massive criminal abuse of Near and Far Eastern peoples being perpetrated primarily by the United States under the fallacious assumption that all these thousands of detained human beings have to be held to prevent them from fighting again. Due to ethnic or religious identity or superficial, false accusation, they have in effect been assumed to be guilty before having been legally proven so—a gross violation of human rights in any society regarding itself as just or civilized. Thus, innumerable detainees—some just children—have been wasting away for years in American torture prisons in gross violation of habeus corpus.

Supposedly the clinching argument for continuing incarceration of "War on Terror" detainees is the "ticking bomb" scenario (discussed in part in the McCoy review). Allegedly, a captive could harbor the secret knowledge of an imminent bomb disaster; so torture to get at the truth is justified. But according to scholars of torture like McCoy and Darius Rejali, author of the authoritative *Torture and Democracy*, such key individuals are very unlikely to get caught. And even if they were captured, torture would most likely produce false information, as the case of al-Libi proved catastrophically. Furthermore, according to experienced FBI agents, most arrested detainees know nothing. Might they fight if released? That probably depends on the kind of treatment they experience during confinement, whether the reputed FBI mode of winning their confidence or the CIA mode of brutalizing alienation.

Meanwhile, where is the presence and pressure of American moral indignation? There certainly were voices of individuals and non-government organizations rising in opposition to Bush-Cheney's administrative savagery. For example, the Center for Constitutional Rights in New York tried to have Rumsfeld served with a warrant when he was in Paris in 2007. But the protest against torture had no swelling of societal condemnation against Bush, Cheney and Rumsfeld being responsible for covert (and later overt) policies in which military and even contracted guards exposed naked detainees to freezing cold and extreme heat, beat them like dogs, punched and kicked their groin, and forced them to stand in place for 24 hours or more until their feet and ankles were swollen to twice their natural size, thereby causing horrible pain and possible kidney failure—and so on and on.

Institutional torture of any individual should torture our conscience. Indifference to the ongoing or excruciating torture of other human beings reduces our essential humanity. When our government tortures in our name, it criminalizes every one of us not only as citizens but as members of a nation traditionally famous for, and rather boastful about, its civil liberties and rule of law. Punishment before judgment, as in Dilawar's case, becomes punishment as illegal and criminal judgment. Dilawar's thigh, rightly understood, deeply felt, is our thigh.

Meanwhile, Diliwars's wife and pre-adolescent daughters, subsisting in an Afghan village, lost a husband and father. If nothing else, one hopes they never hear of a film called *Taxi to the Dark Side*.

"Diliwar's Thigh: Deep Inside the Dark Side" by Donald Gutierrez—*Common Sense*, August 2008; *Humanist Society of New Mexico*, September 2008.

11
Review: Neil Belton, *The Good Listener:*
Helen Bamber, A Life Against Cruelty

The Good Listener: Helen Bamber, A Life Against Cruelty by Neil Belton centers on Helen Bamber and the relation of her life of caring for torture victims to the political cruelty of 20th century states from World War II on. An extraordinary tension emerges in Belton's book between state torturers trying to annihilate a victim's basic sense of self and individuals like Bamber and her organizations trying to re-humanize victims through various techniques of care and healing. Listening to their histories—and to their bodies—as if they are unique and of crucial importance is central to Bamber's therapy.

Bamber was the daughter of Polish Jews fleeing pogroms. The family settled in London, and by the 1930s her father, utterly obsessed by the growing menace of Nazi Germany, would read portions of *Mein Kampf* to his daughter when she was still a child. Her father's inexorable pessimism placed Bamber in the Kafkesque plight of "spend[ing] the rest of her life acknowledging that the situation [of State political cruelty] is indeed hopeless but that it is necessary to do something about it" (187).

Something about dealing with alienated parents and a father overwhelmed by a sense of approaching disaster oriented Bamber towards listening sympathetically to people in pain, extending care, attempting healing and, finally, in 1985 at age sixty, establishing her own organization, the Medical Foundation for the Care of Victims of Torture. The path to this achievement exposed her to enough human suffering, anguish, rage, pain and sordid surroundings to fill half a dozen lives. In 1945, at age twenty, she had volunteered to enter the Belsen concentration camp as part of a British rehabilitation team. Belton explains that, though Belsen was not intended as a death camp, over half of its 60,000 inmates died in the three months before liberation. Being at Belsen exposed Bamber to inmates' profound need to communicate their experiences of horror:

> "Above all else," she said, "there was the need to tell you *everything*, over and over and over again. And this was the most significant thing for me, realizing that you had to take it all. They would need to hold on to you; it was important that you held them, and often you had to rock... you would hold on to them, and they would tell you their story." (89)

For Bamber what was worse about Belsen were stories of individuals already designated for death first being selected for torture. This demonic gesture of thoroughly violating persons internally before killing them horrified and galvanized her.

The demonic certainly figures in *La Question* (1957) by Henri Aleeg, a French-Algerian paratrooper *and* a member of the rebel FLN (National Liberation Front). Aleeg revealed that the French were using "electrocution, half-hanging, drowning and beating" against Algerians during the 1950s France-Algeria Crisis (Aleeg, 172). This practice was theoretically justified in a book entitled *Modern Warfare* by a French paratroops officer named Roger Trinquier. Trinquier identifies rebels as terrorists, who, not operating by usual codes of combatants, can't expect mercy. He extends this status in a sinister metaphor found later in Chile, Argentina and elsewhere since—that subversion is a form of disease, a cancer that needs eradication. Thus, "torture is, properly understood, a kind of rehabilitation" (176).

Belton employs a devastating irony to Trinquier's "rehabilitative" torture by quoting from Aleeg's *La Question*:

> Ja-[a para sergeant], smiling all the time, dangled the clasps at the end of the electrodes before my eyes. These were little shining steel clips, elongated and toothed.... He attached one of them to the lobe of my right ear and the other to a finger on the same side. Suddenly, I leapt in my bonds and shouted with all my might.... Still smiling above me,

> Ja—had attached the pincer to my penis. After a while ... they
> had thrown cold water over me in order to increase the
> intensity of the current. (176-77)

This sense of being in the grip of the demonic, combined with
uncertainty about how much and what kind of torture will occur, or whether
one will live or die, made the Chilean victim Adriana Borquez who was
beaten, electrocuted and assaulted by dogs, prefer death to further torture.
A German who had moved to Chile and joined the Communist party there,
Borquez had been swept up by General Pinochet's military, imprisoned and
tortured at length. She later reached England where Bamber was able to
relate Borquez's experiences in Chile to her work against torture.

Bamber was to deal with many victims undergoing the kinds of horrors
experienced and described by Aleeg and Borquez. She first worked as a
versatile and effective assistant to activist male doctors and administrators,
then was a major activist with the British Amnesty International until 1985,
when she formed her own organization. One of her earlier associations was
with Dr. Maurice Pappworth, who, acutely sensitive to cruelty committed by
doctors, documented enough instances of it, especially in England and the
United States, to establish an archive. According to Belton, "Newborn
babies in the public wards of hospitals, the mentally ill and prisoners asked
to 'volunteer' were most vulnerable" (163). In one particularly egregious
instance in Philadelphia, nine three-year-olds were used for catheterization
experiments. Needles were inserted into their femoral arteries and jugular
veins while they were forced to breathe gas through a mask.

Bamber's involvement with Pappworth and his courageous medical
ethics campaign prompted her to start connecting good medicine with good
listening and human rights activism. She came to realize that one must be
aware of both the abused body *and* of what or who causes the abuse in order
to counter torture effectively. Torture through the world could be stopped
immediately, she maintained, if the major powers acted against it. "The legal
instruments are there to prevent torture. And states could practice practical
pressure, yet nothing is really done by the powerful states to stop it" (322).

The deepening awareness that both torture and its social context need
confronting led to Bamber's gradual departure from Amnesty International
and to the formation of her Medical Foundation. "The Foundation," says
Belton, "works publicly against the existence of torture. Any less
commitment would, in the eyes of its members, turn their efforts into an

after-care service for the tortured" (321). Bamber, according to Benton, didn't revere suffering, nor did she sentimentalize torture victims. Though she had high hopes for them, she also felt that their experience will remain with them forever and affect their families.

The Good Listener ends with an aptly symbolic anecdote concerning Bamber's helping an Iranian man tortured by Khomeini's Revolutionary Guards. Conned by a doctor into admitting that his biggest vulnerability was his back, his back is what the Guards worked over. In Bamber's office, his pain became so bad that he started banging his head hard on her desk. Suddenly, Bamber "put her hands between his head and the table, and before he could stop himself, his forehead hit her hands." She told him that "he'd stood up to Khomeini and he shouldn't be defeated by him now" (350).

Belton offers an engrossing, powerful narrative about how much radical good one woman has created against extreme political evil. Ultimately, *The Good Listener* would make all of us good listeners to a very dark world of unspeakable cruelty, pain and suffering that can be confronted, and perhaps alleviated, through empathic involvement with that agony and ongoing resistance against states that cause it.

"Review: Neil Belton, *Helen Bamber: The Good Listener, A Life Against Cruelty"—Common Sense*, February 2000; *Bloomsbury Review*, 2001.

12
Review: Dianna Ortiz,
The Blindfold's Eyes:
My Journey from Torture to Truth

A torture victim once said that surviving torture is worse than torture. That excruciating perception indicates what much of this book on a torture experience and its psychic and international repercussions involves. Sister Dianna Ortiz is an American Ursuline nun who had been in Guatemala for two years dedicated to helping bring social justice to the brutally repressed poor of that country. As such, and being a Catholic associated with liberation theology, Ortiz was regarded as a subversive by the right wing authorities. It also became clear that she was under military surveillance during those two years. In *The Blindfold's Eyes: My Journey from Torture to Truth*, Ortiz recounts being kidnapped and tortured by Guatemalan army officers with an American named "Alejandro" present and, apparently, in charge. This very long, absorbing memoir attempts, among other things, to understand who the individuals (especially "Alejandro") were, and, crucially, what was "Alejandro's" relation to the United States government.

But *Eyes* is much more than a "Who Is Alejandro?" political mystery, important as that endeavor is. Indeed, *Eyes* might be one of the best accounts ever provided of the psychological impact and after-effects of torture. Some torture victims end up committing suicide because torture often eviscerates one's trust in life. Also, it continues traumatizing the victim for years. Ortiz to this day sleeps with lights on and dreads the onset of night and sleep because flashbacks of her torture and torturers recur then, as well as the screams of Guatemalans being tortured within earshot. Triggered by her kidnapping, she jumps when someone gets close to her unexpectedly. Nor can she stand individuals staring at her. Climactically, she "inherited" a shaving razor from another female torture victim and keeps it under her pillow or otherwise close by. At one point, several years after her November 1989 torture, she cut her wrists. During the numerous interviews and conference speeches and in meeting with American political officials, Ortiz was virtually forced to re-experience flashbacks of her torture and often broke down. Yet part of her enormous courage and integrity is that over the years she continued to endure these overwhelming situations to discover the true identity of her tormentors and, crucially, the ultimate political or institutional context for her torture. Pursuing this harrowing path, her scope of victims was continually enlarged, as she became more aware of, and started condemning, the torture and massacre of the hundreds of thousands of Guatemalans carried out by Guatemalan "security" or Army forces over decades.

Eyes also harbors a theodicy. Being burned on her back one hundred and eleven times by cigarettes no matter what answer she gave to questioning, being gang-raped by three Guatemalans and hung by ropes naked over a lime-covered pit of dead and dying, groaning men, women and children, having rats dropped on her head, her faith was ravaged. Further, the rapes led to impregnation, and, feeling she would give birth to radical evil, Ortiz had an abortion. Now this is an Ursuline nun from a traditional New Mexico Catholic family who not only had made a vow of chastity but now had to face the reaction of priests and her order to her getting an abortion (one priest informed another rape-torture nun that her abortion was a mortal sin). She asked where God was when she was being tortured but gradually felt his presence through the support community she built up and attracted. This community included the noble and courageously persistent Jennifer Harbury, whose Guatemalan guerrilla-officer husband, Everardo Bamaca, was captured, tortured and finally executed by the Guatemalan army—again with Washington's knowledge, pretense of ignorance and tacit approval.

Perhaps Ortiz's most profound form of psychic self-exploration and redemption arose from one of the most horrendous events during the torture. Besides being filmed during the rape from angles that falsely suggested her complicity, Ortiz cut another woman's body with a machete guided by a coercive torturer's hand and feared that she had killed her. She attempted to exorcize this diabolical enforcement by giving archetypal status to this woman in her mind and in all her campaigns to shed light on Guatemalan political victims and the officials and institutions complicit in such terrorization. Further, in an act of propitiatory exorcism, Ortiz dedicated *Eyes* to her "Woman Friend." One of the forces that in fact sustained her sanity and crusade was dedication to that female image, as well as the strength she gathered from her power animal (dolphins) that emerged in a pivotal transformative dream. She certainly needed all the strength she could summon, because she bravely returned twice to Guatemala after her ordeal, once under the compromising auspices of the American Embassy and later with only a few friends when she revisited the site of her kidnapping and torture for investigatory purposes.

Though there were many key figures in the thirteen-year post-torture trauma Ortiz underwent, several especially structured Ortiz's experience. First, there were the two army officer torturers, the "Guate-Man" and the "Policeman" (plus a third, a *campesino* named Jose). Guate-Man and Policeman not only physically molested Ortiz, they attempted to destroy her future by either attacking her faith or by saying no one would believe her account of the torture. They also warned that she would always be in danger from them—not an idle threat.

The primary American obstacle to Ortiz's vindication was the American Ambassador to Guatemala, Thomas Stroock. His office first became sensitive to Ortiz's account of her extreme abuse when she mentioned that "Alejandro" is an American, and that he might have some connection with the State Department. This of course was extremely inflammatory for an embassy head to deal with, and Stroock's reactions from 1989 on, for years, was one of furious outrage that turned into assailing the very basis of Ortiz's torture. His extreme reaction was summed up in an interview in which he claimed that Ortiz was never burned or raped and even questions whether she was or is a nun. (One State Department official, Lew Anselem, claimed that Ortiz's burns and bruises resulted from a rough lesbian sadomasochistic involvement. Anselem also claimed that Ortiz kidnapped herself.)

However, Stroock's rage concealed complicity. Evidence arose that Stroock had played a role in "the secret U.S. support for the Guatemalan army." Stroock "had supervised the CIA station chief [in Guatemala] and had access to the assets list." Having access to such a list would strongly suggest that Stroock's embassy at the very least knew "Alejandro's" identity. Further, seventy-four arms deals from the United States were implemented by Stroock; some of these weapons were, according to the investigatory journalist Allan Nairn, "used in the Santiago Atitlan Massacre of December 1990" (321).

So, this high-placed American diplomat, according to Ortiz, in effect helped cover up American-supported Guatemalan army genocide against its own people. Documents would later be forthcoming showing that Stroock, as ambassador, had no intention of doing justice to Ortiz's case. Ortiz regarded Stroock as being instrumental in aiding and concealing American involvement in horrific human rights abuses by the Guatemalan government. This in turn, according to Ortiz, facilitated the extermination of any critics of a brutally repressive regime favorable to American ideological and big-business interests in Guatemala, and thus lent that country an aspect favorable to its inclusion in NAFTA.

Ortiz sums up the cost of this dissembling by the American government through such representatives as Stroock:

> My experience [her kidnapping and torture] is a daily occurrence in Guatemala. Six people a week are killed for political reasons. The army's counter-insurgency campaign has left an estimated 200,000 dead and another 45,000 disappeared....Some 440 Mayan villages were wiped off the map. Hundreds of people vanished. Their mutilated, charred remains are only now beginning to emerge from secret mass graves. (350)

"What about the U.S.?" she aptly asks. "When will the truth be exhumed?"

Two individuals crucial to moving Ortiz's narrative from torture to truth are Nairn and Jennifer Harbury. At a conference in Washington in the early 1990s on torture in Guatemala, Nairn's well-informed and bold revelations about the White House's complicity accomplished several crucial things for Ortiz: first, it substantiated her certainty that "Alejandro" was not a figment of her imagination. Second, and even more important, Nairn's exposition of Washington's complicity in destroying the democratically elected Arbenz regime of 1954, and in aiding the Guatemalan death squads with CIA lists targeting critics or "enemies" of the new regime and the United Fruit Company, was liberating and energizing for Ortiz. It helped her to view her personal ordeal in context of the genocide being committed by Guatemalan authorities with American backing for decades and strengthened her to conduct her campaign of proving government involvement not only for herself but for all victims of Guatemalan-American violence since the 1950s.

"I didn't want," Ortiz says, poignantly, "to believe my government had betrayed me. I didn't want to believe I lived in a country that had overseen my torture" (181). But it had, and rather than demoralizing Ortiz, Nairn's disclosures further clarified her vision through the "blindfold" of the psychic impact of her torture and the deliberate obfuscation surrounding it that Ortiz claims was spread by Stroock, the American State Department and other political institutions and media, both American and Guatemalan. Nairn put both Ortiz's plight and the horrors experienced by hundreds of thousands of Guatemalans within a just condemnation of the larger context:

> If over the years, the U.S. had adopted different policies toward Guatemala, there would be no need for this conference [on torture in Guatemala]. (181)

Another significant figure in *Eyes* was Harbury who was on a personal crusade to save her husband from torture and execution by the Guatemalan army. Harbury contacted Ortiz as part of a campaign to bring together Americans who have been attacked in Guatemala or had lost relatives there. This involved a two-edged proposition for Ortiz. On the one hand, joining forces with Harbury and others would strengthen her own quest and significantly broaden its impact on both the American and Guatemalan governments. On the other hand, political association with the wife of a Guatemalan revolutionary officer could perilously jeopardize Ortiz's own status; it could intimate that Ortiz was actually a political subversive manipulating her alleged torture experience to persuade Congress to end funding of the Guatemalan military. What made her decide to join Harbury and further publicize their plight was her deep urge not to succumb to ongoing terrorization by the Guatemalan army and, most important, not to abandon the multitudes of Guatemalan victims whose screams resounded in her mind years after her 1989 abduction.

This decision intensified the psychological and emotional pressures Ortiz has had to confront for years. Ortiz was continually menaced externally and internally. Besides the nihilistic presence of her actual torturers, she was implicitly threatened at one point by a president of Guatemala. Further, Guatemalan agents in dark eyeglasses tracked her at Washington conferences and press meetings as well as at a torture treatment center in Chicago called Su Casa. One day a box filled with dried excrement was left at her doorstep; she also received threatening phone calls in Spanish from anonymous Guatemalans. Further, she was frequently bullied and vilified by Stroock and several government agencies during meetings and investigational conferences. It is thus not surprising that she had considered leaving the Ursulines and keeping her "freedom" razor handy. She feels a guilt moreover (deliberately intensified by Stroock) about thinking only of herself during her torture crisis when other victims were undergoing possibly unspeakable torture. And she had to deal with a savage degradation inflicted on her, which included sexual exposure to dogs and a torturer ejaculating in her mouth, both actions videotaped. These experiences, and her abortion, comprise an extremely heavy burden for anyone to bear.

Yet something of her spirit comes across early in *Eyes* when one of her captors, a *campesino* named Jose, begs her for forgiveness when they are alone for an atrocity he committed as part of a paramilitary attack on a village. He feels that Ortiz's religious status can cleanse him and promises to save her. Whether Jose could really have saved or released Ortiz is uncertain; what, however, is certain is the moral stature embodied in Ortiz's refusal to "sell my forgiveness for my freedom" (7). This refusal is followed by her being plunged into torture, but the moral toughness revealed in this instance prefigures the fortitude she will demonstrate in going after the ferocious Guatemalan army and the high-placed American-government officials who at times seem as remote and heartless as officials in Kafka's *The Castle*.

Ambassador Stroock emerges as one of the salient hypocrites in *Eyes*, and the mysterious "Alejandro" (later tentatively identified as one Randy Capister, a CIA operative) still might roam the netherworld of CIA-State Department covert machinations. Yet Ortiz exposes another major scoundrel in the person of the Guatemala Army Vice Chief of Staff Hector Gramajo, who conducted the scorched-earth policy of the 1980s in Guatemala and under whose tenure Ortiz's torture occurred. This key senior officer actually published an article in a Harvard journal (the *International Review*) in which, describing Guatemalan army maneuvers, he wrote:

> You needn't kill everyone to complete the job....We instituted
> Civil Affairs, which provides development for seventy percent
> of the population, while we kill thirty percent. (300-01)

This "Civil-Affairs" plan included, among other atrocities, killing thousands of Guatemalans and annihilating over 600 villages, which involved murdering babies and decapitating eight-year-old children. "Gramajo," Ortiz states, "was personally in charge of and supervised 'the 30 percent aspect of the program'" (301). Asked once if his army had a scorched-earth policy towards regime critics and suspected opponents, he described it as a "scorched-Communist" policy (Gramajo was not just waxing metaphorical; some "suspects" were half burned to death and had flesh sliced off their bodies with machetes).

A School of the Americas graduate, Gramajo, *after* his reign of terror in which his death squads exterminated almost 2,000 civilians and "disappeared" around 500 more, was awarded a scholarship to Harvard by the United States Agency for International Development. Gramajo, once asked on *Prime Times* about his claim that Ortiz's ordeal was actually a rough lesbian affair, backed off. General Gramajo considered running for president of Guatemala in 2004.

This powerful, deeply moving memoir is not without flaws. For one thing, *Eyes* suffers from insufficient use of dates. Important events (such as conferences on torture) are often not put within a time frame, undermining narrative coherence. This flaw might have been mitigated by a chronology as well as by an index, which would have helped in locating key participants, organizations and events in this subjectively complex and intricate memoir. Also, the book could have been somewhat shorter. Though Ortiz records every nuance of her recollections and flashbacks of her ordeal and of her at times tortured relationships with individuals and groups afterwards—and this certainly is an invaluable part of the book's contribution to an ontology of the trauma of torture—almost five hundred pages of this wearies the reader. Finally, *Eyes* is a "with" book. It was written "with Patricia Davis," who gave the book "more than words on paper" and without whom "there would be no book" (x). If Davis helped write the book, what more or less was her contribution to it?

Nevertheless, *Eyes* provides an unforgettable contribution to the literature of the aftereffects of torture. Just as valuable, it also delineates a

torture victim who develops the vitality and courage to pursue and expose
her torturers to the top levels of two savage governments.

"Review: Dianna Ortiz, *The Blindfold's Eyes: My Journey from Torture to Truth*"
by Donald Gutierrez—*Common Sense*, March 2003; *Z Magazine*, January 2004;
Bloomsbury Review, March 2004.

PART II

WAR AND DEMOCRACY

WAR ON DEMOCRACY

13

Patriotism and Country Versus State

War Is the Health of the State
Randolph Bourne, *The State*

War is the State
Kenneth Rexroth, *The Dragon and the Unicorn*

As the U.S. Patriot Act (October 26, 2001) ominously implied that the "true patriot" had best keep his or her mouth shut about his government's actions no matter how evil, patriotism has become a word that would benefit from an iconoclastic embrace. One's immediate definition of patriotism is likely to be love of and dedication to one's country. This definition, though, is less one of instinct than of indoctrination encountered as part of one's upbringing. The indoctrination shifts us into something ultimately darker or narrower when patriotism is further defined or implied to mean the approval of the foreign economic "interests" and political-military authority of one's country. The problem emerging at this point is that the idea of country has subtly changed into another societal concept, the formidable abstraction and reality called "the state."

One can love one's country in the form of, say, San Francisco's cultural liberalism, New Mexico's green chile, climate and mountains, the Midwest's festive sense of Halloween, autumn trees in Vermont, the New

York theatre, art or baseball world—or individuals, such as Thelonius Monk, Theodore Dreiser, Franz Kline, Eugene Debs, Dorothy Day, Susan Farrell, Cesar Chavez or Amy Goodman. If, however, love of one's country means accepting the battle cry "My Country, Right or Wrong!" for example, or American presidents threatening to declare war without congressional authorization or permitting corporation-boardroom decisions that kill jobs for hundreds of thousands of Americans and further poison our air and water, then I am not a patriot. Put another way, one must differentiate "country" and "state" to get at a more satisfactory definition of patriotism, for to have to love John Muir and Amnesty International USA on the one hand and Anthony Scalia and a regressive tax system on the other is to ask of us a love that only a schizophrenic could provide.

To entertain a civilized idea of patriotism, one might reverse conventional or unchallenged acceptances. This reversal could mean viewing as unpatriotic the 1950s House Un-American Activities Committee or the White House's more recent warrantless wiretapping or CEOs receiving bonuses on top of seven-figure salaries for executing mergers that raise product costs for millions of Americans and throw innumerable thousands out of work. Further, were not Trent Lott and Newt Gingrich depriving the American people of immense amounts of public wealth by trying to pass a bill in 1997 to subsidize the tobacco industry with $50 billion? Was that not unpatriotic, even traitorous, behavior because it would have misused the American people's wealth and threatened their health? Or, in 2008, was Treasury Secretary Henry Paulson, the former Goldman Sachs CEO, very possibly committing an act of vast treachery in bailing out Wall Street at the enormous expense of the American people? And, if so, how do we define patriotism and America in terms of those two antithetical elements: Paulson vs. the country?

Was Daniel Ellsberg a patriot in the best sense when he turned over to *The New York Times* the Pentagon Papers, in which it was revealed that LBJ had secret plans for extending the Vietnam War into North Vietnam while telling the public that he was for peace and planned to end the war? Isn't any American president or politician who dishonestly draws the country into an unjust, illegal or unnecessary war unpatriotic, even traitorous? Are not activists like Father Roy Bourgeois and Kathy Kelly splendid American patriots in vigorously condemning the brutal American methods of public control, i.e., state terror, which we exported through Latin American military and police officials via the School of the Americas?

Now if one wants to be a good citizen and a patriot to boot, how does one shape a viable sense of patriotism out of the above melange of diverse, polarized items? What is a patriotic response to an illustrious American painter like Mark Rothko on the one hand, and on the other to John Foster Dulles (roughly contemporaries), our former ice-cold-warrior Secretary of State who, during the 1950s, brought the United States close to precipitating nuclear war against mainland China?

Deciding on these responses could be facilitated by viewing Rothko under the rubric of country and Dulles under that of state, with "state" understood to mean country in its most abstracted, highly concentrated political-military coercive form.

Rothko was a private individual, developing over the years his particular craft and genius as an artist towards the creation of majestic, non-figurative canvases of mystically luminescent and somnolent horizontal planes of color. His work did not glorify the Stars and Stripes or the Pentagon; and yet, suddenly seeing his big canvases as I walked into the American Wing of the Musee National d'Art in Paris in the summer of 1990, I felt a thrill of patriotism.

One could perhaps at least accept what, say, Dulles or former Secretary of State Henry Kissinger stood for—that is, the state—if one felt that their conduct as American statesmen protected or nourished the culture that makes or preserves a Rothko or a Billie Holliday or the Civil Rights Act of 1964 or Habeus Corpus or preserves progressive taxation and aids the young, the poor and the elderly. People like Dulles or Kissinger or former Defense Secretary Donald Rumsfeld would instantly declaim that their foreign policy advice to the president was dedicated to protecting basic American freedom and values and (especially) "National Security."

When high state officials like Dulles, Kissinger and Rumsfeld said that they were acting in the "National Interest" or defending the "Free World" or the "American Way of Life," by, respectively, threatening China with nuclear bombing, massively bombing Cambodia or devastating oil-rich Iraq, they were, again, making the claim that the interest of the state *is* that of the country: They were protecting the country from the Chinese or the Viet Cong or Saddam Hussein—or now, Iran. But this asserted coinciding of the interests of country and state is totally unacceptable. A great deal of the hostility displayed by the American state and mass media towards international communism, whether that of the Soviet Union, Mao's China or Castro's Cuba, was excessive and provocative.

The Cold War was also an enormous windfall for certain sectors of American society whose concerns were not really those of the country, that is, the great majority of Americans unconnected in any way (except income tax and their draftable children) with the state and its political-military plans and multi-trillion-dollar costs. It should be news of undying interest to the country financing it that the American defense industry and its investors profited enormously from the Cold War—and continue to do so in America's current wars.

Dr. Helen Caldicott went so far as to assert, in 2002, that huge armament corporations like Lockheed Martin imperil the world because of the pernicious character of their weapons research programs and the billions in contract money lavished on them by the Pentagon.[1] As the world includes the United States, obviously Americans themselves would have their safety and security imperiled and thus *betrayed* through the blowback consequences of the bellicose foreign policy of the American state.

The Cold War also benefited the state by keeping the general public tractable and wage earners deprived of at least a third to two-fifths of their rightful working income while intimidating the country for decades with warnings of black-booted commissars ruling Los Angeles and New York City or nuking Disneyland. Is it unpatriotic to condemn the powerful individuals and institutions that wasted huge amounts of America's material wealth and emotional energy by first engendering the Cold War in the late 1940s under President Harry S. Truman and then inflating it to seem much worse than in fact it was? Perhaps the Dulleses, Johnsons, Nixons, Kissingers, Reagans, Bill Clintons, Bushes (among others) have been the betrayers—not only of the state, but of the *country.*

Is patriotism the last refuge of a scoundrel? It depends who the patriot is, what he is dedicating himself to, the state or the country, and whether the genuine national interest of country and state converge. As suggested earlier, all too often they don't converge or are even polarized.

Patriotism is in itself a controversial and variable concept. Integral to nationalism, it becomes more and more dangerous in a world that must surmount its jingoism in order to form a comity of nations anchored in subordinating each nation to an authoritative internationalist polity and rule of law. Turning nation against nation, and, thus patriot against patriot, is simply too risky in a world of spreading nuclear arms capacity, increasing poverty and class differentiation, climate warming and its very severe impact on food production, rising religious fanaticism and possibly uncontrollable population growth—and, recently, the global financial meltdown.

Patriotism can embody a fulfilling sense of community if the essential values of state and country sizably and ultimately coincide. That they seldom really do should alert the country to the likelihood that the state could be up to something dubious at best, pernicious and even catastrophic at worst, when it starts fanning the fires of national security, patriotism and war. Hope that Barack Obama would bring state and country into harmony fired his 2008 presidential campaign and a multitude of supporters, but his administration continued to rely heavily on Wall Streeters for economic advice, and the Pentagon has remained close to Obama's ear, so that civil liberties are now more imperiled than even under George W. Bush. One should be concerned that, as before, state is making short shrift of any bonding with country.

---

1. See review of Caldicott's *The New Nuclear Danger*, Ch. 22.

"Patriotism and Country Versus State" by Donald Gutierrez—*Common Sense*, September 2003; *El Tecolote*, November 2003; *El Dorado Sun*, January 2003, *The Humanist Society of New Mexico*, February 2009; *Progressive Populist*, May 2009.

14
Review: Chris Hedges,
War Is a Force That Gives Us Meaning

With the United States still engaged in undeclared wars, Chris Hedges' *War Is a Force That Gives Us Meaning* remains timely. Besides describing the devastation and barbarities of recent wars unflinchingly, *War* bitingly exposes violence committed by the state against civilized values in waging war. Hedges' iconoclastic honesty about the real nature, appeal and horrors of war and the actual motives behind nations going to war is humane and crucial because it could force individuals and, one would hope, national leaders to confront their own bellicosity and self-deceptions, as well as the enormous lies told to a nation by its leaders.

Many of Hedges' insights about the real character of war embody truths most people don't face:

> War exposes the capacity for evil that lurks not far below the surface within all of us. (3)
> Once we sign on for war's crusade, once we see ourselves on the side of the angels,... it is only a matter of how we carry out murder. (9)
> There is nothing redeeming about any war, including the supposed good wars that we might all agree had to be fought. (28)
> War is...organized murder. (23)

As a lead epigraph for the chapter "The Plague of Nationalism," Hedges offers the American anarchist Randolph Bourne's mot: "War is the

Health of the State" (43).

These sentiments are hardly what one would expect from American "embedded" journalists, who, Hedges asserts, have since Gulf War I become the state's cheerleaders of war.

Hedges' war credentials for making such stark declarations are solid. A former *New York Times* war correspondent, he has covered wars and conflicts most of his adult life in El Salvador, Guatemala, Nicaragua, Colombia, Sudan, Yemen, Algeria and Bosnia, as well as the first *Intifada* in the West Bank and Gaza, Sudan, Yemen, Algeria, the Gulf War and the Kurdish rebellion in Turkey, among other places of social violence. He has been ambushed on isolated Central American roads, "beaten by Saudi military police, [captured] for a week by Iraqi Republican Guard....fired upon by Serb snipers" (2). Viewing corpses returned to desperate families in Kosovo, he became accustomed to lifting sheets off bodies and finding gouged-out eyes, broken skulls, castration. Hedges' reportorial perceptions bear the hyper-reality of a rifle-butt smash to the head.

Considering why Hedges would get involved in reporting war provides a key dimension of his distinctive truth-telling:

> The enduring attraction of war is this: Even with its destruction and carnage it can give us what we long for in life. It can give us purpose, meaning, a reason for living. (3)

However, though war can give meaning to people's lives, *War* clearly suggests that ordinary civil society is deficient in meaning and value to many. This is an enormously significant perception, one Hedges might have elaborated. Obviously, many people find vicarious fulfillment as part of a nation united in purpose against an enemy. This deep need for social solidarity is manipulated into a collectivist will by the state, often to distract the populace from critical domestic problems.

War, Hedges asserts, is a drug; it gives its participants a rush (he felt this narcotic power himself). All too many individuals find war, despite its horrors and cruelties, to have been the greatest experience in their lives, the one time they lived most intensely, shared the deepest camaraderie, had the strongest sex drive. Hedges, further, makes it clear he is not a pacifist, and claims he admires professional soldiers.

Hedges exhibits characteristic integrity in suggesting extremity on both sides of most conflicts. In a frightening chapter entitled "The Seduction of Battle and the Perversion of War," he observes that the "god-like empowerment over other human lives and the drug of war combine ... to let our senses command our bodies....Killing unleashes within us... destruction" (89). This murderousness is apparent when Hedges witnesses Israeli soldiers at a Gaza strip refugee camp taunting ten-year-old Palestinian males out into the open by hurling at them such epithets as "son of a whore" and then shooting them "for sport," "their stomach...ripped out" by M-16 bullets. This extreme cruelty has led to the extreme indoctrination apparent in a two-year-old Palestinian child who, asked by his mother what he wants to be in life, says, "A martyr" (68).

Making the crucial point that the myth of war seldom endures for those undergoing combat, Hedges develops a key distinction between what has been termed "mythic reality" and "sensory reality" in war. Mythic reality glamorizes war, sees it in black and white terms morally and reduces each side to objects; it is chiefly spread by the state and the media. Sensory reality in war reveals what the mythic reality does not, "always the lie of omission. The blunders and senseless slaughter by our generals, the executions of prisoners and innocents, and the horrors of wounds are rarely disclosed...to the public" (22). The implication is that if the public knew of the sensory reality of war (as it finally did in Vietnam), it would not tolerate one.

Hedges doesn't pull his punches about American state violence, mentioning our support of the Nicaraguan Contras and of Jonas Savimbi of Angola, who, backed by President Reagan, was responsible for the death of 500,000 Angolans. Considering, however, the direct and indirect carnage Washington has perpetrated abroad for half a century, Hedges could have thrown more punches. There is the massive bombing of Vietnam under Johnson, then Nixon and Secretary of State Kissinger's genocidal involvement in wars from Latin America to Indonesia. In the chapter "The Highjacking and Recovery of Memory," Hedges observes that leaders committing war crimes seldom go to prison (if their side wins). Forces at war often try to destroy the culture of the enemy, including physical aspects such as public buildings, mosques and libraries, and hide the atrocities they commit through covert mass burials and obliterated public records. Thus, the painful but essential process of exhumations in places like Bosnia becomes a literal and symbolic mode of restoring cultural memory and truth.

Restoration of historical truth leads to an important consideration in *War* that involves a crucial opposition between a state set on going to war and the moral resistance to war of the individual. Hedges refers to this individual voice frequently, but most memorably in stating that the first people silenced by the state (often forcibly) when war starts are dissidents:

> They give us an alternate language, one that refuses to define the other as "barbarian" or "evil," that does not condone violence as a form of communication. Such voices are rarely heeded. And until we learn once again to speak in our own voice and reject that handed to us by the state in times of war, we flirt with our own destruction. (15-16)

This passage embodies more than a statement of political free expression; it represents a powerful libertarian thrust against the incessant tendency of the state to centralize power and to control, if not repress, the people.

The championing of the individual voice explains the vital presence of literature in *War*. Hedges not only makes numerous literary references (Virgil, Shakespeare, Homer, Joyce) but deploys them to provide important insights about the character of war and human nature. He discusses how *Troilus and Cressida* conveys Shakespeare's sense of the profound depravity of war. Unlike his *Henry V*, this play attacks the national myth glorifying war, leaders and nation. In presenting a grim view of society and human nature, it underlines the unique power of great literary art to convey the hard truths. And Hedges suggests the truth is the only way to restore the cultural memory and thus societal integrity obliterated by the conquests of war and the subsequent pervasive distortions of the "winner's" historical reality.

Any general book on war is bound to elicit strictures. *War*, instead of mainly castigating murderous Serbian gangster warlords like Milan Lukic, might have condemned the war-criminal decisions of heads of major states like England, Russia, the United States and others that were responsible for the death of many millions of people. Also, *War* presents much on the Balkan conflicts but very little on the Central and South American wars, not to mention World Wars I and II and the Korean and Vietnam wars. Hedges might have researched material about earlier major wars he had not personally encountered; doing so would have provided an even broader base for his reflections.

Nevertheless, *War* unforgettably illustrates the deeply corrupting psychological and physical impact of combat. Additionally, it provides bold insights into war's deep rootedness in human nature and the state's tenacious, if dissembling, commitment to war. *War* also suggests that in the enormous opposing forces of destructiveness and love, we survive as individuals—and, it is implied, as civilized communities—through love, which "alone [unlike war] gives us meaning that endures" (184-85). The consequences of accepting destructiveness, given modern technological sophistication, is to thrust us all towards self-annihilation.

"Review: Chris Hedges, *War Is a Force that Gives Us Meaning*" by Donald Gutierrez—*Common Sense*, May 2003; *Eldorado Sun*, May 2003.

15
Review: Jonathan Glover,
Humanity: A Moral History of the Twentieth Century

Jonathan Glover's *Humanity: A Moral History of the Twentieth Century* might also have been entitled *Humanity: A History of the Immoral Twentieth Century*. Early in the book he cites the estimate that 86 million people were killed by war in the period from 1900 to 1989. Despite speculative complications about the proportions of populations to war deaths in past centuries compared to the 20th century, 86 million war deaths is a stunning figure. Glover's book attempts to look at the psychology of how wars occur and the atrocities they cause. He demonstrates cogently that this psychology is present as much in civilians as in military leaders. Over half the book is devoted to societies like Nazi Germany, Stalin's Soviet Union, Mao's China and Pol Pot's Cambodia that have committed mass atrocities.

Glover's aim in part is to consider "the psychology which has contributed to this set of man-made disasters" (43). Indeed, he scarcely misses a disaster. They may not all be here but the reader will likely feel that there's more than enough—World Wars I and II (including a sizable chapter on Hiroshima), Vietnam (mainly My Lai), the Nixon-Kissinger bombing of Cambodia (which, Glover argues convincingly, helped the Khmer Rouge take power), Rwanda, Bosnia and the hell created for their societies by Hitler, Stalin, Mao and Pol Pot.

Glover frames his usually detailed discussions of these disasters by discussing Friedrich Nietzsche's contribution to the erosion of an external moral law and of humane responsiveness. "To see others suffer," says Nietzsche in *The Genealogy of Morals*, "does one good; to make others suffer

even more; this is a hard saying but....without cruelty there is no festival"
(17). Glover does not hold Nietzsche responsible for all the mass brutalities
of the 20th century, but he does connect the presence of elements of cruelty
in his work to a unique feature in the Nazi perspective on subject peoples:
"There was an intensity of positive hatred in those who planned the
genocide, which was not matched in the Stalinist exterminations" (396).
That is a chilling statement, considering that one estimate puts the number
of political deaths under Stalin at over 20 million.

Glover, in a long, brilliant section titled "The Moral Psychology of
Waging War," presents a crucial concept that he calls the "moral slide."
The moral slide involves moving downward from one immoral or evil act to
the next, the second step or slide made possible and easier by having begun
the first:

> The blockade [of Germany near the end of World War I,
> which led to the starvation of anywhere from 462,000 to
> 762,000 German *civilians*] slid by degrees from having a
> slight effect to having a devastating impact. The blockade
> made area bombing seem acceptable. Area bombing was
> reached by a gentle slide from military bombing. The bombing
> of German cities made acceptable the bombing of Japanese
> ones, which in turn allowed the slide to the atomic bomb. The
> slide went on from the Hiroshima bomb to Nagasaki. (115)

Glover suggests another form of the moral slide that seems particularly
relevant to 20th century modes of technology, industrialization, bureau-
cratism: "There is another form of disconnection between what people do
and their sense of moral identity. The division of labor can make the
contribution of any single person seem unimportant" (403). On the other
hand, Glover cites the atomic bomb as a project so divided up among
scientists, politicians, military brass and others that no one could feel
exclusively or even personally responsible for it. General Leslie Groves was
jubilant on hearing about the explosion. According to President Truman,
"This [dropping the Bomb] is the greatest thing in history" (101).

What strikes this reviewer as extraordinary in *Humanity* is less
Glover's ideas about the need for a sense of moral identity to be connected
with human responses than the dozens of scenes and events of incredible
cruelty and terror imposed by governments on their own citizens and on

other peoples: Mao's Great Leap Forward, causing a famine killing 20 to 30 million; a seventeen-year-old Red Guard male beating up a kneeling, bleeding woman; Kulak peasants forced by the Stalin regime into barren, icy regions near the arctic, "left, with no food or tools, on bits of land in the middle of marshes. The paths back were guarded with machine guns. Everyone died" (238); Nazi officers trampling on the heads of Polish Jewish children; the Khmer Rouge murdering one fourth of Cambodia's entire population.

There were redeeming acts: Helicopter pilot Hugh Thompson saved villagers at My Lai from Captain Medina's crazed soldiers; *German-allied* Italian officers protected Jews from the Nazis; nuns, despite the Pope's passivity to the Nazi regime, hid Jewish children in their convents throughout Europe. Thrilling and wonderful as these acts were, they fail to balance the appallingly huge quantity of social brutality and murder committed mostly by the state during the 20th century. Glover feels there is hope for humanity in the future in the acceptance of international legal authority by the superpowers like the United States and China. Optimism on this score is at best moderate. (See Ch. 19, "Universal Jurisdiction and the Bush Administration," for more discussion of this issue.)

One shortcoming in Glover's otherwise deeply moving, magnanimous and courageous book is his ignoring the role of commercial forces in shaping 20th century social violence. It is not, as he claims, only ideology, belief and the erosion of a universal moral law that has led to the 20th century wars, but the rapacious, unrelenting drive to control markets by dominating rival imperialist nations and subjugating vulnerable or smaller societies by military force or overwhelming economic pressures. Commercial greed has played its part in the brutalization and deaths of millions.

"Review: Jonathan Glover, *Humanity: A Moral History of the Twentieth Century*" by Donald Gutierrez—*Bloomsbury Review*, May 2001; *Common Sense*, November 2001; *Justice Xpress*, Summer 2002.

16
George Orwell and Washington's War Rhetoric

Political language is designed to make
lies sound truthful and murder respectable...
George Orwell, "Politics and the English Language"

One reason George Orwell remains an essayist of force is the significant relevance of his political insights into the relationship between the state and lying. Phrases and terms used by Washington to justify and render acceptable the Iraq War and the war in Afghanistan, such as "securing the peace," "liberating Iraq," "Coalition forces" and "war of necessity" evoke Orwell's famous sentiment that, "In our time, political speech and writing are largely the defense of the indefensible." Political speech and prose coming out of Washington today, because they defend the indefensible, require a diction or rhetoric that makes the real goals of American presidents and our War Department acceptable.

Both Presidents George W. Bush and Barack Obama, their Cabinets and the Pentagon have implemented a subterfuge rhetoric of concealment and euphemism that deceives and thus seriously misinforms the public. Expressions like "liberating Iraq," "the War on Terrorism," "destroying weapons of mass destruction," hollow at best and hypocritical and genocidal at worst, were key to Bush's war propaganda. To "secure the peace" really meant invading Iraq illegally and without provocation from that country. Words like "secure" and "peace" provide a tranquilizing, pacific sense hiding the fact that this "secured" peace is achieved not only by the United States engaging in a criminal war but in the particularly brutal mode of "overwhelming force."

"Overwhelming force" exhibits another verbal dishonesty in which "force" really means spectacular, high-tech violence, the "spectacle" aspect meant to intimidate other nations harboring subversive thoughts of not obeying Washington. A corollary term for this sort of collateral intimidation is "shock and awe." This fearsome phrase is meant not only to terrify the nation about to be attacked (or, more accurately, massacred) unless it follows orders or even if, as in the case of Iraq, it *does* what it's told to do. It is also designed to terrify other nations, such as Afghanistan, Pakistan, Iran, Yemen, Somalia, that might have America's annihilative "democracy" bombed on their hospitals, public bridges, TV stations, museums, electricity grids and water systems. The American journalist Paul Farth said some years back that the Pentagon's "shock and awe" plan resembled Nazi Germany's "blitzkrieg." "Blitzkrieg" or "lightning war" certainly sounds like the "father" of all brutal military threats, of which "shock and awe" is the ineffably brutal "son."

"Collateral intimidation" comes to mind from that all-time Pentagon favorite mollifier, "collateral damage." *Democracy Now*'s Amy Goodman has observed that the White House or the Department of Defense would never allow that phrase to be applied to American civilians killed by a foreign attacker of America. The fact that the Pentagon does not hesitate to use this term regarding human casualties in nations it assaults suggests a dehumanizing, implicitly racist attitude towards the civilians of what are usually Third World countries. Reduced to the status of trees, cars or house walls, these victims of cluster bombs, fuel air-explosive bombs, Bunker Busters, carpet bombing, and drones guided towards Pakistan from Nevada are stripped of their humanity, and thus their deaths are not really deaths in the minds of the high-ranking politicians, generals and admirals planning their "*theatre* of operations" murder while ensconced in their bunkers.

This reductive dehumanization underscores Orwell's point in his essay "Politics" that "the writer is not seeing a mental image of the object he is naming; in other words, he is not really thinking" (164-65). It is also true that these leaders deliberately use terms like "collateral damage" and other euphemisms to conceal from the public the horrific impact of war on the human body. Indeed, Washington's war-propaganda machine thinks carefully about how to deflect the public from experiencing mental images of war so as to prevent it from thinking that "liberating Iraq" or "stabilizing Afghanistan" is in reality an egregious assault on either country.

When Orwell claims in "Politics" that "to think clearly is a necessary first step towards political regeneration," he incisively relates the moral function of language to its political use. However, it is difficult to deal with institutions like the American state and the media that deliberately use vague or misleading language—and withhold essential information—to hide the truth about the nature or necessity of the many wars American presidents have triggered. How does the public get the government to think clearly, that is, honestly? Why *doesn't* it think honestly? And why doesn't the media stand up to government disinformation and insist on or convey the truth? These important questions have obvious answers that need not be pursued here. More challenging is countering the forces and motives that compelled the Bush administration and the media to lie about why the United States invaded Iraq and Afghanistan. Of course a point can arise and perhaps has arisen when political leaders believe their own lies, but then one is witnessing a country's leadership veering dangerously out of control.

When Orwell says, "The writer is not seeing a mental image of the objects he is naming," it should nevertheless be clear that a major function of contemporary war language, like "job," "collateral damage," "surgical air strikes" and "Daisy Cutters" is precisely to make readers as well as writers *not* see the real image hidden at the heart of such diction; to do so could appall the public and alienate it from the war. Some Americans to this day claim that "we" didn't finish the "job" both in Vietnam and in the first Gulf War. *Job*? What a profound desecration of the basic civilizational value of work. Should we really call America's use of napalm, cluster bombs, depleted uranium shells, the CIA's genocidal Operation Phoenix program carried out during the Vietnam War, the total destruction of millions of human beings and homes and the turning of innumerable people into permanently grief-stricken refugees in Vietnam, Iraq, Afghanistan and Pakistan, a "job"?

Another vilely dishonest phrase is "Coalition forces." Of course the actual coalition against Iraq was the United States and England. Some African nations were surprised to find themselves on the list. Apparently, there has been no level of lying to which Washington will hesitate to sink to give the impression it was not being unilateralist or immoral in waging its "preventive" wars. As for "*surgical* air strikes," the "body" supposedly healed through some of the American bombing of Baghdad, Afghanistan and elsewhere was anything but medically benefited; civilians up to 200 meters away from the bomb site were killed or mutilated.

Finally, there is the ineffably misleading phrase "Daisy Cutter." The initial impression that this bomb is a kind of super lawn mower changes radically on reading Dr. Helen Caldicott's *The New Nuclear Danger*. FAE (Fuel Air Explosives) bombs "detonate just above the ground, creating a wide area of destruction." Undergoing two fuel-ignited explosions:

> The second charge then detonates [a] fuel-air cloud, creating a massive blast....Near the ignition point people are obliterated, crushed to death with overpressures of 427 pounds per square inch, and incinerated at temperatures of 2500 to 3000 degrees of centigrade. Another wave of low pressure—a vacuum effect—then ensues. People in the second zone of destruction are severely burned and suffer massive internal organ injuries before they die. A third zone of destruction ruptures lungs and ear drums, while the fuel itself is extremely poisonous. (x-xi)

There are other FAE "side effects," but Caldicott's description graphically exhibits the diabolic irony of the euphemism "Daisy Cutter" with its implied bottomless contempt for the "daisies" that are "cut."

Further, war imagery is not only visual, it is also aural and provides as spectacular and overwhelming a dimension of war as the visual—and of course is integral to the visual. The noise of aerial bombardment is horrific, especially that of our high-tech wars, in which bombs weighing thousands of pounds are dropped; and the United States made one thousand sorties over Baghdad in a matter of hours. (According to John Pilger in *The New Rulers of the World*, the United States in 2001 dropped over ten thousand *tons* of bombs on Afghanistan—some heavy surgery there.) Aggravating the terrible din of war is the relentless, maddening frequency of bombing and the visceral knowledge of people in the vicinity of bombing that the intensifying whistling and roar of bombs descending and exploding represent a force that could blow them and their loved ones to bits—this has been part of "liberating" Iraq and Afghanistan. It is not certain whether generals and political leaders safe in Washington or at a base in Qatar realize the actual impact and consequences of bombs on the human body, but the Pentagon brass (not to mention American presidents) have shown no interest in finding out, and that says a lot. General William Tecumseh Sherman's famous remark "War is Hell" never prevented him from carrying out his conception of total war during the American Civil War, then applying it to the lives and lands of Plains Indians. The United States "employing" FAEs, cluster bombs and cruise missiles may fit the Pentagon's idea of "surgical air strikes" but to the bombed victims of "collateral damage" it must seem more like Sherman's "total war."

Two phrases under which all those mentioned in this essay could be subsumed are "Pax Americana" and "Manifest Destiny." The United States "securing the peace" by either attacking or threatening any—and every—nation that either disobeys its commercial "interests" or tries to equal its military supremacy, leads, if successful, to a "Pax Americana," a world dominated for an American military, political and mega-corporation agenda. This is "pax." And an even larger contextual euphemism with pseudo mystical and pseudo religious overtones is "Manifest Destiny." What this phrase included was the United States violently acquiring one-third of Mexico in the mid-19th century and Cuba and the Philippines at the end of that century. Such imperialist expansion led in the 20th century to over 700 American military bases (some the size of small cities) positioned all over the world as well as formidable American naval fleets in every ocean. What emerges from all this excessive military power abroad is a sense of the "Destiny of America" being to intimidate and overpower every nation in the world, spreading "Free Trade" by the threat of FAEs, bunker busters, depleted uranium ammo and Apache helicopters. The "Destiny" in America's "Manifest Destiny" became "Manifest" when President Bush asserted in a Bob Woodward interview, "We will export death and violence to the four corners of the Earth in defense of our great nation." President Obama, once the great hope of many Americans who want a leader who will work for world peace, appears to be pursuing Bush's global exporting of war.

America's unilateral rigidification of the world's future to its own liking bodes ill both for the world and for the United States itself. One vital way to prevent our government from plunging the country into nihilistic war-making is to be vigilant about how our centers of power use and misuse language, a linguistic and moral sensitivity for which we are indebted to Orwell.

"George Orwell and Washington's War Rhetoric" by Donald Gutierrez—*Common Sense*, April 2002; *Bloomsbury Review*, September 2002; *Eldorado Sun*, July 2003.

17
Review: Christopher Hitchens,
The Trial of Henry Kissinger

Does Henry Kissinger, like Franz Kafka's Joseph K in his novel *The Trial*, wonder why people are knocking on his door? He would claim the reasons for *his* arrest would be lies. According, however, to Christopher Hitchen's book, *The Trial of Henry Kissinger*, there are good reasons for our former secretary of state to be arrested and tried. Hitchens presents a list of offenses:

> The deliberate mass killing of civilian populations in Indochina,
> Deliberate collusion in mass murder, and later assassination, in Bangladesh,
> The personal suborning and planning of murder of a senior constitutional officer in a democratic nation—Chile—with which the United States was not at war,
> Personal involvement in a plan to murder the head of state in the democratic nation of Cyprus.
> The incitement and enabling of genocide in East Timor.
> Personal involvement in a plan to kidnap and murder a journalist living in Washington, DC.

Not exactly minor indictments. "The above allegations," Hitchens continues, "are not exhaustive. And some of them can only be constructed *prima facie*, since Mr. Kissinger...has caused large tranches of evidence to be withheld or destroyed" (xi).

To what extent *prima facie* evidence weakens Hitchens's case against Kissinger is obviously hard to determine. Apparently, Kissinger has either made evidence of his role in catastrophic events inaccessible, not mentioned them in his memoirs or has lied about his involvement in them.

Space doesn't permit doing justice to the intricacy of Hitchens' analysis and judgment of Kissinger's role in the disastrous events presented in *Trial.* I will focus instead on his treatment of Kissinger's involvement in the Vietnam War and touch briefly on his alleged complicity in the horrors of Bangladesh, Chile and East Timor, war crimes all.

Hitchens claims that Kissinger and President Richard Nixon prolonged the war in Vietnam four years more by secretly sabotaging the Democrats' Paris Peace Talks in 1968. They made a secret deal with the South Vietnamese junta that they could offer a "better deal than they would get from the democrats." The junta then pulled out of the Paris talks, leading to four more years of war with "the same terms and conditions as had been on the table in…1968" (15). The consequences of this secret Kissinger-Nixon plotting were 31,205 American casualties between 1968 and 1972, not to mention almost half a million Vietnamese casualties and the obliteration of much of their land by incredibly heavy bombing and chemical defoliation.

This covert violation—cynically carried out for tactical advantage in the presidential election—was then magnified by the American aerial attack on Laos and Cambodia in which up to 350,000 *civilians* in Laos, and 600,000 in Cambodia, were killed. These bombings were also executed in secret, rationalized by the claim that the Viet Cong supposedly had supply lines into these two countries. Though Kissinger habitually claims he was not in the loop in these and others acts of massive state violence by the United States, Hitchens indicates time after time that Kissinger was very much involved in them. With Nixon he picked out bombing sites and was keenly attentive to all the resultant "data."

Hitchens argues that Kissinger knew of and was involved in these illegal acts of war and terrorism. Using the evidence of a Saigon bureau chief named Kevin Buckley, Hitchens shows that Kissinger was indifferent to the 5,000 or more noncombatant civilians killed by the United States in the Mekong Delta province. Hitchens' dependence on *prima facie* evidence emerges here:

> [T]he degree of micro-management revealed in Kissinger's memoirs forbids the idea that anything of importance took place without his knowledge or permission. Of nothing is this more true than his own involvement in the bombing and invasion of neutral Cambodia and Laos. (33)

Prima facie evidence is evidence that establishes a fact or that is immediately plain or looks convincing on first appearance. This definition suggests that more evidence could be needed to make the case for Kissinger's criminal involvement in Indochina complete. Such additional evidence resides in a short section of *Trial* subtitled "A Brief Note on the 40 Committee." Hitchens refers to this committee as "a semi-clandestine body of which Henry Kissinger was the chairman between 1969 and 1976" (16). He defines it as "a committee which maintained ultimate supervision over United States covert actions overseas during this period" (16). Hitchens then draws the implication from Kissinger's position in this powerful committee that he can be assumed to have had "direct knowledge of and responsibility" (18) for covert actions. Although this may not be smoking-gun evidence, when Hitchens combines it with other instances of almost certain involvement by Kissinger in mass atrocities and the lethal violation of heads of state in nations the United States was at peace with, Kissinger's culpability for war crimes appears even more likely.

Hitchens buttresses his indictment by referring to General Telford Taylor (chief prosecuting counsel at the Nuremberg Trials) and his book *Nuremberg and Vietnam* (1991). Taylor claims that if the American leaders designing the Vietnam War were judged by the same criteria as Japan's World War II chief militarist, General Tomoyoki Yamashita, they too would be hanged. According to Taylor, the United States in Vietnam seriously violated the Nuremberg principle that it was legally committed to uphold. If this is true and if the evidence is *sufficient* (as it seems to be) that Kissinger was a primary participant in masterminding acts of "negligent homicide" against Vietnam (as well as against Indonesia, Chile, Bangladesh and East Timor), then he qualifies, according to both Hitchens and Taylor, as a war criminal. General Taylor gives a specific edge to the charge in describing "the practice of air strikes against hamlets suspected of harboring Vietnamese guerrillas as 'flagrant violations of the Geneva Convention on Civilian Protection'" (30).

In the case of Bangladesh, where anywhere from one-half million to three million Hindu civilians were murdered by Pakistani troops, the deliberate non-interference of the United States was, according to Hitchens, due to Nixon and Kissinger using Pakistan as an intermediary to an economic rapprochement that the White House wanted with China. General Yahah Khan, the man mainly responsible for the massacre of Bengalis, felt free to pursue his genocidal policy because of his middleman role in American-Chinese diplomacy. Thus, urges Hitchens, "the collusion with him [Khan] in the matter of China *increases* the direct complicity of Nixon and Kissinger in the massacres" (48).

In the case of Chile, Nixon was determined to oust the Democratic socialist government of Salvador Allende because American corporations such as ITT and Pepsi Cola were hostile to it. Nixon wanted Allende out by any means, and to achieve that, it was necessary to get rid of the one powerful Chilean official, General Rene Schneider, who firmly opposed military involvement in the election procedure. Schneider was kidnapped and murdered, and the legitimate Allende government was overthrown with the connivance of the White House. A Kissinger cable to the CIA station in Santiago dated 18 October 1970 indicates, "sub-machine guns and ammo being sent...leaving Washington 0700 Oct due Santiago late evening 20 Oct" (59).

This secret message, along with other incriminating ones, more than suggests to Hitchens that Kissinger was at the center of this deadly clandestine activity. Writing to an extremist right wing general named Roberto Viaux, who carried out the murder of Schneider, Kissinger says, "The time will come when you with all your friends can do something. You will continue to have our support" (61). Thus, according to this chain of evidence, Kissinger and Nixon opened the way to the toppling of the Allende government and, consequently, to the torture and killing by the regime of Augusto Pinochet. All that Kissinger has to say to Pinochet about Pinochet's murderous repression of thousands of Chilean citizens is that "your greatest sin was that you overthrew a government that was going Communist" (70). As one would expect, Kissinger failed to repeat this remark in his memoirs.

Finally, Hitchens charges Kissinger with complicity in the 1975 invasion of East Timor by Indonesia. Kissinger and President Gerald Ford left Jakarta one day before the invasion. Though Kissinger denies discussing anything of importance with President Suharto, Ford in effect contradicts this. Not only did the United States supply Indonesia with 90 percent of its military weapons (a violation of American law), but it also gave the green light to the invasion which killed at least 200,000 East Timorans. Such examples of Kissinger's complicity and cover-ups appear to underline the ruthlessness of a frequently practiced realpolitik that put a lust for power above all ethical considerations.

International courts of law now exist that are capable of ruling upon cases involving assassination, terrorism and kidnapping despite the doctrine of sovereign immunity. Judges in France have tried to summon Kissinger for questioning in regard to "disappeared" French nationals in Chile, as have judges in Chile in regard to the many Chilean "disappeared." What is highly significant in Kissinger's case is the possibility of indicting a famous *American* as a war criminal. A key barrier to whatever justice Kissinger might deserve is the incomplete accessibility of State Department, CIA and National Security Council memos dealing with the international crises mentioned above. Within these limitations, Hitchens does a scrupulously analytical and morally impassioned job of showing that available evidence, as well as what might some day become available to public perusal, suggests why Kissinger hesitates to travel abroad these days.

"Review: Christopher Hitchens, *The Trial of Henry Kissinger*" by Donald Gutierrez—*Bloomsbury Review*, September 2001; *Common Sense*, April 2002.

18
Review: Vincent Bugliosi,
The Prosecution of George W. Bush for Murder

The title of Vincent Bugliosi's *The Prosecution of George W. Bush for Murder* might at first appear audacious or even outrageous. What is really outrageous, though, is that, according to Bugliosi, President Bush and his administration have gotten away with lies and executive actions based on deception massively criminal in character without anyone—until Bugliosi—legally holding Bush to account. Congress, the media and the public have given Bush a free ride, which infuriates Bugliosi. This shocking societal irresponsibility embodies an ethical catastrophe for the nation and the world. For this Bugliosi holds Bush accountable litigiously with an unparalleled ferocity.

Bugliosi's prosecutorial qualifications are impressive. He has won 21 out of 22 murder convictions, the most famous of course being the Manson case. He has also won 105 out of 106 felony jury cases. To F. Lee Bailey, Bugliosi is "the quintessential prosecutor." How then does he handle this "case"?

Prosecution operates on two rhetorical levels. First, it projects an intensely personal approach at the reader, which is compelling but also occasionally off-putting. Bugliosi brings home the horror of losing a son in the war by recounting a horrific account of his death, then asks how you would feel if it were your son. On the other hand, he'll address the reader with, "Hey, Estupido, I'm talking to you!" to be sure one gets the point of some stricture of Bush that he regards as obviously major. *Prosecution* attempts to reach as many people as possible with this direct, righteously angry, common-decency strategy. This is often effective as polemic, considering the subject and the dramatic nature of his indictment.

On a more formal yet accessible level of discourse, Bugliosi presents a methodical, detailed account of Bush's reasons and alleged lies to justify starting the war on Iraq. This is followed by an imaginary court prosecution of former President Bush with a crucial definition of the charge of murder in regard to Bush's initiating the war. This is the legal core of *Prosecution*, which is supplemented by other crucial concerns. These include the seriousness of Bush's crimes; the various costs of the war; what kind of judgment should be rendered Bush; Bush's terrible performance in combating terrorism; Bush's not being held responsible for 9/11 occurring on his watch but, instead, heroizing himself by transforming that event into cause for a "War on Terrorism;" Dick Cheney and Condoleezza Rice as Bush's co-conspirators in murder; and Bugliosi's sharp disapproval of Congress, the media and the public for accepting Bush's war.

Bugliosi presents Bush's chief initial reasons for attacking Iraq: Saddam Hussein's alleged Weapons of Mass Destruction and his tie-in with Bin Laden in regard to 9/11. Bush insisted that Saddam's WMDs constituted an imminent threat to the United States despite the fact, as Bugliosi observes, that sixteen American intelligence agencies stated that Saddam was not a threat. Further, a White House White Paper misrepresented the claim of the State Department's Intelligence and Research Bureau that Iraq was not moving forward on nuclear arms research. There is also the demonstrated Uranium-from-Niger lie and the 2002 "Downing Street Memo," which indicated that the intelligence was "being fixed around the policy" by the White House.

Bugliosi continues examining Bush's lies, but enough serious ones have been cited here to allow us to consider Bugliosi's legal procedure for indicting Bush for murder. Bush, Bugliosi claims, "took this nation to war under false pretenses" (116). The president's lies led to the death of thousands of American soldiers and many thousands of Iraqi civilians. In the most riveting part of *Prosecution*, Bugliosi sets up his idea of Bush's defense against these charges and then, in a formidably entrapping style of prosecutorial interrogation, proceeds to demolish it. Bush's argument of self-defense—based on his claim that he was defending America from imminent Iraqi attack—can, Bugliosi asserts, be disproved by carefully demonstrating his lies and contradictions under relentlessly logical interrogation. And if Bush next claimed that in 2002 Congress authorized the war, a prosecutor would assert that "consent is not a defense to the crime of murder" (92).

Further, with regard to Bush's alleged lies to justify attacking Iraq, "fraud vitiates consent."

Bugliosi next attempts to show how all this lying and misrepresentation by the former president constitutes murder. The prosecution would need to prove that Bush did harbor "a criminal state of mind" (94); and, by Bugliosi's line of argument, this proof would be found in Bush's lies leading to the death of American soldiers. Did Bush want those deaths? No, but he committed actions making them all but unavoidable by declaring a preemptive, not preventive, war. This crucial distinction was underlined to a significant degree by his false WMDs defense claim, which made it clear that Iraq was not preparing to attack the United States.

At this point, Bugliosi examines the legal character of murder and relates it to defendant Bush. For the legal charge of murder to be valid, it must, states Bugliosi, contain two elements, the prohibited act, *actus reus*, which has to be accompanied by *mens reus*, criminal intent.

> In this case, the "act" by Bush would be ordering his military to invade Iraq with American soldiers, 4000 of whom have already died....The necessary intent that would have to be shown, as indicated, is malice aforethought, satisfied if Bush either intended to kill the soldiers by ordering them to war, or he started the war with reckless and wanton disregard for the consequences and indifference to human life. (93)

Bush's defense would be that he was acting in (national) self-defense. But, as his self-contradicting chain of lies would reveal this to be totally untrue, he would, asserts Bugliosi, be shown to have a "criminal state of mind" and thus to be guilty of murder. And if his defense claimed that Bush would never have wished American soldiers to be killed in a war, the (Bugliosi) prosecution would argue that ordering Americans into a war (especially an illegal and unjust one) would inevitably result in American military deaths, thus sealing the case against Bush.

Bugliosi points out, further, that Bush could be liable to what in law is called the felony murder rule whereby certain felonies are "so inherently dangerous, in and of themselves, and the risk of death was so high" (97) that there could be an indictment of first degree murder, "even though there was no malice." According to Bugliosi, such a ruling can be administered, "even where the defendant is not the killer" (98).

Bugliosi, not a prosecutor likely to stop halfway, stunningly pushes the legal possibilities to their climax. He states that although Bush could be indicted for second-degree murder, which carries a life sentence, "Bush's alleged crime is so prodigious and on such a grand scale that it would greatly dishonor those in their graves who paid the ultimate price because of it if he were not to pay the ultimate penalty. This is why all attempts should be made to prosecute him for first degree murder" (99). The prosecution of Bush could (should, Bugliosi argues) be for first-degree murder, for which he could receive the death penalty. Moreover, Bugliosi asserts that "most first-degree murder cases are based on circumstantial evidence" (100); there need not be a smoking gun (or a mushroom cloud). Finally, proving that Bush did not act in self-defense by declaring war on Iraq requires proof only beyond a reasonable doubt.

Is Bugliosi's "prosecution" of Bush merely a vindictive fantasy lacking serious grounds for pursuing legal justice? Certainly not according to Bugliosi, who, after detailing Bush's lies in office, further attempts to strengthen his case by discussing some terrible consequences of Bush's war. As of 2007, the money for the war could have financed health care for all insured Americans for perhaps thirty years. Further, most of the world loathed or feared Bush, and thus, to some extent, the country. Consequently, according to a 2006 National Intelligence Estimate Report, the United States was less safe under Bush than it was before the war. American casualties, as Bugliosi repeatedly states, are well over 4,000. He claims Iraqi casualties come to somewhat over 100,000, which is generally considered a conservative estimate. And he points out that millions of Iraqis have been dislocated from their homes and country. Of course, the loss of many billions of dollars for America's social needs (such as health care, education and bridges) is another area of outrageous negligence caused by the war and occupation.

Bugliosi suggests effective venues in which Bush could be tried, the best being in a federal court; failing that, the case could go to a state court. And because soldiers killed in the war came from every state in the nation, any state attorney would have the right to indict Bush. If Bush's indictment still seems improbable, Bugliosi reminds us that in 2004, General Pinochet at age 89 was finally indicted by his country. Bugliosi, moreover, cannily remarks that in any trial proceeding all potential jurors be asked under oath whether trying a president of the United States would be acceptable to them; if not, they would be dismissed from the jury.

Prosecution contains a "Photographic Brief," seven pages of photos divided into two shockingly contrastive sections. The first shows both Americans and Iraqis ravaged with grief for family and friends killed or wounded in the war. The second exhibits eight photos, taken from 2002 on, of Bush broadly smiling, grinning from ear to ear, looking like he's having (as he had himself declared) the time of his life. Bugliosi repeatedly presses on the reader Bush's insensitive personal happiness. This is usually shown in juxtaposition to such incidents as one soldier in Iraq writing to his folks to let them know he's okay and that he worries about them, only the next day to be found dead and decapitated, with evidence indicating he had been tortured.

Bugliosi also discusses in detail how Bush vacationed 977 days or over one-third of his 2,923 days as president. While other American presidents, whatever their own war-mongering (a relevant, important consideration Bugliosi ignores), are seen even in private looking grim and concerned about a given war during their watch, Bush apparently is mainly grieved because, for example, the White House running track is not long enough for his daily workout.

Prosecution has its flaws. Bugliosi's righteous if pugnacious anger might occasionally seem excessive. For example, he calls Bush a son of a bitch and a coward, and the American public the living dead for not responding to the Bush administration's malfeasance. He also whitewashes some former presidents, which makes Bush look even worse. (Richard Nixon's secret bombing of Cambodia is not mentioned.) Many of his quotes lack a source listing and there is no bibliography. On the other hand, *Prosecution* includes 74 pages of notes, one of which is ten pages long. Many of the notes are important to key ideas in his legal, prosecutorial and polemical argumentation.

Bugliosi can be repetitive to a fault; but then incremental repetition is how a good prosecutor proceeds, and Bugliosi is clearly a formidable prosecutor. Finally, Bugliosi would have further strengthened his indictment of the massive damage Bush's illegal war did to the country had he cited war profits made by the defense industry. The public money paid by the Pentagon to Boeing and the rest of the ordnance manufacturers amounted to hundreds of billions of dollars. As Chris Hedges puts it pungently in his book *Death of the Liberal Class*, "war, after all, is primarily a business" (Hedges, 51).

Nevertheless, actualizing the prosecution of President Bush could be very difficult, to say the least. Enormous institutional pressures would surely be brought to bear—relayed through the Supreme Court, Congress, the corporatized media and conservative think tanks—to prevent this extraordinary legal action, even if a sizable number of Americans favored it. The pro-Bush forces would, falsely but energetically, claim that such an indictment would seriously denigrate the office of the American presidency itself, using that prestigious shield to defend a felonious president. Furthermore, Bush has been virtually pardoned by the Obama administration's refusal to indict senior officials in the preceding administration for alleged crimes while in office.

Still, it is momentous that Vincent Bugliosi has thrust this bold and cogently argued "case" into the public arena. Prosecuting former President Bush could become a potent seed in the American mind. And who knows what young, morally inflamed state or federal attorney might one day take up the challenge of imposing justice on George W. Bush—and carry it through.

"Review: Vincent Bugliosi, *The Prosecution of George W. Bush for Murder*" by Donald Gutierrez—*Humanist Society of New Mexico*, November 2008; *Progressive Populist*, December 2008.

19
Universal Jurisdiction and the Bush Administration

Is Donald Rumsfeld a war criminal? If so, can he or other senior Administration officials be prosecuted? Can the prosecution be effectuated, the ex-Defense Secretary put behind bars? These are crucial and intriguing questions to anyone who feels that the ex-Secretary of State not only bore major responsibility for the secret torturing of Mid- and Far Eastern detainees, but was guilty of war crimes for his part (along with President Bush and Vice President Cheney) in implementing an illegal and unjust attack on a sovereign nation, Iraq.

These considerations invite some reflections on the legal concept of Universal Jurisdiction. According to an article published in the November 2006 issue of *The Nation*, the legal analyst Brendan Smith and the historian Jeremy Brecher claim that this "doctrine allows domestic courts to prosecute international crimes regardless of where the crime was committed, the nationality of the perpetrator, or the nationality of the victim. It is reserved for only the most heinous offenses: genocide, war crimes and crimes against humanity, including torture."

More than a few unconstitutional laws and covert practices hammered or sneaked through by the Bush administration possibly make Universal Jurisdiction an increasingly relevant and dramatic juridical protection against the enlarging authoritarian proclivities in White House governance. These pernicious developments have included, among others, the U.S. Patriot Act, warrantless surveillance of Americans, the Abu Ghraib, Guantanamo and extraordinary rendition scandals, and, more recently, the terrifying Military Commissions Act of 2006 and barely noticed Defense

Authorization Act of 2007 (Public Law 109-364). This last Act, undercutting *Posse Comitatus*, enables the President to introduce martial law. Possibly the most sinister of all these proto-totalitarian measures, this Act would impose military domination over civil institutions and civilian life, and easily slide into targeting ultimately anyone as an "illegal enemy combatant," to be dealt with accordingly.

All of the above could embody grave illegal conduct by the state, but the act most likely to lead to future war crimes by high-placed officials is the Military Commissions Act. The reason that Act especially could lead to future war crimes is that it exonerates war crimes already committed. This Act in effect provides legal protection for, among other transgressions, the White House's violation of habeus corpus, denial of access by detainees to evidence acquired from them coercively, and the imposition of torture and indefinite confinement. The White House can now do punitively whatever it wants to *anyone*, including any American.

It is worthwhile then to consider both the potential and the actual power of Universal Jurisdiction in relation to war crimes committed by government officials. Also called the Universality Principle, Universal Jurisdiction fits neatly into such American-backed global ideals and institutions as the United Nations Charter and the post-WWII Universal Declaration of Human Rights. The United States is a signatory to both. Initially designed to end the "scourge of war," the Declaration is expansive enough to stigmatize high-placed political leaders who commit war crimes, crimes against humanity, torture and genocide. Accordingly, such an American-supported international ideal could re-enforce Universal Jurisdiction in condemning specific acts and individuals (American or otherwise) who violate these formalized ideals.

Still, these are only ideals and moral sanctions. They seem to lack force against powerful government officials whose unrelenting obstinacy and arrogance are based on their tunnel-vision sense of being right through the privilege of power and inaccessibility to indictment. Top-level American officials like Bush II, Cheney, Rumsfeld, and Rice would not likely have been arrested and detained anywhere through Universal Jurisdiction. If Germany, for example, had arrested any one of the above while in their country, Washington might well have threatened Germany formidably. Could it, however, threaten a Germany, Belgium, or Spain serving as the vehicle of international, even global, authority?

The possible confrontation of a super state and an international institution leads to the thorny problem and concept of state sovereignty. Theoretically, this doctrine means that all states, no matter how tiny, are, according to the United Nations Charter, entitled to have not only their borders safeguarded but their leaders as well. What, then, gives one state (Germany, Belgium, the United States, etc.) the right—let alone the power—to try a key state official of another nation?

That right could be based on a sufficient number of significant states responsibly accepting the concept of Universal Jurisdiction either as a United Nations resolution or through some other grassroots international institution such as the World Social Forum, with its powerful drive for global social-economic egalitarianism and its potential for worldwide grassroots organization promoting peace, justice and environmental sustainability. If Universal Jurisdiction is truly universal, then it's not only a matter of, say, Germany indicting an American statesman (or vice versa) but of the international community *through* Germany (Spain, etc.) indicting a Rumsfeld, Pinochet, Putin for crimes against humanity or indicting a Bush or Obama for initiating war crimes. This would put the massed weight of the international community upon a transgressor state—again, a primary design of the Universal Declaration of Human Rights.

Washington, granted, has often shown scant respect for international institutions and directives. When, for example, the Reagan administration mined Managua's harbors and financed and trained the Contras, it was condemned almost unanimously by the U.N. and penalized by the International Criminal Court. Washington totally ignored these two expressions of virtually universal censure.

A contemporary U.N., however, that included not only a united Europe but powerful states like China, Japan and Russia, not to mention rising economic powers like India and South Korea, could wield sizable influence against absolutist state sovereignty, especially if these nations were to recognize that their own best interests resided in a flexible balance between sovereignty and just international allegiance and world harmony. Acting on this awareness could lead to some diminution of states committing war crimes.

Christopher Hitchens in *The Trial of Henry Kissinger* argues that "the defense of 'sovereign immunity' for state crimes has been held to be void." Mentioning the landmark case of the Pinochet verdict in England, Hitchens continues, "There is now no reason why a warrant for the trial of Kissinger may not be issued, *in any one of a dozen of jurisdictions* [emphasis added], and why he may not be compelled to answer it" (xi). Amnesty International reports that the United States is one of a dozen nations undertaking investigations, prosecutions and trials employing Universal Jurisdiction to extradite individuals for crimes including torture. Amnesty International also insists that genocide, crimes against humanity, war crimes and torture fall under international jurisdiction. Washington shouldn't have it all its own way; if it utilizes Universal Jurisdiction to charge foreigners for war crimes abroad (let alone invading nations that allegedly harbor terrorists), it should accept extradition or detention of Americans indicted by other nations for war crimes as well.

Hitchens' and Amnesty's position is reinforced by a team of lawyers from the Center for Constitutional Rights (New York) formally serving notice in Germany that Rumsfeld committed crimes relevant to international jurisdiction, which suggests that Universal Jurisdiction could indeed harbor some potency. Realistically, the test of the value of Universal Jurisdiction boils down to might versus right. Though Washington may not tolerate any nation arresting, or international court indicting, Kissinger, Rumsfeld or Cheney for violations of international law while such individuals are in office, their vulnerability out of office could be another matter. They would not be protected by the armor of official status. General Pinochet once held absolute power over Chile; by 2000, he was stripped of legal immunity by his own country for being accused of committing crimes against humanity.

Furthermore, labeling a Rumsfeld as a war criminal subject to at least virtual trial and legal guilt could have significant symbolic, psychological and deterrent force. Both Rumsfeld and Kissinger have been known to contact foreign states to make sure they wouldn't be detained during a visit; detainment, and what it stands for, could prey on their minds.[1] More significantly, other powerful leaders could feel more restrained if their foreign policy might acquire criminal status or liability internationally. Deterring the war crimes of statesmen would require concerted international condemnation, and that might take time and persistence, especially in view of the seemingly invincible nationalistic arrogance and unilateralism of a super state like the United States. If such inhibiting action reduced even just torture internationally, this would still be an enormous advancement towards extending human decency universally.

The more nations that support international condemnation of war crimes and crimes against humanity, the more impact such censure would likely have. And there is always the possibility that someone acquiring central political authority in Washington will realize that the most desirable foreign policy for creating global comity and *thus* security for America is through a policy promoting international humaneness and generosity rather than ruthless domineering. The consequences of strong states going their own way are so dangerous to the world that, if nothing else, the instinct of survival should make such nations come to terms with the crucial value of their international interdependence through such institutions as Universal Jurisdiction.

---

1. It is thought by some law authorities, such as the Center for Constitutional Rights (U.S.) and the European Center for Constitutional and Human Rights, that former President George W. Bush canceled his planned trip to Geneva, Switzerland in February 2011 out of concern that he would be detained through the agency of Universal Jurisdiction on charges of war crimes and crimes against humanity (including torture).

"Universal Jurisdiction and the Bush Administration" by Donald Gutierrez— *Common Sense*, April 2007; *Progressive Populist*, August 2007; *The Humanist*, March 2007.

20

Review: Naomi Wolf, *The End of America:*
Letters of Warning to a Young Patriot

Naomi Wolf's book *The End of America* begins with these words: "I am writing because we have an emergency." This warning is preceded by a quote from Justice William O. Douglas: "A nightfall does not come all at once, neither does oppression. In both instances, there is a twilight where everything remains seemingly unchanged. And it is in such a twilight that we all must be aware of change in the air—however slight—lest we become unwilling victims of the darkness."

Douglas's warning goes to the heart of Wolf's book, which asserts that a society can be in the process of moving from a democratic to a fascist society (that "twilight") without most people realizing it. Wolf uses parallel examples from Fascist Italy and Germany to show that dictators like Mussolini and Hitler came to absolute power within democratic institutions. She terms this process a "fascist shift."

"Both Italian and German fascisms came to power legally and incrementally in functioning democracies; both used legislation, cultural pressure and baseless imprisonment and torture, progressively to consolidate power.... both aggressively used the law to subvert the law"(21).

This process, Wolf claims, is what is happening in our country right now. Though Brown Shirts are not storming through Greenwich Village beating up NYU student activists or left wing professors, there are signs that America is becoming a closed society. *End* exhibits this ominous process as ten steps: Invoke an External Threat, Establish Secret Prisons, Develop a

Paramilitary Force, Surveil Ordinary Citizens, Infiltrate Citizen Groups, Arbitrarily Detain and Release Citizens, Target Key Individuals, Restrict the Press, Cast Criticism as "Espionage'"and Dissent as "Treason," and Subvert the Rule of Law. Just eight of these steps turned Thailand into a police state within a few days, and the same process, Wolf warns, is under way here, if more subtly and gradually.

End is a wake-up call to make us citizens realize that we reside in Justice Douglas's "twilight" and are moving towards the darkness of fascism: hence, the relative brevity of the book and the rousing effectiveness of these elaborated ten chilling steps. It is hard to decide which of these steps are more pernicious, but it would seem that step ten, The End of the Rule of Law, embodies the preceding nine in a terrifying climax. As Wolf states, the ten steps interplay and enhance one another in such a way that the whole is more than the sum of its parts, each contributing to, and climaxing in, fascism. I will deal here only with some of the most crucial points among them.

Regarding a government invoking an external and internal threat, Wolf cites totalitarian Italy, Germany and Russia as justifying their existence—and their increasing and finally totally illegal power—by claiming a dangerous external enemy. To perpetuate the threat, these regimes covertly wanted that enemy sustained. In the case of the Bush administration, its "War on Terrorism" fixation lent itself to this end. Having a dangerous external enemy turns internal dissent into treason, making valid criticism ultimately condemnable as treason. Such a fraudulent emergency, Wolf demonstrates, led to Hitler's Enabling Act of 1933 and President George W. Bush's innumerable Signing Statements, both crucial stratagems for circumventing their respective parliamentary and congressional checks and balances.

Perhaps more dramatically frightening of Wolf's ten steps towards fascism is the establishing of secret government prisons—Guantanamo military base in Cuba, Abu Ghraib prison in Iraq and numerous Black Cells stretched around the world. Wolf, at this juncture, formulates a potent insight about the "fascist shift": "A secret prison system without habeus corpus is the cornerstone of every dictatorship" (46). Stalin's gulags in Soviet Russia and Hitler's concentration camps in Nazi Germany come to mind. Wolf's point is that Guantanamo ultimately threatens *us*. A case in point is Bush's National Defense Authorization Act of 2007, which endangers all Americans by putting civil society under martial law, thereby allowing for detentionary treatment of critics—"traitors"—of the regime. (Earlier, Ronald Reagan had plans, according to a 2009 *Progressive Populist* piece by Ted Rall, to place almost half a million dissidents in concentration camps.)

Wolf's paramilitary-forces step suggests both Mussolini's and Hitler's gaggle of thugs organized to commit targeted violence against enemies. Citing material from Jeremy Scahill's brilliant work on the military contractor Blackwater (now called Academi), Wolf sees a parallel in this paramilitary operation. She notes their disturbing presence and even criminal conduct on the streets of New Orleans following Hurricane Katrina. Wolf might have developed the implication here that Blackwater could evolve into an American version of the German Nazi S.A., patrolling the streets of American cities and towns, attacking dissident demonstrators and so on.

Continuing down Wolf's steps lands the reader at surveillance. The supposedly discontinued Bush Administration's TIPS (Terrorism Information and Prevention System program), whereby mail carriers and others would report "suspicious" people, is just one of numerous recent examples in America of surveillance today. Not mentioned in *End* is the enormous degree of surveillance going on at college campuses today, as well as the far more lethal ordnance carried by campus cops. Wolf's haunting quotation, "Surveillance leads to fear and fear leads to silence" (88), pinpoints a central insight about any police state. Today one's e-mail, phone calls and web activity could be under government scrutiny. Individuals are even afraid to sign petitions to avoid being on some "list."

Infiltration of citizens groups is a particularly menacing step because it exhibits the government behaving in an underhanded way that crucially violates the democratic ideal of an open society. Government spies infiltrate dissident organizations, even including Veterans for Peace, which also violates the First Amendment ("the right of a people to assemble"). As happened in 2010 in Minneapolis, FBI agents not only infiltrated an anti-war group, but even became leaders in the organization, thus serving as a wedge to put the group at the mercy of full government intervention. Wolf observes that spies infiltrated labor unions in fascist Italy and that Stalin's spies kept an eye on Russia's intellectuals and dissidents. Examples from Nazi Germany, Pinochet's Chile, the Stasi in East Germany follow. Again, after the illegal COINTEL surveillance against peace activists of the 1960s, America is falling into this pattern of government surveillance. As Wolf notes, "Since 2000, there has been a sharp increase of U.S. citizens that are being harassed and infiltrated by police and federal agents, often in illegal ways" (90).

One might say that such surveillance, though disturbing and illegal, is not quite the same thing as arbitrarily arresting, then (sometimes) releasing citizens. However, it can lead to that. Arbitrary detention and release, another step with parallels to totalitarian societies, is observable in the 75,000 Americans on the "No Fly List"—one of whom is Naomi Wolf. Wolf cites the No Fly List as an example of such arbitrary power by the state.

Such immobilizing of one's freedom of movement obviously violates both the Constitution and the very essence of a free society. But it harbors more sinister implications when a state becomes more despotic and hostile to critics, rebels, dissidents. Being on such a list makes one aware, as it did Wolf, that one is being tracked—not just watched—by the state. Wolf doesn't pursue the consequences of what can happen to such individuals in a tyrannic society, but in a closed society, being on the government's suspect list can sooner or later lead to imprisonment, torture and even death. And a major step towards this destiny is, as Wolf indicates, "Making it more difficult for people out of favor with the state to travel back and forth across borders....a classic part of the fascist play book" (98). This, Wolf points out, occurred in Nazi Germany and the Soviet Union.

Restricting the Press is a crucial process. Wolf cites the Bush Administration's attempt to slide PBS to the right by pressing for fewer allegedly liberal programs. A more lethal example was the U.S. military threatening to fire on independent journalists (including Americans) if they transmitted stories from Iraq electronically, as well as forcing them to reveal their political attitude towards the Iraq War. The broadest example of press restriction was the manipulation of the press by the White House to convey lies to justify the 2003 invasion.

Criticism as espionage and dissent as treason imply an advanced phase of Wolf's "fascist shift" that could destroy key areas protected by the Constitution. The proposed H.R. 1955, though passed by the House by a huge margin, did not pass in the Senate. Had it done so, the bill would have virtually indicted and thus repressed any public expression of "suspicious" ideas or thoughts. Right wing publicists like Anne Coulter and William Kristol have attacked liberals as well as media like *The New York Times* as traitorous, helping to establish a public mindset consonant with the repressive outlook of the Bush administration towards dissent.

As in all of Wolf's preceding steps towards a fascist or totalitarian state, she offers vivid parallels of dissent arbitrarily interpreted as treason in Stalinist Russia of the 1930s and Hitler's 1934 law criminalizing dissent. These autocratic tendencies appear ominously similar to such American hunts for "traitors" as were evident in the savage 1917 Espionage and Trading with the Enemy Act that outlawed anti-war expression, and, following World War I, in the Mitchell Palmer raids on thousands of citizens and immigrants without warrants for arrest. In 2006, a San Francisco talk-radio host urged execution for *Times* editor Bill Keller if it were proven he had legally treasonous intimates. The government's transformation of dissent, an essential facet of an open society, into treason could finally subvert law itself. This pernicious process is paralleled by Wolf with Hitler's thorough corroding of law *within a legal context.*

All of this climaxes darkly in the subversion of the rule of law. As with Hitler, this process, which Wolf claims can occur quite quickly, involves a series of increasing demands by a leader for more power, more rights. Finally a tipping point is reached at which a checks-and-balances system collapses and the president/leader becomes the "Supreme Leader." One recalls the numerous instances of contempt for and dismissal of Congress, and thus of the public, exhibited by the Bush administration after 2001. The Military Commissions Act of 2006 and the National Defense Authorization Act of 2007 further subverted the institutions designed to promote representative democracy and protect the public from government autocracy. In a short final chapter, "The Patriot's Task," Wolf implores all Americans to demand accountability from the government and restore democracy.

Wolf's book would have benefited from an index, as there are many significant names and events one would like quick referral to. More seriously, Wolf says virtually nothing about the Pentagon's increasing and extremely expensive militarism involved in maintaining a global imperialism, which might be considered a major force in a "fascist shift."[1]

Despite these shortcomings, *The End of America* is a rousing call to activism. Instead of focusing merely on one or two serious violations of our social contract with Washington, it piles up ten to arrive at a powerful condemnation of dangerous White House malfeasance. If her bold comparisons of the Bush administration with the solidification of tyranny achieved by Hitler, Stalin and Mussolini might appear excessive to some, it is nevertheless the very disturbing similitude of those comparisons that should sound a wake-up call. Americans should subordinate their daily concerns and begin taking action against a government regime that is taking their freedom and ultimately their country away from them.

---

1. This is discussed authoritatively in Chalmers Johnson's "blowback" series: *Blowback: the Costs and Consequences of American Empire* (2000), *The Sorrows of Empire: Militarism, Secrecy, and the End of the Republic* (2004) and *Nemesis: the Last Days of the American Republic* (2006). *Sorrows* is reviewed in Ch. 27.

"Review: Naomi Wolf, *The End of America: Letters of Warning to a Young Patriot*" by Donald Gutierrez—*Common Sense*, October 2008; *The Humanist Society of New Mexico*, June 2008; *Progressive Populist*, August 2008; *ABQ Trial Balloon*, June 2008; *Chiron Review*, Autumn 2008.

21
Feeling the Unthinkable

The title of one of the great 19th century European novels, Gustave Flaubert's *L'Education Sentimentale*, is particularly important today in our Nuclear Age. The novel's title points to a frightening gap in the sensibility of some people in positions of substantial power—defense corporation heads, top military officials, politicians, scientists and others. What I refer to is the apparent inability of these individuals to *feel* the medical, physical, and ecological consequences of nuclear and conventional war.

In 1962, the Rand Corporation futurist Herman Kahn wrote a book called *Thinking About the Unthinkable* (updated in 1983). It attempted to justify approaching the phenomenom of nuclear war in rational, objective terms: the different "scenarios" leading to nuclear war; various kinds of deterence; civil defense; possibilities for recovery (assuming recovery from major nuclear war would even be possible, which many experts deny); and so on. What has shocked some about the Khanian perspective on conceiving of nuclear war is the heavy emphasis on the rational, a word too readily regarded as a synonym for terms like sane, decent, even humane. I suggest that within the context of nuclear catastrophe, appraising nuclear warheads and their total effects *only* rationally or objectively is indecent, inhumane—and insane.

Dr. Helen Caldicott memorably articulates the nature of the evil role of nuclear scientists, R&D technicians and others, past and present, in her powerful 1984 book *Missile Envy: The Arms Race and Nuclear War*:

> In fact, most of the strategic theories used today are recycled RAND theories developed years ago by those scientists whose professional aim was to develop credible

plans to fight a nuclear war with the Russians, often talking
about first strike. The trouble was that they never could,
despite their toil during all these years, devise a scenario
where they could win without the deaths of millions of people.
Yet they persisted tenaciously with their theories, and they are
still at it today... their terminology allowed them to
contemplate ghastly scenarios without permitting those stark
facts to penetrate their emotions and their souls. The trouble
is that these people taught everyone else how to practice this
scientific psychic numbing by rational elimination of human
emotions from the equation of mass genocide. These men were
above all else rational! What a disservice to humanity they
performed! (222-23)

In contrast to the scientists' rational, objective assessment of the
results of nuclear war, Caldicott's ghastly scenarios would mean, among
other things, millions of people annihilated by the incredibly intense heat,
blast pressure and radiation unleashed by these diabolical bombs. Now,
people with Kahn's mentality are ignoring or repressing the emotional,
bodily—and thus crucially human—aspects of nuclear destructivity; they
do not envisage or, key word, *imagine* in the most intensely felt way what the
actual physical results of nuclear war would be. No awareness seems to exist
in these people of what it could physically and mentally feel like to have
millions of human beings instantly transformed into radioactive dust in
dozens of major cities in the Soviet Union and the United States (for of
course the nuclear fate of the two largest nuclear nations is tightly
interlinked). There is little or no felt consideration among well-subsidized
Think Tank rationalists like Kahn about the pain, terror, depression,
suicidal and homicidal drives—in short, the mass psychic breakdown—that
would likely be induced in nuclear "survivors." A former Soviet Premier put
the consequences of nuclear war with memorable succinctness: After a
nuclear war, Nikita Khrushchev once said, "the living will envy the dead."

There is a whole world of private sensibility—of feeling (both
emotional and sensory), intimate consciousness and self-consciousness—
that we all sizably experience about our own being and body, and about our
external surroundings to which Kahnian objectivity is totally insensitive. The
old prejudice that men mainly think and women mostly feel might harbor
truth in the vital sense expressed by Caldicott that women relate more
profoundly to life-nurturing values than men do. This orientation of course

is not just a matter of culturally defined roles. Women are more inclined than men to promote life because they are biologically as well as culturally involved directly in raising and caring for the young.

Whether or not women are really more expert than men at relating to others, they are more skillful at relating to their own and to other people's feelings and at interpreting their emotions, their inner life. Women, that is, are generally better students of *l'education sentimentale* than men. This implies that women usually possess a greater, deeper sense than do men of the crucial humanistic culture of the emotions (Rosseau, Proust, D.H. Lawrence notwithstanding). Women consequently are possibly more proficient than men at relating emotion and its special significance to the affective or feeling aspects of nuclear war and "scenarios" about it.

Thus, two alternative interpretations follow. Either, only women can humanly perceive the utter horror of nuclear war, and are thus a kind of different, perhaps superior sensibility in the area of a humanistic psychology of nuclear war and all its demonic consequences. Or, what some, perhaps many, women can feel about nuclear war is something men may also feel, or, if they don't, must learn to feel, if human society and life and indeed the earth itself are to survive.

Obviously, men too possess this vital emotional or subjective sense of nuclear annihilation; neither Jonathan Schell's *The Fate of the Earth* nor Robert Scheer's *With Enough Shovels: Reagan, Bush, and Nuclear War* could have been written without this sense. Also, there are men (doctors, artists, scientists, teachers, even retired military officers) who are deeply engaged in the anti-nuclear-war movement. But the authoritative fact remains that most of the individuals carrying out the nuclear weapons experimentation, testing, arms sales and build-up since World War II have been men. Men conceived the H-bomb, such as its proud father, Edward Teller. Men run the highly profitable defense corporations and the think tanks and the pivotal Congressional committees and power defense industry lobbies and money-lending banks that have created in the United States and the Soviet Union approximately 50,000 warheads. (Though sizably reduced in number by both countries in 2011, experts claim it would take only 300 warheads to destroy both nations, and far more than that remain as of 2012.)

It is then, I submit, primarily men who are moving the world towards possible nuclear annihilation, partly because they are not imagining nuclear war in terms of feeling. Granted, there are other factors for the arms buildup and nuclear war threat: our induced paranoiac fear and hatred of other powers such as China and Russia; greed and careerism among politicians, arms contractors, scientists, military professionals; the Pentagon's virtually unlimited budget; the American "City-on-the-Hill" missionary obsession; and so on. Aside from these factors, it is usually men, adult males, who justify preparing for nuclear war by the pernicious rationalization that destabilizing, escalating strategies like deterrence and SDI (Strategic Defense Initiative) will prevent it, and who ignore realizing its horror and insanity in human terms.

This does not necessarily mean that all or most women are anti-nuclear-war, peace-oriented stalwarts. I don't recall any protest from Mrs. Reagan, Mrs. Weinberger (wife of Reagan's Secretary of Defense), Mrs. George Bush or the wives of the powerful war corporation moguls to the devastatingly expensive and dangerous arms buildup that their husbands have been perpetrating for years, nor does an Aristophanic "scenario" like *Lysistrata* seem likely in their bedrooms (desirable as it might indeed be for such wives to declare to their death-oriented husbands, "No Peace, No Sex!"). Further, it was also our female Secretary of State, Hillary Clinton, who a few years ago thundered that the United States would "nuke" Iran if it attacked Israel. And Margaret Thatcher, England's prime minister from 1979 to 1990, earned the sobriquet "Iron Maiden."

One reason for emotionally minimizing the real catastrophic horror of nuclear war possibly relates to Robert Jay Lifton's concept of psychic numbing. Nuclear war and annihilation are so unimaginably ghastly that many people—both men *and* women—refuse to face them emotionally; instead, we "novocaine" ourselves to any feeling about such a catastrophe. It is not only the Herman Kahns, the generals and admirals and hawk Congressmen and defense corporation chiefs who consider the prospect of nuclear war only "objectively." Many of us do so because an emotional realization of nuclear weapon destructiveness is too frightening to undergo. The imagination cannot tolerate such a massive horror, but the rational mind lobotomized of affect can. Yet, as Schell, Lifton, Caldicott, Lord Zuckerman, Scheer and a growing number of scientists have been saying now for years, the consequences of this numbing of feeling about nuclear war—along with other factors, nationalistic and ideological paranoia, financial greed, computer or human error, political machismo—are the increasing likelihood of conventional war and of war threats escalating to nuclear war.

The implicit danger of warning about the unprecedented horror of nuclear war is to make conventional arms buildup and conventional war seem "safe" by comparison. This is an extremely dangerous delusion. The adage that all is fair in love and war harbors an ominous dimension in the Nuclear Age. For, though the world and the earth might at first appear to survive a conventional weapons war, one must take the emotional and vindictive propensities of war confrontation and fortunes to their logical conclusion in order to realize that in our era conventional war and thermo-nuclear war are inextricably connected realities. How many heads of state and General Staffs, faced with national defeat and disaster, and possessing nuclear weaponry, are humanely going to concede defeat rather than go *all the way* to preserve "national integrity"? We are all too familiar with the remorseless voices in the Pentagon (and certainly elsewhere) who felt that the United States should have finished the Vietnam War "properly" by using thermonuclear warheads in that already war-pulverized little country. Can we really believe that modern education about the global perils of nuclear war is so prevalently and thoroughly understood that militarists and zealots would not encourage the use of nuclear devices (under, of course, "justifiable" circumstances)?

Further, the basic military (let alone human) tendency to "try out" new and magically powerful weapons—especially considering all the money they cost to devise—provides another impetus; one is itching to see how (and how effectively) the thing *works*. And conventional arms development is of course not cheap; in all its multifarious forms, the production and distribution of such material impose another drain on the national budget. With regard to nuclear plant "pollution," Colonel John Barr has observed:

> Since World War II, hundreds of nuclear power plants have been constructed around the world. Subjected to attack by conventional weapons, each is a potential source of nuclear debris far in excess of the relatively mild conflagration at Chernobyl. In addition to nuclear plant installations, thousands of industrial plants now use or manufacture lethal chemicals. (*The Peacebuilder*, February 1990, p.11)

Colonel Barr's point is devastatingly apt, for it corroborates the crucial point that conventional and nuclear cannot and must not be conceptually isolated; they are, terrifyingly, one. As argued earlier, conventional war can and likely would lead to nuclear war in one way or another. 20th century people knew all too well that genocide can result from conventional warfare; when it includes insidiously vicious practices like chemical warfare, the ecological consequences can be grim.

When conventional and nuclear war are regarded, as they should be, as two sides of the same coin, the genocide resulting from conventional war methods and aims can then be placed on the level of virtually total, global catastrophe. It is imperative for humanity to assume that all war is potentially disastrous and even literally catastrophic to itself and to the earth, because escalation from conventional to nuclear war or "China Syndrome" vulnerability and effects are sufficiently probable to rank very high among factors leading to the actualization of Herman Kahn's "Unthinkable."

Thus, it is utterly essential that more males and more females, especially those in key areas of power in American, Soviet, and other societies, learn to feel about both conventional and nuclear war—to imagine what it would mean to trigger missiles whose weaponry on explosion would release heat the temperature of the sun, with the blast and radiation effects that would dwarf in destructive power and scope the fury of natural calamities like hurricanes, tornadoes and earthquakes.

What would life be like in a post-nuclear world with mostly contaminated water, soil, fauna and flora, and no communications media, no heat, electricity, transportation? How would we care for the millions of surviving burn victims when our present medical burn facilities (which are very expensive to maintain) can at most take care of a few thousand people nationally? How would survivors be fed for weeks or months, when most food not destroyed by the blasts would likely be ruined by radiation? Who would care for the millions of the physically and mentally ill people, convulsed with complex, organic sicknesses deriving from the effects of the bombs, and who would administer to their extreme state of mind? What about the impact of pandemic diseases carried by radiation-resistant insects and pests? How would we be able simply to cope with our loved ones dead or (perhaps slowly) dying before our eyes? The novel by Cormac McCarthy, *The Road*, offers one graphic version of what post-nuclear devastation might really look and, therefore, feel like.

All of these hellish conditions, which constitute only part of the unprecedented horror of nuclear war, and which are far from adequately described by nuclear "scenarists" like Kahn, represent what continued psychic numbing and a rationality severed from emotional sensibility could lead to. When theorists like Kahn write about nuclear war, its impact and results, they think in quantitative, "objective" diction and media—tables, ratios, megatonnage, etc.—rather than in emotional, human terms, the intimate language of what our flesh, blood and minds experience and can bear. Their mode of thinking applied to nuclear devastation constitutes potentially one of the most genocidal betrayals of human values by professional men in history. Nuclear physicists like the brilliant and sentimentalized Robert Oppenheimer have talked of nuclear-bomb theorization as being "technically sweet"—an appalling phrase. More recent scientists such as MIT computer science professor Joe Weitzenbaum have told Helen Caldicott that the theoretical problems behind devising nuclear weaponry are "incredible fun" to work on.

Applied to nuclear devastation, such a mode of thinking is brutally insensitive. On the other hand, more and more scientists are coming out strongly against SDI, nuclear arms, and nuclear war as viable or ethically acceptable modes of warfare. This development suggests an increasing sanity in a key sector of American thinking about the "Unthinkable." Theorizing about nuclear war devoid of a deep feeling for the human body, human being and human society—let alone flora and fauna—moves the world towards doom.

"Feeling the Unthinkable" by Donald Gutierrez—*The Peacebuilder*, September 1990.

22
Review: Helen Caldicott, *The New Nuclear Danger:*
George W. Bush's Military-Industrial Complex

Dr. Helen Caldicott is not a person to take lightly. Besides igniting the movement in Australia to force France to halt nuclear testing in the South Pacific, she founded the Physicians for Social Responsibility and has been a powerful peace advocate for over thirty years. Perhaps her most important contribution to peace and global safety, however, has been the professional knowledge and humanity she brings as a physician to the medical consequences of nuclear warfare. Having already written two invaluable books dealing with the global peril of nuclear war, *Nuclear Madness* and *Missile Envy*, she now adds a third. *The New Nuclear Danger: George W. Bush's Military-Industrial Complex* passionately contends with persuasive evidence and analysis that the world is in a thermonuclear crisis mostly generated by the outlook and policies of American political, military and war-industry leaders.

The title and subtitle of Caldicott's book indicate why there has been a nuclear crisis in our time. The presidency of George W. Bush saw the consolidation of a right wing, corporation controlled, hyper-militaristic, unilateralist foreign policy perspective that rendered its plans of military preparedness potentially lethal for the entire world. According to Caldicott, the government was erecting and developing a structure of nuclear weaponry power which, combined with Bush's very costly National Missile Defense program, imperiled an already highly unstable world. Thus, it was extremely ironic that Bush had accused Saddam Hussein of Iraq of being a global destabilizer, for, judging by the cogent, well documented case Caldicott makes in *Nuclear Danger*, the United States, with its massive arsenal of weapons of mass destruction (WMDs), was—and remains—the most subversive threat to world amity.

Although every chapter is arresting, those particularly engrossing deal with subjects the public should be informed about: the privileged secrecy in which American nuclear scientists have worked for decades and the extraordinary amount of nuclear weaponry they have created (65 types of nuclear weapons and over 70,000 bombs); the huge role of weapons industries like Lockheed Douglas in both shaping American foreign policy and in receiving billions of the public's dollars for war research contracts; the grave environmental hazards, expensiveness and perniciousness of current research and development in nuclear facilities and weaponry; and the Pentagon plans to monopolize and militarize space.

Caldicott also discusses at considerable length the history of American research on uranium weaponry and the use of depleted uranium weaponry by the United States in the Gulf and Kosovo wars. Here she makes the essential point that such weaponry constitutes a Weapon of Mass Destruction when evaluated by four key criteria: the effects of the weaponry over a period of time, environmental safety, humaneness (a crucially ignored standard in modern weapon design) and geographical dispersal limits.

In Chapter 2, entitled "The Reality of Nuclear War," Caldicott is rightly unsparing in presenting the impact of nuclear explosion on the human body. She also explains what such blasts do to the surrounding building materials (glass, stone, metal), which thus impinge on the human body. Most American cities over 100,000 in population are likely targeted by Russia today; many cities in Russia are probably targeted by the United States as well. According to Caldicott, most people in a city struck by a bomb would be transformed into radioactive dust, and the area of lethal fallout would cover thousands of square miles.

Exposure to radiation would cause a variety of horrific ailments (such as the extreme swelling of brain cells) leading to death. America's 104 nuclear power plants could be transformed into thermonuclear catastrophes. Diseases would spread from contaminated natural resources and trillions of infectious, radiation resistant insects. Finally, nuclear winter would likely result from the black, radioactive smoke from burning cities, forests and oil wells, reducing sunlight to 17 percent of normal. Consequently, sub-freezing temperatures could destroy the earth's biological support system, leading to global starvation.

Against this terrifying backdrop, Caldicott discusses our present nuclear danger. In a long chapter called "Manhattan 11," she describes the Stockpile Stewardship and Management Program, an enterprise that involves ongoing nuclear weaponry research by New Mexico's Los Alamos and Sandia laboratories. The supposed purpose of this new project is to guarantee the adequate functioning of the United States' stockpile of nuclear weapons. Caldicott's highly detailed exposition and critique of the SSM program is strikingly different: "Nuclear scientists are actually designing, developing, testing and constructing new nuclear weapons at an annual cost of five billion dollars over the next ten to fifteen years" (43).

One of the serious problems with SSM research, she observes, is that it violates international arms control treaties like the Comprehensive Test Ban Treaty and START II by concealing nuclear research that constitutes nuclear weapons testing. Arms-control treaties would also be violated by establishing a national defensive system, National Missile Defense, that would render it invulnerable to foreign missiles and thus enable a war offensive by the United States. Aside from authoritative evidence that the NMD wouldn't work, such a defense destroys the mutually assured destruction (MAD) agreement that prevented the two superpowers from destroying the world during the Cold War era.

Another instance of America's violating international standards of limits to nuclear weapons research involves the National Ignition Facility. Located at the California Lawrence Livermore laboratory, this stadium-size facility, costing billions of dollars, is designed to "stimulate the development of a pure fusion bomb" (53). The lack of a fission product in nuclear weapons, however, renders their construction undetectable, thus preventing arms control verification by other nations. Such deviousness was the very thing over which the Bush administration threatened Saddam Hussein with war.

Two financial citations in *Nuclear Danger* exemplify how heavily oriented Washington is towards war. According to a publication called *The Defense Monitor* that is put out by retired military officers, the Pentagon is spending $589,802 a *minute*. The second figure implies a major indictment of the military-industrial complex:

> Globally the annual military expenditure stands at 780 billion dollars. The total amount required to provide global health care, eliminate starvation and malnutrition, provide

clear water and shelter for all, remove land mines, eliminate nuclear weapons, stop deforestation, prevent global warming, ozone depletion and acid rain, retire the paralyzing debt of developing nations, prevent soil erosion, produce safe, clean energy, stop overpopulation and eliminate illiteracy is only one third that amount—$237.5 billion dollars. (185-86)

Two important chapters deal with the National Missile Defense and Washington's plans to militarize space. According to one American military official, "With regard to space dominance, we have it, we like it, and we're going to keep it" (115). Air Force General Ralph E. Eberhart, head of the Space Command, speaks just as bluntly: "Space has proven itself vital to our national interests" (125). Caldicott presents the historical background of NMD, then elaborates medical, problematic rocketry aspects and critical environmental hazards of the anti-missile concept, including plutonium from exploded enemy missiles and National Association for Space Agency rockets falling through space to earth. Caldicott views America's attempt to dominate space as part of a larger strategy to sustain the global disparity between rich and poor, a major thesis she unfortunately doesn't elaborate.

Although President Bush's National Missile Defense program could thus have been regarded as integral to this space-control scheme, it harbored another, atrocious, facet—American pre-emptive first strike capacity. Caldicott's ideas about this capacity, which she relates to NMD and the Pentagon's space imperialism designs, deserves very serious attention. She thinks the real war targets of America are not "rogue" nations like North Korea but Russia and especially China. The location and upgrading of American early-warning radar facilities are in places like Thule, Greenland, and Clear, Alaska, which strongly suggest Russia and China as targets. Moreover, a sophisticated imaging intelligence gathering radar is situated in northern Norway only forty miles from the Russian border. And Pentagon strategists repeatedly mention China as the main future foe.

The final chapter of *Nuclear Danger* focuses on Lockheed Martin's deep involvement in the star wars industry. Caldicott's assertion that this corporation "literally controls the fate of the earth" (163) might at first seem extreme. However, when one considers the levels of funding LM receives from Washington ($15.1 billion in 2000 alone)[1], the enormous influence of its lobbyists, the entrenchment of its personnel on influential conservative think tanks like the Heritage Foundation and, most insidiously, the number of direct ties to Bush staff personnel, it becomes clear why this chapter is titled "The Lockheed Martin Presidency and the Star-Wars Administration." Lockheed Martin, TRW, Boeing and other weapons manufacturing corporations have enormous clout in Washington and sell far more weaponry abroad than do many countries combined. Further, they often sell to both sides at war—Turkey and Greece, India and Pakistan, Taiwan and China, Iran and Iraq.

What comes across in *Nuclear Danger* as most disturbing was the extreme involvement by the military and the big arms corporations in formulating American foreign policy, the intense bellicosity and unilateralism of that policy under former President George W. Bush and his administration's continual warnings to the public of perpetual war. America's defense and nuclear arms plans under the Bush administration represented a crisis for the world *and* the earth. They evoke the words of another woman, who, like Helen Caldicott, also embodied a dire warning to America and the world: "No civilization," urged Rachel Carson, "can wage relentless war on life without destroying itself and without losing the right to be called civilized."

---

1. As of 2010, Lockheed Martin was to be financed \$323.6 billion to build 2,413 F-35 Lightning 11 war planes. Though a modest portion of the cost would be borne by a few other countries, this project comprises the most costly U. S. defensive plan to date.

"Review: Helen Caldicott, *The New Nuclear Danger: George W. Bush's Military-Industrial Complex*" by Donald Gutierrez—*The Justice Xpress*, Winter 2002, v. II, no. 1; *Eldorado Sun*, November 2002.

23

The Great Military-Defense Industry Swindle of America

The Pentagon is like a black hole; what goes in
is forever lost to us, and no new wealth is created.
Gore Vidal, *The Decline and Fall of the American Empire*

Americans are paying far too much for the military budget. Moreover, one gets the impression that most Americans haven't really absorbed this extremely significant fact. The kind of monies being expended for ordnance are so preposterously large as to make one think of the infinite spaces of astronomy. Furthermore, most of us have little idea of what, say, a Joint Strike Fighter costs (or is), how many JSFs a given armed service wants, and whether it is even a legitimate war need.

Moreover, our political representatives marginalize their constituencies in matters of military costs and needs. This results in an enormous gap between the money spent by our government on ordnance and the capacity of the public and even of Congress to evaluate and control that expenditure, let alone to shift it towards vital civic needs. If one asks why all the stupendous amount of ordnance and the monies needed to implement it are necessary, a variety of rationales—or rationalizations—are announced. Defending Freedom is crucial—and expensive. President George W. Bush insisted that our enemies hate us for our freedom but said nothing about how that hatred might be explained by Washington destroying *their* freedom.

It's a dangerous world out there, we are informed, but some, such as Noam Chomsky, Robert Fisk, John Pilger, William Blum, Tom Englehardt,

Andrew J. Bacevich and Chris Hedges, hold that the American State has much to do with making that world dangerous. They claim that the United States is *the* rogue state in the world. Anyone who really believes that the United States wants to extend democracy and freedom throughout the world has to explain why the major corporations always seem to be present in a region or country invaded and "stabilized" by the American military and why Washington spends so much time, energy and money pursuing that imperial stabilization. What such domination leads to, besides widespread enmity towards the United States, even by the populations of European and other allies, is perpetual and widening war and, thus, perpetual and enormous drain on the monies of the American public.

A major part of what results from a virtual policy of perpetual war is something called the "War-On-Two-Fronts" thesis: America must have the capacity to wage two full-scale wars simultaneously. Further, it must have a missile defense system which, according to the *Bulletin of Science for Democratic Action* (February 2000), has already cost the nation almost one trillion dollars of "the cumulative nuclear weapons expenditure of $5.5 trillion: a defense system which any self-respecting terrorist can evade." According to Cecil Heftel, Hawaii's five-term congressman, "Over the years, trillions of tax-payers' dollars have gone to the Pentagon" (*End Legalized Bribery*, 1998). This tells us nothing about the size of public monies that get sucked into the Pentagon's shadow budget, but it is likely massive. Finally, the State (America in its war dimension) must keep ahead of its potential enemies—and, of course, its allies, who (you never know!) may one day *be* enemies.

These three "musts," as all "musts" from the Pentagon, should be rigorously questioned. My thrust here will be to underscore the staggering costs of these Pentagon "musts." I suggest that such necessities are vastly exaggerated and do grave damage to such critical civil needs of our country as education, decent health coverage, help for the poor and the elderly, infrastructure, protection of the nation's water and food, and so on.

If it is financially advantageous to the American defense industry CEOs and the communities depending on this sector for work and income, then, of course, America needs an enemy. Indeed, two or three would be even better because that would justify further military expansion and expenditure and be great for the defense industry and for war jobs. Furthermore, having an enemy or two makes the public even more fearful. The mainstream media would justify the increased expenses of an American "crusade" against "global terrorism" or a genuine nationalist libertarian leader who had decided to terminate his or her nation's client status to the United States and opt for economic independence. The full battery of American libertarian rhetoric would be discharged throughout the country to incriminate the new, extremely threatening "rogue" nation. First it was Iraq, now Iran, with Venezuela and other South American nations targeted for becoming less cooperative with the imperatives of the Washington consensus. In the process of this expensive, paranoiac belligerence by the state, essential civic needs get, at most, lip service from Washington.

Americans need to realize the annual total sum of military expenditures which, from 1975 to 2000, possibly came to eight trillion dollars. If broken down into a few categories, the military budget would reveal expenditures that are shocking, even in terms of any likely external threats. Granted, being precise about Pentagon expenditures is difficult for the average civilian. The Pentagon itself apparently has serious difficulties in keeping track of costs, considering that its financial ledgers in 1999 needed almost seven trillion dollars in adjustments and "could not show receipts for $2.3 trillion of those changes" (*Albuquerque Journal*, March 4, 2000).

In a book published in 1998 called *Fortress America: the American Military and the Consequences of Peace*, the economist William Greider provides a crucial context for the ordnance costs, which I will selectively detail here: "[T]he U.S. Military-industrial complex… is in the process of devouring itself, literally and tangibly. The awesome interlocking structure of armed forces, industrial interests, and political alliances that have sprawled across American public life and purpose for two generations cannot endure for long, not in its familiar shape and size" (ix).

Greider's next point segues into the focus of this essay:

> [A]nother imperative of the Cold War [is] the endless search for invention. The military and industry remain united in their desire to invent and produce new generations of high-tech weapons that will trump superior numbers of less sophisticated armaments fielded by a less advanced industrial society. Indeed, the brilliant new weapons systems to be produced by the United States seem most threatening to the already brilliant existing weapons systems in the U.S. Arsenal, since those are themselves without peer anywhere in the world. (xv)

Particularly striking in Greider's book are the operational costs of ordnance. The M-1 Tank, for example, costs $147 a *mile* in fuel and repairs. Multiply that basic formula by the 2,400 M-1 Tanks (not to mention Bradleys and other kinds of tracked vehicles) at Fort Hood in Killeen, Texas, and the expense amounts to at least $267,000 to run these tanks just *one* mile. And that was more than ten years ago. More recently, according to *Jane's Armour and Artillery*, the M1A2 Abrams Tank costs $21 million each, and the army has 3,000 of them. And this is just one kind of tank; there are thousands on thousands of Bradleys, trucks, tankers, Humvees and other heavy vehicles spread over the 900 domestic bases and the 735 to 1,200 bases (depending on what defines a base) distributed throughout the world. No wonder Washington, the pentagon and the American oil industry want endless amounts of oil—they can't make and sustain wars without it.

Going from tanks to ships, from Army to Navy, places us on some very expensive vessels. According to Greider (30), Arleigh-Burke-class destroyers cost $850 million each. The Navy has acquired 17 since 1971, which amounts to an approximate total sum of $11 billion. A more recent estimate, which includes seven more Burke destroyers being planned, cites a figure of $33 billion. These destroyers cost around $30,000 a day to operate or $11 million each a year, plus almost $2 million each solely for various training activities.

And destroyers are small fry. Consider the cost of aircraft carriers: In 2007, the *Harry S Truman* cost around $4.5 billion. The *Ronald Reagan* was built in 1999 at a cost of $5 billion. There is a certain sinister appropriateness in these huge mechanisms that provide such horrific aerial destruction being named after American presidents—political executives notorious for plunging the nation into unnecessary wars. These two presidents in particular were (in)famous for, respectively, igniting the Atomic Age and fueling the Cold War to new heights of national exorbitance. "Harry" and "Ronnie" combined cost *us*—and one should always bear that "us" in mind—almost $10 billion.

Purchase costs of ordnance might also thin American wallets thanks to the Air Force—but not just them, as the other services want wings, too, *new* ones. All these weapons also entail operational costs, despite the fact that many sit idly on the ground for long periods of time. (Some even sit underwater. One hundred old Sherman M-60s were donated by the Pentagon to form artificial reefs for fish in Mobile Bay off the Alabama coast.) This does not even include the much larger bomber planes, like the B-52 and others, which presumably have been and remain more costly in flying time than fighter planes.

This point leads to a far larger, more complex consideration—the very expensive Pentagon practice of selling supposedly outmoded, superfluous or excess ordnance to other nations (including "rogue" ones). The Pentagon often just gives them away to justify buying updated versions of the same weaponry, or entirely new planes or warships or combat helicopters. As Greider sagely observes, this extremely costly habit leads to the United States basically being in competition with itself. Its "outmoded" ordnance sold, for example, to an Iran might need to be superseded because the enemy—or potential enemy—now has a (our) dangerous weapon. We must keep ahead of "Iran's" F-4s.

This tricky rationale suggests that if Iran—let alone North Korea—is a potential enemy to the American people, it is a good friend indeed of the American defense industry, whose huge cash register it keeps ringing merrily. In this peculiarly twisted sense, Iran is also a good friend to the Pentagon, which, with adroitly staged anxiety, pressures already paranoid or opportunistically patriotic members of Congress and our presidents into sustaining the defense budget at the level of the Cold War era, if not higher.

Granted, many members of Congress are kept in the dark about the basic budgetary realities of the Pentagon's ordnance requests. Congressman Heftel claims,

> Congressional oversight does not enter into the picture until after Pentagon needs have been discussed with industry representatives and often with sympathetic members of Congress. By the time Congress votes on the defense budget, most of the discussions about military priorities have already taken place. Most of the contractual agreements have been discussed, if not sealed as well. (75)

In *The American Way of War: Guided Missiles, Misguided Men, and a Republic in Peril*, Eugene Jarecki points out that defense contractors successfully urge congressmen to spread the contracts to as many states as possible. The strategy for such expanded coverage is to gain public approval of the public's money supporting defense-ordnance jobs, a given war, the defense industry and, consequently, a congressman's own popularity with his or her constituents.

Why do these horrific weapons of destruction cost so much money? If there is some kind of direct ratio between their degree of destructiveness and their cost, the public might ponder financial—if not ethical—reservations about the extreme degree of technical sophistication needed and implemented to create these planes. This is especially worth considering in view, for example, of how grossly overrated the touted performance of America's stealth bombers were during the engagements with Iraq and Afghanistan.

Moving ahead, one should not overlook what new Navy planes cost. Not content with ships costing enough money possibly to provide free health coverage for all Americans for at least one or two years, the Navy wants F/A-18EF fighter bombers. Aptly called "Super Hornets," these metal, wasplike, vicious-looking planes sagging with red and light gray missiles bear a price tag of $80 million each. As the Navy wants 1,000 of them, the cost approximates $80 billion (Greider, 40). And in case the Navy somehow runs out of F/A-18Es, Boeing has thoughtfully supplied F/A-18Es, F/A-18Fs *and* F/A-18Ds. As for the Army, it needs new helicopters, specifically 1,292 Comanche armed recon copters that cost a total of $45 billion.

Perhaps the most expensive ordnance of all might be the Joint-Strike Fighter. The Services want to buy 2,978 of them. The JSF, described by *Jane's All the World's Aircraft, 1999-2000* as a lightweight fighter, was figured to reach a heavyweight total cost of $300 billion (*Jane's*, 569). And then last but hardly least in expense and superfluousness are the B-2 long-range bombers. As of 2008, these behemoths cost two billion dollars *each*.

What emerges from the above only *partial, selective* list of ordnance expenses is that our government is spending in the trillions of dollars on military preparedness and undeclared offensive wars, even though the nation is deeply in debt. Further, among the developed nations, our country is lowest in providing for the well-being of the large majority of its population, and is highest, courtesy of Reagan, Bill Clinton and Bush Jr., in its extreme financial generosity to its ruling upper class.

In the meantime, the Pentagon and its allies in Congress continue to seek rationalizations for the mammoth military budget. Partly this is needed to conceal the enormous contradictions between legitimate military preparedness and the irony of keeping unused defense factories open by designating perfectly suitable ordnance as outmoded to justify spending further billions for ever more high-tech killing weapons. Thus, the worst thing that could happen to the Pentagon and America's war industry is peace. A more fitting definition of a society led by lunatics and greed would be hard to find, at least among nations describing themselves as democratic.

So what is done with all that enormous ordnance when the very bad news called peace occurs is to find enemies and initiate wars called "police actions" or "interventions." If a nation builds an arsenal, especially a formidable one like America's, the temptation to use it becomes overwhelming, especially when driven by powerful market incentives.

Few people in the different sectors of the American defense community seem to be concerned about the expense of the endless ordnance they crave, or its unbelievably horrible destructiveness. They appear totally insensitive to the kind of agony that weapons inflict on other human beings, whose nerves, veins, arteries, bones, muscles, vital organs and blood are just as sensitive and vulnerable to exploding, fragmenting, burning metal-sharp shards and poisonous gases and chemicals as are the bodies of their own wives, husbands, mothers, fathers, sons and daughters. These Iraqi, Afghans, Palestinians and other Middle Eastern people are also wives and husbands and mothers and fathers and daughters and sons.[1]

The special New York City Police Department unit that killed Amidou Diallo some years ago had an operational motto: "We own the Street." Americans must take back not just the street but the country from the Iron Quadrangle—the White House, Congress, the Defense industry and the Pentagon—and restore the nation's wealth to the imperatives of a civilized, peace-oriented society. If this is not done, the increasingly interlocking structure in America of military-industrial-political forces will sooner than we think coagulate into a full-fledged fascist society.

---

1. See Robert Fisk *The Great War for Civilization: the Conquest of the Middle East*, Chapter 13, "Now Thrives the Armourer." This stunning chapter narrates Fisk's acquiring a fragment of a Hellfire missile fired by an Israeli Apache helicopter at a Lebanese Muslim ambulance that killed several children. The rocket fragment contained code numbers identifying as its maker American munitions manufacturers Martin-Marietta and Rockwell International. Fisk takes the rocket fragment to Rockwell to exhibit to its company CEOs what the rocket had done to Arab children.

"The Great Military Defense-Industry Swindle of America" by Donald Gutierrez— *Sun Monthly*, September 2001.

24
American Global Democracy and the Militarization of America

Why are the American people being led to think that the militarization of women is a valid form of equality? This idea is both false and pernicious, not because females have less stamina or are less reliable under pressure than males (they're not) but because it further entrenches American society in a militaristic mindset. The increasing militarization of America consolidates a vertical American power structure already almost omnipresent in such key areas as business corporations, academe and civil service. After all, being a "good soldier" means not only being generally disciplined but becoming conditioned to deep obedience. No doubt these qualities are to a degree valuable for combat, but to have increasing numbers of young people repressing their instinctual life and civic mentality subverts a democratic, open society.

America is the most massive military superpower in the world. If this immense force strikes the Pentagon's military experts as having a deficient number of troops, this is due to the spurious drive to assert a global American military presence. This presence can be seen as necessary on one or two mutually irreconcilable grounds: to protect democracy worldwide or to protect and extend the interests of the major American banks, investors, corporations and transnational companies. One cannot take seriously claims by American politicians and our media that America and its military (and monies) are needed globally to stabilize the world for democracy in a world already destabilized by the CIA and the client nations' moneyed Overclass. America's vast armed services and military technology are basically needed to protect what in the old days was called Vested Interests.

But to make this protection of the interests of high finance, major corporations and the war industry seem more democratic, it must appear that we are preserving stability for world peace and equitable international free-trade conditions. If the United States pulverizes Iraq and imposes a brutal ten-year sanction that is virtually killing or maiming Iraqi civilians from babies to old people, that is justified by "our" need not only for access to oil in the Near East, but, as Noam Chomsky has observed, to assert a permanent control of those resources amounting to ownership.

I broach this military-economic background to suggest a few motivations behind why America supposedly needs an overwhelming military and endless funding for the Pentagon. "Someone has to keep the world in order," goes the egotistic nationalistic reasoning, "and it might as well be us." Of course there is also the military mindset in the United States that has enlarged and hardened alarmingly since World War II. Having—and partly inflating—an "Evil Empire" like the Soviet Union, and our American penchant for developing ideological xenophobia, worked handily with the patriotic greed of defense contractors, corporation-oriented politicians and bureaucrats (such as former Secretary of State Henry Kissinger) who were going into lucrative private consulting. And, as always, the banks and Wall Street financiers unfailingly got their hands into any huge military buildup, arms-making and international arms-selling business (this last category, according to *Parade Magazine* [Nov. 10, 1996], amounting to $135 billion for 1988-95). Obviously not just the Pentagon benefits from the $48 billion dollars it is requesting from Congress for nearly 1,300 Comanche helicopters —and the helicopters are only one item on the military's endless list.

America in the past fifty-plus years has so militarized its culture that the average American has come to accept this conditioning in the passive way Germans accepted the increasing militarization and authoritarian centralization by Hitler in the 1930s. American presidents violate the law with hardly a qualm, such as Reagan and associates did in the Iran-Contra deal. More significant and sinister was George W. Bush's eagerness as President to attack Iraq militarily. His threat to start the war without Congress's approval was a clear-cut violation of the Constitution for which he would have deserved impeachment, or, according to Vincent Bugliosi, imprisonment [see Ch. 18 for Bugliosi review].

Our military budget in 1998 was well over $200 billion, and has increased sizably since—and this after the Cold War has ended. The military, however, keeps clamoring for more and more money, and Congress eagerly obliges.

Part of this intensifying (and extremely expensive) militarization of the nation is persuading females to enter the Armed Services. First, such a resource would add a huge dimension of womanpower to the military. Females can do all kinds of work in the military: typing, clerking, cooking, data entry and other computer tasks, commanding female and male units, carpentry, mechanical work—and engaging in combat. (Women can't stand or handle combat? They certainly can. In 2010, a top Pentagon board advised allowing female soldiers into combat. Though presented as an issue of gender egalitarianism, the real motive surely has to do with increasing the number of "boots on the ground" for firefights and, basically, for invading weaker nations.)

In recent decades it has become obvious that females are capable of far more physical strength, violence and endurance than was previously conceded. It is also conceivable that females are just as capable of being conditioned to commit military-combat murder as males. Of course much of the differentiation between males and females traditionally was at root cultural with the intention of denying females the life of full and varied possibility that males (some males) had access to. The more females (and males) enter the military, the more exit the civilian work force, unemployment or prison, the more America becomes a garrison state.

If the fundamental idea—and ideal—is to demilitarize America to sane proportions of military preparedness by reducing the numbers of females and males entering the Armed Services (among other things), would this put the nation at risk? This sort of question, Pentagon experts will instantly inform us, can be understood and answered only by experts—military or Rand Corporation or Heritage Foundation experts. But a society defined and run mainly by experts is or is becoming the kind of technocracy that subtly becomes authoritarian. Granted, societies with sophisticated, complex systems of organization seem to need sophisticated personnel conversant with complex techniques of management, operation and control. But this sort of arrangement almost invariably leads to political and economic hierarchy, and such vertical orderings usually undermine the equalitarian, libertarian substructures essential in work and culture to a truly vital, open democratic society. These "technical experts"—including media-commentator "celebs" like Sam Donaldson and Cokie Roberts—are pampered and grossly overpaid, and thus form a social-economic class significantly separated from the income and general experience of the average American.

This is precisely why the military as a model of social ordering is a sinister symptom. Its increasingly pervasive influence over and authority within American civilian society fosters a militarization and hierarchic rigidification of American civilian culture, and, as such, represents another sizable step towards a high-tech, closed, virtually fascistic society. Legally and ideally, the civilian sector in our society is supposed to wield authority over the military sector. In view, however, of the power, the wealth, the arrogance, the outrageously inflated budget and prestige of the Pentagon, its so secretive allies like the CIA and the NSA, and such servile funders and boosters as Congress and the media, who can really believe that civilian authority over the military is registered forcefully enough in our national life to assure the public that the military is really subordinate to civilian society? We should recall that when the Nixon presidency was sinking in the crisis of Watergate, a military man, General Alexander Haig, was about ready to "step in," as he later stated. And in the 1930s, a conspiratorial attempt was afoot by a few military officers and Wall Street financiers to overthrow President Franklin Delano Roosevelt's administration—until retired Marine General Smedley Butler exposed this plot.

Television ads exhibit the army advising young people to "be all you can be" by joining up. And of course one beholds young, attractive female and male soldiers (i.e., models) happily manning computer-filled "war rooms," armored tanks, fighter planes. What is omitted from this TV glamorization of Service life is the symptomatic crime of sexual harassment and rape of female military personnel, of which the Navy's Tailgate incident is only one example.

Serious as such sexual transgressions are, one has to subsume that outrage under the broader evil of the regimentation of gender and sensibility represented by the spurious equalitarianism of militarizing both sexes. Is the alternative to induct only, and more, males whom our society has failed to accommodate with a decent education and civilian work? Obviously, there is a need to investigate how this military juggernaut of ours has assumed its present excessively overprivileged and overextended global dimensions. A good start would be absorbing the meaning of James Carroll's magnificent study, *House of War: the Pentagon and the Disastrous Rise of American Power*.

The American public needs to de-sanctify and rein in its military. Moreover, it needs to expose and de-power all the economic and political institutions and individuals feeding off or expanding the military's luxuriant estate. The nation needs to control and delimit the military and the State. Otherwise the State (represented by the White House, Congress, the Pentagon, the CIA, NSA, FBI and the other dozen or more intelligence agencies) could finally turn on American society through an increasingly synergetic, centralized authoritarian power and do to it what Nazi Germany or the Soviet Union did to their—and other—societies. As Naomi Wolf has pointed out (see Ch. 20 for Wolf review), an open society can shut down with alarming rapidity. A key agent in such a catastrophe for civil society is a superpower military. And now, thanks to President Obama, that we have the National Defense Authorization Act looming over the country, the real possibility of the American military assisting in the subjugation of the American populace is a terrifying threat to a democratic, free society.

"American Global Democracy and the Militarization of America" by Donald Gutierrez—*Sun Monthly*, September 2001.

25

"Fuck" and Death Metals

War is "the cataclysmic ecstasy of violence"
General George S. Patton, Jr.

In D. H. Lawrence's 1920s novel *Lady Chatterley's Lover*, a minor male character expresses his ideal of self-liberation by wanting to feel free to say "shit" in the presence of "ladies." Well, it is now the year 2012, and young (even very young) ladies feel free themselves to say "shit" in the company of gents. In turn, more than a few gents—and some women—sprinkle the word "fucking" on their daily social discourse the way many cover a dish of spaghetti with grated Parmesan. That "fuck" is overused today in certain quarters—like high and junior high schools, not to mention kindergarten— is obvious. The average blockbuster movie apparently is not regarded by Hollywood studios as suitable for audiences ages 18 to 80 unless "fuck"—"fuck you," "fuckin" (watered down by the timorous to "friggin"), "dumb fuck" (Joe Pesci characters' favorite) or, expression of choice, "motherfuckin" (or just "mother" for the verbally lazy)—is not only packed into practically every sentence of dialogue but, preferably, into every conceivable syntactical niche within a sentence.

I haven't counted the number of times "fucking" (and its melodious variants) appears in recent highly rated as well as low-rated movies, but what happens when movie-goers become so "fucking"desensitized that that kind of language almost seems bland? Do we get to the point when it becomes necessary to place the F-word in contexts of escalated violence to give it its old, and now more and more enfeebled, kick?

"Fuck"—not to mention its verbal affiliates—has been one of the premier smash-mouth words of electrifying force. It should be used, if used at all, only for special occasions—an unexpected flat tire when going out (all dressed up) for a night on the town, a bar or dark-alley brawl, the sudden appearance on TV of Henry Kissinger, Bushes Sr. and Jr., Cheney, Rumsfeld, Robert Rubin, Henry Paulson, Lloyd Blankfein, General Petraeus (some of my choices). By using the big "F" as virtually a ninth part of speech, we not only reduce its shock power, we also reduce the vibrancy, force and color of all words, because "fuck" and all its variants have traditionally registered like a screech that obliterates a conversation—one can't hear the other words. (Though, granted, people who depend heavily on "fuck" or "fucking" usually don't command a large vocabulary by which to balance their "F"s.)

Why, then, all the "fuck"s and "fucking"s in popular culture, in schools, colleges, movies, sports venues, garage shops and elsewhere? Verbal violence comes at you like a hardball pitched by a pro, so shock remains one intent of using the word, expressing anger, mindless defiance and contempt. Another is domination. "Fuck" always contained a sizable dimension of violence; it is a word edged with harshness, sharpness, hostile penetrativeness.

According to *The Dictionary of Contemporary Slang*, "fuck" may have been borrowed from Norse ("fukker" in Norwegian, "fokker" in Swedish). *The Random House Unabridged Dictionary* offers "fokken" from Middle Dutch and "focha" from the Swedes. One is not exactly surprised to hear from this source that "the age and origin of the word is obscure"—considering its dark character, this would seem appropriate. It is relevant, further, that a common aspect of its meaning is to strike, push or prick. (How often is "prick" employed as a polite noun?) Partridge's *Dictionary of Slang* mentions the appearance of the Italian "fottore" as early as the 16th century which, it asserts, is predated by the Latin verb "pungere," to strike, but how much the Latin usage predates the others is not stated. "Fuck," according to Spears, may have appeared as early as the 15th century and might have had a Scots origin. There is also a German derivative, "ficken," but no reliable information is available about its earliest usage. The Italian variant also means to penetrate, and another etymological dimension, the French "foutere," means to strike.

D. H. Lawrence tries to humanize and, in his iconoclastic sense, civilize "fuck" in *Chatterley*. In his splendid long essay "A Propos of *Lady Chatterley's Lover*," he says:

> The mind has to catch up, in sex: indeed, in all physical
> acts. Mentally, we lag behind in our sexual thought, in a
> dimness, a lurking, groveling fear....Get the two in harmony.
> It means being able to use the so-called obscene words,
> because these are a natural part of the mind's consciousness
> and body. Obscenity only comes in when the mind despises
> and fears the body, and the body hates and resists the mind.

But the resistance that Lawrence protests has melted in the heat and speed of contemporary media sensationalism and the enlarged margins today of linguistic license. As Lawrence Panas has it in his very amusing book, *The Erotic Tongue: A Sexual Lexicon*, "Freed at last by the U.S. Supreme Court decision on *Lady Chatterley's Lover* in 1951 [sic, the year was 1961], the word soon gained new life....We had rediscovered the f..k with a vengeance."

Further, the word has too long a history of its own intentionally harsh lasciviousness to be gentrified even by Lawrence's gamekeeper, let alone by Lawrence's iconoclastic idealism. Rather, it lends itself more naturally—unfortunately—to the contemporary nihilistic imagery of Death Metal musician-lyricist Chris Barnes' *Cannibal Corpse* CD "F...... With a Knife" which, despite the title's six ellipses, conveys much more than most people not only want to hear but even conceive of. What follows after wielding "fuck" in all of its variations gets boring or just seems inadequate? In examining Death Metal lyrics, it becomes clear that "fuck" has become heavily underlined by an elaboration of graphic violence reaching extremes of pornographically sadistic torture and murder.

Some psychologists sanitize the excessive use of extreme slang by claiming it provides alienated youths with a comforting area of psychic darkness that is good for their health. A related theory is that it provides an escape valve for young people who have been abused or ignored by parents and other authorities—except when it doesn't, and a bunch of mosh-pit louts, bored by just banging each other's bodies in the Pit, go out and brutally kill someone at random (one murdered convenience store employee had her head bashed in by a Death Metal inspired bunch).

A more relevant insight by such psychological experts might be that the violence of so many "F"s spit out in the movies and its obnoxious implementation in Death Metal lyrics reflects not only the obsession with sex

and violence in our society at large but their sinister blending. This blending
is spelled out forcefully in Dr. Helen Caldicott's book *Missile Envy: The
Arms Race and Nuclear War*:

> These hideous weapons of killing and mass genocide may
> be a symptom of several male emotions: inadequate sexuality
> and a need to continually prove their virility plus a primitive
> fascination with killing. I recently watched a filmed launching
> of an MX missile. It rose slowly out of ground, surrounded by
> smoke and flames and elongated into the air—it was indeed
> a very sexual sight, and when armed with the ten [nuclear]
> warheads it will explode with the most almighty orgasm. The
> names that the military uses are laden with psychosexual
> overtones: missile erector, thrust-to-weight ratio, soft lay
> down, deep penetration, hard line and soft line. (319)

American politicians felt compelled during the Cold War to be
"tough" or "hard" on the Soviet Union; to be "soft" suggested not only being
pacifistic or conciliatory but impotent. (Caldicott also mentions how
American generals who informed Congressmen that America "has these
small blue [nuclear] missiles and Russia has these great big red missiles"
always got the funding they'd requested.) And John F. Kennedy, when he
made Nikita Kruschchev back down during the American-Cuban Missile
Crisis (to the credit of the Russian leader, it would seem), made himself look
psychosexually hard and Kruschchev "soft" by saying, "I cut his balls off."

Think about a country like ours whose state—the White House,
Congress, the Pentagon, the CIA and the sixteen other intelligence
agencies—employs overwhelming military force as its basic form of
diplomacy towards other countries and allows easy access to guns; highlights
and dramatizes guns, violence, explosions in so many of its movies, TV
programs and Nintendo games; affirms violence and belligerence as
credentials of manhood; sells more arms abroad by far than any other nation
in the world; and is continually at war. The likely outcome will be alienated
young (and not so young) people evolving their own cultist forms and
expressions of violence. And one aspect of this will be the most nihilistic use
conceivable of the most intimate word of sexual aggression in human
relations—"fuck."

Death Metal lyrics, then, are not merely an extreme type of hard-metal
rock. Death metal is also America's stealth bombers and laser-guided

rockets and uranium depleted shells and cluster bombs and B-52 bombers (and their tens of thousands of bombs dropping) and Apache helicopters and F-16 and F-22 fighters and dozens of other types of ordnance—all firing, releasing, projecting, ejaculating their death metals. One might say that Chris Barnes' lyrics and the Pentagon's "lyrics" relate in the way that Barnes drops "F-bombs" as a mode of surprise profanity attack, his "Shock and Awe." Here are the concluding lines from Barnes' lyric "Torture Killer": "I'll tear you up—and fuck the / holes I cut in you / cut into you / Murderer—I rape the dead / One sick fuck." And here is a description of a weapon in *American Fighters and Attack Aircraft* by Mike Spick and Barry Wheeler:

> GAU-8/A Avenger 30 mm cannon. With a length of 21 feet without the magazine drum and a round which is larger than the normal 30mm shell, this gun is the most powerful weapon of its kind now flying. Projecting menacingly from the nose of the A-10A Thunderbolt, the GAU-8/A can fire depleted uranium-cored, *armour-piercing* rounds at a rate of 2,000 or 4,000 per minute [emphasis added] from its seven barrels. The shells are fed from a large drum in the body of the fuselage via a winding conveyor system, the drum accommodating 1,174 rounds of linkless ammunition.

This is just one of hundreds of ordnance described in an almost 200-page book, which gets virtually lyrical about the killing capacity of certain ammunition, weapons, and fighter and bomber aircraft.

Barnes' last line above, "One sick fuck," suggests a "narrator" distancing himself from the preceding four lines, but the sheer horrific brutality of these lines makes one suspect a dodge to conceal Barnes' own heinous attitude. From another Barnes lyric titled "Bone Saw": "Dying slow and painfully—a / gasping breath escapes from you / I rip the flesh and cut through bone / you are bleeding." Here we have no externalized narrator; Barnes clearly appears to be one with his "fictional" sex-torturer killer. (According to a July 2000 issue of *The Nation*, some women's rock groups have apparently been matching Barnes' verbal violence slice for stab. One band in San Francisco called Tribe 8 flings rallying cries around like "Castrating Bitches Unite" and "Don't Leave a Stump; It Can Be Reattached.")

Barnes has said in an interview that he would never want people to go

out and commit the acts he describes in his pathologically violent lyrics, that
he is just trying to entertain people (though one wonders what kind of people
would find Barnes' incredibly misogynist lyrics entertaining). In view,
however, of the extremity of his lyrics, one feels that he is being
disingenuous in polarizing words from deed, because public (and private)
words can be a form of deed, or lead to deeds, some horrifying (Hitler's
speeches, for example, or rabble-rousing tirades igniting a lynching). The
Barneses of Death Metal type lyrics may disavow responsibility for their
violent words but they coarsen the minds of some fans to a point that has led
to homicidal violence.

How could two such seemingly separate and different American
phenomena as a band's lyrics and American military firepower be
interrelated? The American literary critic and scholar Lionel Trilling once
defined culture as the hum and buzz of implication—and his critics scoffed
at the almost comical breadth of the famous Columbia University professor's
definition. But perhaps Trilling had something. The enormous capacity for
destructiveness of the American state—like a mega-nuclear explosion—
permeates everything, especially when it experiences its orgiastic release in
"police action," intervention or other forms of unauthorized warfare. The
state's images of international violence can be found on every major TV
network, as well as in the major newspapers and magazines, and though its
technical marvels are gloatingly dwelled on by tech experts, the consequences of devastated human flesh and bone and mind are totally ignored.

Apologists for Barnes' appalling lyrics—as well as Barnes himself—
claim that the lyrics are an inside joke, short horror stories, camp. "It's
almost so crazy it's funny," a Metal Blade Record company CEO claims. But
CEO Brian Slagel also admits that "the fans are often angry and rebellious."
I'm certainly not protesting the right or need of young people to be angry or
rebellious, let alone to have their own culture or counter-culture. There's
plenty for the young—and the rest of us—to be furious and rebellious about
in regard to social, economic and political realities of American society and
the genocidal conduct abroad of the American state. But writing lyrics for
public exhibition and consumption about carving a female lover's vagina out
with a knife or enjoying causing and watching her "dying slowly and
painfully" then knifing the flesh to the bone, takes us to a region of insane
sadistic fantasizing having nothing to do with humor, camp, "entertainment"
or the privileges of cult within even the most generous libertarian
boundaries.

Rather, as a level of unlimited brutality, Barnes' lyrics are commensurate in quality if not in quantity with American predator drones committing "collateral damage" as they massacre Afghan/Pakistani women and children as well (perhaps) as Taliban, or American Gulf War bulldozers burying Iraqi and Sadaam-dragooned Kurdish prisoners of war alive in miles-long trenches, or killing close to four million Vietnamese in a war the United States should never have engaged in. A lot of the killing in these engagements (not to mention others) was expedited by penetrative metal whose conception, efficacy and implementation were brought about by "normal," law-abiding, well-paid citizens working in highly secretive, politically protected places like Sandia Lab (Albuquerque), Los Alamos and the Lawrence-Livermore laboratory in California. One suspects that these people, who, unlike some Death Metallers, would never think of themselves as being satanic, possess a sensibility like Chris Barnes', if more covert and indirect; apparently they too don't come to terms morally with the real, bloody consequences of their work.

I am not necessarily suggesting a direct cause-effect connection between the ongoing, massive violence carried out by the American state and the violence implied by Death Metal lyrics. I do suggest, however, that whatever its official rationalization, the state's publicly sanctioned, immoral violence, by its own essential gratuitousness, encourages this other, cultist violence. As yet, the songs of Six Feet Under band's Chris Barnes, while overtly misogynist, don't lyricize the extermination of both sexes, young and old, as America's National Security State does globally.

It is possible, even likely, that state violence and the excessive media depiction of violence encourage the potential for violence in smaller, disaffected groups towards their own particular object of hatred or fear: "Hey!" Chris Barnes might shriek (and Barnes, author of "Hammer Smashed Face," "Strapped, Raped and Strangled" and similar lyrics, is known for a vocal style consisting of raspy screams and snarled death grunts) "like, if the fuckin Pentagon can fuckin bomb Iraq and Afghanistan every fuckin time they feel like it, I can say what I fuckin think about the fuckin bitches." Perhaps males like Barnes don't think the matter through along such lines; more likely, it is subconsciously evolved, a mind resembling one of Jonathan Swift's Yahoos wandering through its own dark, brutal maze. Yet this subconscious route does not make the end result any the less virulent; it might even make Barnes' unspeakable lyrics worse than they might have been had he consciously worked the process through, and thus given a little play to the control of conscience—assuming he and his recording company have one.

If the parallel I am presenting is valid, who is to blame—the state or the Chris Barneses and Death Metal record companies? All three are. American stealth-bomber-diplomacy in Pakistan, Afghanistan and Yemen; Washington's willingness to define global-imperial "interests" through orgasmic ordnance and nuclear threats; the abiding if subtler violence of racist and class tensions and prejudices—all pervade the body social, ethically repelling some against it, but for others providing a green light to their own violent, nihilistic rebellion. And that is what Chris Barnes' "fuck"—the most vicious usage of the word that one is likely to encounter in the public arena—is essentially grounded in. "War is the health of the State," once said the American anarchist and literary critic Randolph Bourne; "War *is* the State," wrote the poet Kenneth Rexroth decades later. If so, violence propels the blood of its body. People like Barnes, instead of rebelling against the bomb-dropping American state and its complicit society, actually sustain and confirm it through the character of their own pathological verbal violence. The Chris Barneses are the fake rebels against a society screeching, through Barnes' metal-death-fuck lyrics, the American state's own murderous obscenities.

"'Fuck' and Death Metals" by Donald Gutierrez—*On the Bus*, v. 17-18 [2002].

26
Review: Seymour Hersh, *Against All Enemies: Gulf War Syndrome; the War Between America's Ailing Veterans and Their Government*

Seymour Hersh begins his book *Against All Enemies: Gulf War Syndrome; the War between America's Ailing Veterans and Their Government* by quoting the Oath of Office taken by all American Army officers: "I...do solemnly swear...that I will support and defend the Constitution of the United States against all enemies, foreign and domestic; that I will bear true faith and allegiance to the same; that I take this obligation freely, without any mental reservation or purpose of evasion..." The gist of Hersh's book relates to this Oath ironically, for, in effect, the "enemy" of the officers (including generals and other top brass) appears to be the American soldiers who did the real fighting in the war that made them vulnerable to the Syndrome. What this vulnerability consisted of and how it came about rounds out Hersh's short but compelling study of the Gulf War Syndrome.

In 1991 Gulf War veterans began complaining of symptoms of illness: rashes, stomach distress and memory loss. One vet, Jerry Wheat, complained of "abdominal pains that would drop me to the ground, and I could barely eat" (28). Steve Robertson, besieged by nausea, fever, chills, diarrhea, memory loss and aching joints, was given Prozac. Like other vets, they were told they were victims of "stress," a military code word for cowardice. This was the common response of the military authorities, reminding some of the brazen neglect accorded Vietnam War veteran victims of the toxic defoliant Agent Orange. By 1998, more than 90,000 Gulf War vets were complaining of illnesses related to something encountered on active duty.

Hersh proceeds to chart the possible causes of such widespread sickness. First, he mentions that Iraq possessed what we now call bioweaponry, which was assumed to be pulmonary anthrax. Next he considers Pyridostigmine Bromide, or PB, an experimental drug regarded as protection against the nerve agent Soman. This is one of several key points in the book in which the irony of Hersh's main title comes into play. Though there was evidence that ingesting PB induced "a neurological response known as bromide intoxication, the symptoms of which included confusion, tremor, memory loss, stupor and coma" (22), the Pentagon forced American soldiers to take PB. The FDA had given the Pentagon permission to administer the antitoxin *if* the Pentagon gave relevant information to all military personnel. Though the military promised to do so, they did not.

This is only one instance in a pattern of indifference, denial, suppression and repression exhibited by both the Pentagon and the Veterans Administration. Physicians who observed real nerve damage in veterans were not encouraged by their superiors to recommend significant benefits. When information appeared that "depleted uranium is a highly toxic, heavy-metal by-product of the uranium enrichment process for producing weapons-grade nuclear material" with a half-life of 4.5 billion years, and that the American military had fired more than 600,000 pounds of DU shells and bombs at Iraqi troops and tanks, irradiating much of the battlefield, the Pentagon was insisting—as late as the mid 1990s—"that there was no evidence linking the use of DU munitions to the Gulf-War syndrome. *Those who tried to raise the issue were rebuffed* [emphasis added]" (61). As one Gulf War medical unit commander, Dr. Asof Durchovic, stated, the VA had no interest in these seriously ill veterans; the Department of Defense suggested to Durachovic that his work on the Syndrome be discontinued; the VA later fired him (62). The Washington Press Corps, Hersh informs us, gave virtually no attention to the plight of the sick veterans.

Several revelations make the entire history of the Syndrome truly heinous. Congressional Hearings conducted in 1992 revealed that the American government between 1985 and 1990 licensed at least 771 sales to Iraq "of sensitive dual-use equipment—including missile guidance gear, high-tech computers for targeting, *and toxic precursor chemicals that, when mixed together, create nerve gas*" [emphasis added]. That investigation also discovered that the Department of Commerce "had authorized the sale to Iraq of lethal biological pathogens, such as anthrax, suitable for military use" (51-52).

It is no wonder that when General Colin Powell informed President Bush Sr. that hitting Iraqi plants could *release* Iraqi bioweaponry, Bush was agitated. Apparently Powell was not. He not only said it was a necessary gamble but one he would make again (18). The callous indifference of top brass flashes out here, not only in Powell's willingness to seriously endanger the well-being of hundreds of thousands of American and Iraqi troops and Iraqi civilians, but in their total distancing of themselves from their sick soldiers, claiming they were (by late 1991) retired and thus out of the loop. Sent a letter by the executive director of the National Gulf War Research Center in Washington asking to meet, Powell said he had no time. (This is not surprising coming from the officer who, told of the huge number of Iraqi children casualties, said that matter was of no interest to him). Ret. Major General Don Edwards of the National Guard, trying to explain the seriously irresponsible behavior of vaunted military "heroes" such as Powell towards their own troops, said, "It's all about ego, self-success and playing the game" (91).

According to Hersh,

> the most dramatic disclosure by the Congressional Committee investigating the Syndrome was the following: the American intelligence community had known since 1986 of nerve-gas weapons in the Iraq weapons depot at Khamisiyah. This information, found in CIA files, was somehow not conveyed to the military units involved before the complex was destroyed in March of 1991. (68)

It was revealed by studies that perhaps as many as 100,000 American soldiers might have been contaminated by Iraqi bioweaponry set loose by American bombs. The American troops in effect seemed to be treated as the enemy—and not only by their own military chain of command. This gross mistreatment also was due to the indifference, stonewalling and suppression—bordering claims Hersh, on criminal negligence—of the Pentagon, the media and ultimately President Clinton who, as Commander in Chief, could and should have stood up for the afflicted veterans—and did not (76).

Why the Pentagon's years of resistance to acknowledging the alarming sickness of American troops? According to Congressman James C. Turner, "Nothing [including Khamisiyah] was going to be allowed to soil the great victory" (68).

A few more observations by Hersh should be stressed. As the war with Iraq approached, President Bush made it clear through Secretary of State James Baker that any Iraqi chemical or biological warfare would lead to an American nuclear response (14). As Air Force General Charles A. Horner put it later, "if there's collateral damage in Iraq, perhaps that's not all bad. There has to be a penalty for building and storing these weapons" (18). One wonders what would or should be the penalty for America's dropping the first atom bombs, and possessing thousands of nuclear devices to this day, as well as "more than one billion pounds of excess depleted uranium in the United States" (87). What emerges here is the willingness of a President of the United States, seconded by a general, to commit nuclear genocide against a helpless and innocent civilian population. Hersh ends his short but pungent study of virtual betrayal of American soldiers by our military leaders with the chilling statement that DU ordnance is now being sold around the world and sales are going very well.

My main stricture of Hersh's important book is that it is too short; it could have expanded its perspective by considering the revelatory position of Ramsey Clark's study *The Fire This Time: U.S. War Crimes in the Gulf.* Clark's book not only underscores the massive brutalization of Iraqi military and civilians by the American military, which violated conventions of ethical conduct in war going back over a century, and amounted in Clark's mind to American war crimes. It also describes in persuasive and thoroughly documented detail the history of the West's relations with Iraq and the Middle East in such a sophisticated mosaic of overt and covert economic and political aims as to show that the Gulf War was actually provoked by the United States. Considering Clark's broader perspective would have enriched and humanized Hersh's study and made its case even more weighted in tragic evil than he indicates. Nevertheless, *Against All Enemies* is a little book of major importance because it implies convincingly that America's worst enemy might well be the people running the country.

"Review: Seymour Hersh, *Against All Enemies: Gulf War Syndrome: the War Between America's Ailing Veterans and Their Government*" by Donald Gutierrez— *Common Sense*, October 1999; *Bloomsbury Review*, v. 20, Issue 1, January 2000.

27
Review: Chalmers Johnson, *The Sorrows of Empire: Militarism, Secrecy and the End of the Republic*

The political philosopher Hannah Arendt, author of *The Origins of Totalitarianism*, once wrote that "The central political idea of imperialism ... is expansion as a permanent and supreme aim of politics." This quotation could serve as the cardinal thesis of Chalmers Johnson's latest book *The Sorrows of Empire: Militarism, Secrecy and the End of the Republic*. Johnson, author and editor of fifteen scholarly books, is considered the American Dean of Asian-Pacific Studies.[1] His *Blowback: The Costs and Consequences of American Empire*, and now *Sorrows*, should also establish Johnson as the authority on contemporary American imperialism. From 1967 to 1973 Johnson was a consultant to the CIA's Office of National Estimates. "Thus began my introduction to the secret world," he says ominously in *Sorrows* (9).

The book's subtitle, "Militarism, Secrecy and the End of the Republic," intimates its thematic direction. Johnson defines militarism as "the phenomenon by which a nation's armed services .... begins to displace all other institutions within a government devoted to conducting relations with other nations" and puts its own institutional self-preservation above all else (23-24).

Johnson lists and discusses the major signs of militarism:

> 1. The emergence of a professional military class and the subsequent glorification of its ideals
> 2. "the preponderance of military officers or representatives of the arms industry in high government positions"

> 3. "A devotion to policies in which military preparedness
> becomes the highest priority of the state" (58-63)

Although these attributes fit the current White House administration snugly, Johnson indicates at length that both American militarism and imperialism have a long history. Further, and even more important, he elaborates in cogent detail the modern configuration of imperialism in military bases spread globally, the sizable role of privatization of military activity, the impact of American imperialism and militarism on other nations, the elaborate institutional secrecy to advance militarism and thus imperialism, the impact of American imperialism (or neo-Colonialism) on globalization and, finally, the erosion of American democracy under what has been called a "Pentagonized Presidency."

How did all this begin? Johnson begins his explanation of imperialism back to the early 19th century when the United States indicated its "interest" in all of Latin America and usurped Indian and Mexican territory. The American takeover of the Caribbean and ultimately the Philippines was made possible through exploiting the sinking of the *Maine* and liberating Cubans and Filipinos not only from Spain but from themselves at the cost of possibly 100,000 Filipino lives. This evolving imperialism also exhibited itself in Indiana's Senator Beveridge announcing that "the Pacific Ocean is ours" (43). And while the Pacific Campaign in World War II was designed to end Japan's imperialism, winning that war also allowed the United States to dominate the Pacific.

As the 20th century and the Cold War developed, the United States had an excellent excuse for spreading its imperialistic wings to defend its national (i.e., financial) interests against the Soviet Union by claiming to defend the Free World. This insistence rings hollow considering that Washington supported repressive regimes in virtually every country it could. Johnson makes it emphatically clear that this pretense of noble intentions has continued in our time. Despite such rationalizations, Johnson contends that American intervention in Kosovo and the two wars against Saddam Hussein, rather than embodying humanitarian intervention and the freeing of a repressed people, were in fact essentially imperialistic.

Johnson's discussion of American military bases provides stunning information and insight into what the Pentagon is up to globally. There are at least 725 bases abroad. The political corollary to this condition is that uniformed American military officers far outnumber American civilian officials abroad, suggesting force rather than diplomacy in dealing with other nations. To Johnson, these bases embody a kind of American second government, a "vast complex of interests, commitments and projects… paralleling civilian society" and consisting of "*permanent* [emphasis added], naval bases, military airfields, army garrisons, espionage listening posts, and strategic enclaves on every continent of the globe" (22-23). What makes all of this sinister is the extraordinary secrecy of this global military macrocosm, not to mention its incredible expensiveness.

A prime example of this secrecy and expense is Camp Bondsteel in Kosovo. According to Johnson, Bondsteel, constructed by a private company, is the largest and most expensive base erected since the Vietnam War, costing over $36 million to build and $180 million annually to run. Significantly, this supercamp with its six-mile perimeter, nine observation towers and its mass of attack helicopters and communications paraphernalia, looks permanent. Johnson climaxes his discussion of imperialistic base-building and secrecy by asserting that "Bondsteel is intended to play a role in a grand strategy to secure for us Middle Eastern and central Asian oil supplies and to control oil going to other countries" (145).

America has its own share of military bases, 969, an extraordinary number which partly explains why our contemporary military consists of 1.4 million troops and possesses a defense budget "larger than most national budgets" (189). Further, despite the rhetoric about having no dealings with tyrants and terrorists, Washington (Cheney in particular) readily fraternized with utterly savage heads of regimes like Uzbekistan and Kyrgyzstan in order to establish bases in Central Asia, which in turn leads to a massive lethal spiraling: "The creation of new bases requires more new bases to protect the ones already established, producing ever-tighter cycles of militarism, wars, arms sales and base expansions" (214). Johnson exemplifies his claim by citing bases not only in Oman and the United Arab Emirates, but in Turkey, Egypt, Israel and Djibouti as well as in four Central Asian third world countries. This proliferation of bases in the Near and Middle East compels Johnson to ask whether this heavy American military presence is designed to dominate the oil regions or whether the bases have taken on a life of their own.

Given that domineering the world directly is too strenuous even for America's resources, developing proxy militaries has become attractive to Washington. This practice has led to two expensive and politically pernicious programs: the State Department's IMET (International Military and Education Training Program) and the Pentagon's FMF (Foreign Military Financing). Formed in 1994, the IMET "offers military instruction to the armies of 96 countries ..." (132). By 2002, it was 133 countries at a cost, reported in 2003, of $80 million. The FMF, which in 2001 received over $3.5 billion (and in 2003 requested over $4 billion) "gives money to countries to buy American weapons and then supplies training in how to use them" (137). That most of these countries have brutal regimes does not appear to concern Washington.

When a government harbors a second, militaristic and exorbitant shadow government, secrecy becomes essential. The Bush-Cheney administration was, however, not the first presidency to harbor covert government enterprises or institutions: "The White House has always kept the 'intelligence agencies' budgets secret, and deceptions in the defense budget date back to the Manhattan Project of World War II..." (12). Secrecy, claims Johnson, is integral to bureaucracy; the less informed Congress, the media and the public are, the better. The most effective way of providing White House/Pentagon secrecy is through the "Black Budget" which has financed such "Black Programs" as the atomic bomb in World War II. Washington continued to operate in secrecy, evidenced by Truman's National Security Agency, Eisenhower's National Reconnaissance Office, Kennedy's Defense Intelligence Agency and Clinton's National Imagery and Mapping Agency. None of these agencies had published budgets but apparently they amounted to multi-billions of dollars. (The General Accounting Office, moreover, has discovered at least 185 Black Programs).

Of special interest to all Americans should be the top secret ECHELON program, an arrangement between English-speaking governments to intercept and share "non-military communications of governments, private organizations, businesses and individuals..." (165). ECHELON enables Washington to snoop on Americans indirectly, as no laws prohibit this sort of intelligence-swapping, and, in any event, no mechanisms of accountability exist. The Pentagon has more than once been willing to go far beyond spying on the nation it is supposed to defend. Johnson cites a 1960s Joint Chief of Staff proposal to Secretary of Defense Robert McNamara called Operation Northwoods, in which the American military would "shoot innocent people on American streets, sink boats carrying refugees from Cuba, carry out terrorist acts in Washington, Miami and elsewhere, and then pin the blame on Cuban agents" to justify another invasion of Cuba (301).

Considering the ponderous American military presence throughout the world, Johnson's CIA concept of blowback becomes frighteningly relevant. Regarding 9/11 as blowback, Johnson then makes a statement that would shock only Americans ignorant of the genocidal aspects of American foreign policy for the last half-century: "…I myself thought that the attacks could be blowback from American policies in any number of places, including Chile, Argentina, Indonesia, Greece, all of Central America, or Okinawa, not to mention Palestine and Iran…" (227).

Johnson thinks that Washington's policy on globalization both undermines it and at the same time provides yet another potential cause of blowback. Such Washington-controlled programs as the undemocratic IMF and the World Bank have had a massively deleterious impact on third world nations; while these countries struggle to survive economically, the IMF-imposed SAPs (structural adjustment programs) severely undercut their essential social programs so as to repay high-interest foreign bank and transnational corporation loans. Such an "adjustment" increases the gap between the rich and poor in these countries, further fueling anti-West hatred. Yet, as Johnson crucially perceives, the expense of Washington's militarism and of its gargantuan foreign debts (possibly $3.5 trillion in the current decade) both undermines globalization while putting the United States dangerously at risk of economic collapse should foreign investors decide to pull their investments, a development Johnson relates directly to Washington's military unilateralist imperialism.

Johnson concludes *Sorrows* with a chapter itemizing and elaborating discussion of four sorrows of America's imperialism and militarism:

> —"a state of perpetual war, leading to more terrorism against Americans…" (285),
> —"a loss of democracy and constitutional rights…" in an increasingly authoritarian presidency,
> —the annihilation of principles of truth to disinformation and a celebration of war and power, and
> —national bankruptcy and dismemberment of social programs to finance ongoing military projects.

Sorrows describes an American military imperialism in which the Pentagon has most of the world (ominously including the United States) divided up into five "Commands," in which an American general, Anthony

Zinni, in charge of the Mid-East Command, has twenty American ambassadors *under* his direction and in which President Bush had targeted sixty (Cheney, forty) nations for terrorist status, who thus merited "preemptive" attack.

Johnson's declaration, "I fear that we will lose our country," (12) seems prescient, after Bush's eight years in the White House and a foreign policy by the Obama Administration that appears to be similar to Bush's. *Sorrows* convincingly envisions the disaster that lies ahead for the United States and the world if the juggernaut of American imperial militarism is not somehow stopped.

---

1. Johnson died in 2010.

"Review: Chalmers Johnson, *The Sorrows of Empire: Militarism, Secrecy and the End of the Republic*" by Donald Gutierrez—*Common Sense*, January 2005; *Eldorado Sun*, January 2005.

PART III

BUSINESS AS USUAL

GREED, RACISM AND GENOCIDE

28

"When Were You Last in Mexico?"
Ethnic Identity and a 1950s Bus Trip Through the South

In early January of 1958 my wife Marlene and I left Berkeley, California on a Greyhound bus trip to New York City where I was to begin a new life as a professional Librarian armed with a University of California Berkeley Master of Librarianship degree. Marlene in turn hoped to expand in her development as a young modernist artist in the energy and stimulation of the New York art scene. We were both weary of Berkeley and the Bay Area after seven and a half years there, and New York seemed attractive in being over 3,000 miles east and in being, well, New York. We had to travel by bus because we had no car and little money, and Greyhound was then the cheapest way to get anywhere. Choosing the southerly route turned out to be a significant mistake but it certainly dramatized for me the maze of ethnic and personal identity.

Had we taken a northerly route, my experiences via bus might perhaps have been markedly different and less disturbing, but we decided to go South, through the Southwest, Texas and the Gulf Coast states partly to avoid bad winter weather but also to say goodbye to Marlene's parents who lived in Inglewood, a municipality southwest of Los Angeles. After spending a day or two with her parents, we got on the bus, outfitted with a straw bag bulging with Marlene's mother's sandwiches, fruit, pickles, crackers and cheese.

Taking this bag might also have been a mistake, as it made us look suspiciously poorer than we were.

When we reached San Diego and got off the bus to stretch our legs, I was approached by an official-looking middle-aged man who asked me for identification. I was so surprised and offended by this unexpected and unwelcome intrusion on my privacy that I angrily refused to cooperate with the request, instead, just walking away. The man, apparently an immigration official, curiously didn't persist and I boarded the bus with feathers a bit ruffled but my identity still unscathed. I had undergone bouts of high anxiety during my seven years at U.C. Berkeley. On one occasion I had fled from a Shakespeare class of perhaps over a hundred students despite sitting in the front row only about ten yards away from a distinguished Shakepeare scholar; and I had experienced a major panic attack in 1957 during my bus trip down to the Oakland Draft Board for possible induction. Consequently, the possibility of feeling "trapped" and thus panicky on a bus for well over 3,000 miles might have left phobias circulating through my inner self like snakes preparing to strike. Given the circumstances, ruffled feathers was a mild reaction for me—so far.

A more sinister questioning of my identity occurred the next evening in a small town in the middle of nowhere in Texas, a place that by its drabness, meanness and ugliness suggested an appropriate setting for lynchings. Marlene and I had gotten off the bus during its coffee-break stop to take a walk around the block and get a little exercise. The block was littered with nondescript houses and vacant lots full of weeds, the sort of place T. S. Eliot might have had in mind for some of those dreary poems of modern urban, spiritual desolation written early in his career.

When we reached the fourth side of the block, we suddenly became aware that an old black pickup was slowly following us, actually driving down the desolate street on the wrong side so as to be close to us, perhaps four or five yards away. A tall, middle-aged Black male was at the steering wheel; at his side was another male, probably middle-aged and Mexican. The latter began speaking to me in Spanish. Not knowing Spanish (despite having Central American parents), I didn't understand what he was saying, but his tone sounded somewhat derisive, perhaps a tad challenging or even menacing. However, I couldn't be sure. Was he, driven by envy, verbally assaulting or insulting me ("Mexican" Don) for accompanying a White Woman? Was he, instead, warning me like an ethnic comrade against the grave danger I was running by strolling along in public with a young, blue-eyed blonde? Decades later, when I mentioned the encounter to a liberal colleague at my southern New Mexico college who had once lived in the deep South, he said I indeed could have been attacked, even killed in both the South and Texas for this association (reminiscences of the violent treatment accorded young Mexican males by the Texas Rangers came to mind later, one young "wetback" drowned in a river while in Rangers custody). Glancing a second time at the front car door, I noticed the top of the barrel of a rifle by the window side of the Black man. After a few minutes, the car drove slowly on ahead of us, disappearing around the corner, to my relief. When Marlene and I reached and entered the bus depot, we saw the same Black man. He either didn't see us or did but ignored us.

What did this road encounter mean? What did it say about an external perception of me, or of anyone? Of course, as with all stereotyping, one's inner or complex personal being is reduced to a few traits, hardly personal or individualized; rather, one becomes victim of a minimalist depiction that is not a self but a derogated or despised type. Were these two men, both members of minorities savaged in America, trying to protect me, or even us? They obviously didn't know—how could they?—that I was an American-born citizen of Nicaraguan and Guatemalan ancestry with two college degrees from a distinguished university. So what? All that was brutally clear—if anything was clear in the somewhat sinister murkiness of the moment, situation and national atmosphere—is that I was a Brown young man walking with a White young woman in a region probably rabidly hostile to even the mild association of us two strolling along together. I had come from Berkeley and the Bay Area, a cultural milieu in which it was taken for granted that Brown, White, Black, Yellow, Red were all equally acceptable colors. Certainly this ideal was often enough not achieved in the Bay Area but at least it embodied a general cultural consciousness and ideal probably not readily found in this Texas town, in the South and for that matter in other parts of the United States, North as well as South.

So instead of having my self-identification confirmed as an individualized libertarian radical and young fellow with intellectual aspirations whose ethnic identity was not a central issue or concern in my daily life, I now had a dark perception on the road South that I could instantly be regarded as an outlaw figure. Emmit Till, the fourteen-year-old Black lad from Chicago, had been brutally beaten and murdered in Mississippi just three years earlier for whistling at and briefly flirting with a White Woman on a bet with friends, and my colleague at Western New Mexico U. had said *I* could have been murdered for my proximity to my wife, my *wife*. So there—possibly? probably?—was a very serious gap between my customary "Berkeley" sense of self and the "Texas-Southern" sense or definition of "Mexican Don," which, if not ethnically accurate about me, nevertheless bore all the reality thrust of a hard smack to the side of the head. As Robert Caro mentions in his formidable biography *Lyndon Johnson: Master of the Senate*, Mexican males at the time were being told, "We don't serve Mexicans," in barber shops in southern Texas while at the same time being told who they *had* to vote for in the senatorial race won by Lyndon Johnson.

But there was another conundrum of identity. I had not emerged from an Hispanic community and thus could not identify with and be empowered by such an identification. My Nicaraguan mother and Guatemalan father divorced when I was around nine or ten, and an Anglo stepfather entered the scene a few years later. For better or worse, I spent the years of youth and young manhood with no connection with a Latin community (except for my mother who was estranged from her family in Nicaragua). Thus, I lacked any sense of ethnic identification with any group. Moreover, being identified over the decades variously as a Mexican, Spaniard, Frenchman, Italian, Greek, Black (by a Black acquaintance) Sephardic Jew (by my German-Irish stepfather) and Arab hardly clarified my sense of identity, but occasionally amused me—I'm surprised no one identified me as an Eskimo or a Laotian. In any event, there seemed little doubt in the minds of American border officials ("La Migra") that I was some species of Mexican or Latin, possibly illegal, maybe dangerous, and certainly meriting investigation.

At our next stop, in New Orleans, I was again approached by an immigration officer or border cop or at least someone official-looking flashing his credentials and asking me for an I.D. This time I complied, simply showing my driver's license, and thus ending the queries. Some might say, well, that's what you should have done all along, without any resistance or emotional fuss about it. That probably would have made things neater, simpler, clear-cut emotionally. Yet surely not only people of color resist or resent having their identity questioned or challenged. The issue of identity obviously goes far deeper than skin color or whatever misguided essentialness we attach to our particular ethnic or racial being. But when the challenge to prove our identity appears to question our ethnic or racial aspect in a way that also invades our deeper sense of our self, we might almost feel—rightly or wrongly—that psychic survival is at hand, that our ethnicity or race is not only as basic as blood but as the very cells of the body.

I certainly had not felt challenged on that fundamental level, but how do we measure the depths to which ethnic or racial identity define us? For that matter, what *is* our most essential being, or deepest individual (if it *is* individual) essence? Is it ultimately psychic, instinctive, even physiological? Put another way, when do we cross from our individualistic being into the rudimentary complexity of our physico-chemical-electrical-fluidic components that comprise our organic essence? Perhaps I could have felt grateful to these questioning officials in their inadvertently driving me to experience the gamut from my ethnic sense of self to my elemental being. I felt no gratitude though, and, curiously, little anxiety and no panic.

Deciding to partake of the Big Easy's popular culture, we boarded a New Orleans street car where I encountered a more subtle form of ethnic ambiguity, semi-comic in retrospect. Getting into the car, we noticed that there were "front" and "back" sections: front, Whites; back, "colored." Now, that sectioning posed some problems and soul-searching, not for my wife who is German, but for me, with my Guat-Nic ethnicity. The crux of the matter was skin color; I was neither black nor white, but sort of in-between, brownish. (This reminds me, later in life, of the graduated racism of "White—all right, Brown—stick around, Black—stay back.")

My dilemma resulted from both a certain lack of confidence about myself psychologically and racially as well as a sizable sympathy for and identity with Black people and their atrocious treatment by White institutions and individuals. I couldn't sit in the back Black area, not being Black (not to mention my blonde , blue-eyed wife), yet I felt guilt at sitting with the Whites. Possibly the best thing to have done under these confused and confusing circumstances, would have been to exit the streetcar, but that didn't occur to me, and Marlene would likely have opposed it.

So I made a "compromise." We sat in the White section seat adjoining the Black section, almost a kind of border. However, it was not border enough. A relatively young Black woman sat right behind us, and, as I put my arm around my wife's shoulders—thus unintentionally crossing the border—my left arm was suddenly and rather violently knocked forward. The woman behind us had abruptly put up her "Colored Only" seat sign, knocking my arm off of her territory. I'm darker than some Blacks but to this woman I was "white" or at least not black and my intrusion was fair game for a little payback, whatever my attempt at compromise, which she couldn't have known or, likely, cared about.

Back on the road the next day, our bus stopped for a meal break in Mobile, Alabama during the evening. After all us passengers had consumed our "Eats" Restaurant fare and gotten on the bus, and everyone including the driver was ready to hit the road again, the driver suddenly turned the engine off and opened the door, allowing another person onto the bus. My first reaction was—well, just another late passenger. But the man was somewhat formally dressed (tie and coat) and seemed bent on a mission. In fact, looking at him more carefully, I began to feel he was not coming towards but *to* me. *I* was his mission.

Again, after the badge display bit, he asked if I was a citizen of the United States. When I said yes, he requested an I.D. Looking carefully at my now frequently handled driver's license, he still wasn't satisfied and asked when or if I had been in Mexico. This seemed an odd question in view of my showing a valid American identity credential and I regretted afterwards that I lacked the presence of mind to challenge the propriety of the question. After all, what business was it of his when or if I had been to Mexico?

I wondered why I hadn't challenged him. Was it lack of presence of mind? Was it some kind of anxiety or fear that if I didn't cooperate with his question there could be unpleasant consequences, perhaps even being "detained"? Was I being too compliant? Was my own sense of identity, of my rights, citizen or personal, dissolving? Or was my cooperation based on not wanting to hold up the other passengers, surely eager to get on with their trip—thus my community-spirited side emerging?

It's hard to be sure—almost fifty years later—of my real motivation(s), but it made me wonder whether those Americans who take their civil liberties so for granted would find their layer of citizen self-assurance much thinner if confronted by hostile or even physically violent interrogation by "detainers." I should add, to do journalistic justice to that incident, that Marlene to this day insists that I was taken off the bus and questioned outside. This scared her, because she thought I could be separated from her out in (again) "the middle of Nowhere"—a sense of place not just Blacks might have felt about southern Alabama in the 1950s. I don't recall being taken off the bus, and thus a long-standing matrimonial disagreement about the past.

Surely, many Middle Eastern Americans today must feel intensely exposed and nervous about their fundamental identity and even the security of their person. They must worry about how that identity is perceived by the hostile American authorities, let alone the average American. For an innocent person (but who is innocent, and in regard to what?) to be seen by some authoritative individual or institution as an outsider, an alien, possibly an enemy, even a suspect Terrorist, is a radical attack not only on one's self but on one's deepest sense of being.

My last border/immigration challenge occurred in Jacksonville, Florida, hardly an international border town. This again suggests (as did the stop in Mobile) that my confrontations by officials might have had less to do with a concern about illegal immigration than with something else. It later occurred to Marlene and I that perhaps Cuba had something to do with my being questioned on our trip east. Fidel Castro overturned the Batista regime about a year later; perhaps Washington was already on the lookout for Fidelista agents flooding the States disguised as poor post-college travelers. But maybe not. Perhaps Marlene was a coyote cleverly using the Greyhound Bus instead of a van for the trip North.

When we finally arrived in cold, wintry New York, I experienced a deep sense of relief. New York being New York, I felt no one here would care who I was, when I had last been in Mexico, or where I was going. The main concern one picked up in the pulsating, brutal yet exhilarating atmosphere of Manhattan was to get out of people's way—they had to Get somewhere, and if you fell down or had a heart attack, just don't block their path. This attitude, common enough in New York, was for the time being liberating to someone uncertain and uneasy about what identity others would project on him. It was a strange and unsettling kind of liberation but liberation it was. I now walked down the cold, blackened-snow streets of the most callously indifferent city in the United States feeling like a free man.

Free—but how free? Two years later in New York I applied for a job as the Head Librarian in the private and posh University Club on Fifth Avenue. I was offered the job, a professional position, but was told that—unlike the Club members (Senators, CEO heads, university and bank presidents, etc.)—I would have to enter the Club by the back door of the regal building. I turned the job offer down.

"When Were You Last in Mexico?" by Donald Gutierrez—*Progressive Populist* June 2007; *Common Sense*, October 2007.

29

Attending College Must Be Free Again
(For the Country's Own Good)

College students sunk deeply in debt due to extremely costly tuition rates represent a grave threat both to America's democracy and to the country's future. A yearly public college debt of $22,000 is not uncommon. The debts of students going into pre-professional graduate programs are much higher, sometimes amounting to several hundred thousand dollars. Individuals in circumstances preventing prompt repayment to usurious student-loan companies (single parent, loss of job or residence, health-crisis costs) not only get interest added to interest but receive bad credit ratings and endless, badgering calls from collection agencies. (President Barack Obama's Education Reconciliation Act of April 4, 2010 was designed to protect students from predatory lending institutions, but years of using usury against students had already been dangerously contributive to increasing class stratification.)

When I attended the University of California, Berkeley, in the early 1950s, there was no tuition. Something called an "Incidental Fee" ($35.00 per semester) covered such privileges or needs as use of gym facilities or the campus hospital (as well as free psychiatric services!) and of course a first-rate scholarly library. Course books were relatively inexpensive, and used copies were readily available at local bookstores. Recently, even at a state university like Berkeley, the cost per year for an undergraduate, according to the U. C. Office of the Registrar, is almost $5,000 a semester (over $16,000 for a nonresident of the state), while enrolling in Berkeley's Boalt

Hall School of Law costs almost $18,000 per semester, including living expenses and expensive books.

Although private colleges are far more expensive, even state school fees, such as Berkeley's, have entailed debts that can imprison students financially for years, decades in fact. It is common knowledge that medical students, for example, are going into higher paying specializations rather than becoming general practitioners in order to pay off six-figure college debts, though the nation badly needs GPs. A quick check of other public universities, such as the University of Michigan and City University of New York, reveals similar high tuition rates. In California, moreover, at least twice as much money is utilized towards building and sustaining penal institutions as is directed towards the state's educational needs.

Extreme financial stress on responsible college students is not only unjust, it is dangerous to the country's future. Higher education should be free to all young people who show an aptitude for and aspire to advanced learning and professional or technical training. Society needs doctors, nurses, dentists, teachers, scholars, engineers, lawyers, economists, philosophers, historians, architects, anthropologists, scientists, artists, novelists, poets, and social, political and cultural critics and other experts—now and in the future. If, however, those high college debt hurdles remain, the consequences are obvious and pernicious: For the most part, only youths from wealthy or comfortable families will be able to afford college, especially quality colleges. The result will be not only a class-based educational structure—Yale vs. Flatsburg City College—but the hardening of a class-structured society. The crucial ideal and reality of democratic, egalitarian institutions of higher education open to all who qualify on the basis of intelligence, aspiration and dedication will have dissolved.

Essential to creating a genuine participative democracy is the fundamental obligation of a society to educate as many of its inhabitants as possible in critical and imaginative thinking. Such an education could allow a broad segment of the population, rather than only an elite, to participate significantly in shaping its society. Without this kind of educated populace, a democracy can lurch into a combination of despotisms, from control—overt or covert—by an imperial presidency or the Pentagon and its congressional boosters to the plutocratic totalitarianism of Wall Street.

Though I am a first-generation American of Central American parentage and from an upper lower-class bohemian family, I was able to attend a major university not only because I received two different scholarships, but because, as a state resident, I could attend a school like Berkeley at small cost. One big reason for this was that wealthy Californians paid a sizable, progressive share of property taxes. This changed in 1978 with the California "revolution" brought about by an anti-property-tax activist named Howard Jarvis. Strongly appealing to the rich and to landlords, Jarvis's Proposition 13 cut property taxes by 57 percent and allowed property to be taxed only during a sale, no longer annually.

This "relief" to the state's wealthy made millionaires and multi-millionaires even richer, and also had a devastating impact on California's county and city budgets. Consequently, among other things, public libraries in the state were unable to expand and, thus, unable to meet the reading needs and interests—especially among poorer families—of a rapidly enlarging population. University and grade school budgets were also affected, due in part to sizable cuts in state educational budgets as well, which were made by Republican Governor Pete Wilson. And though U. C. Berkeley continues to have full enrollments and high ranking nationally, not everyone who merits attendance can afford to attend. With federal Pell Grants having been reduced almost by half in recent years, the debt burden for many students is further intensified.

Thus, the rich, directly and indirectly, have made their own contribution to class-structured higher education in California (and elsewhere), either in effect closing college gates to many children from families of moderate and low income or seriously burdening those who get into school with preposterously large school debts. Jarvis's Proposition 13, which remains a disaster for the state's public funds, is considered to be a major factor in California's continuing budget crisis.

Americans raging about the costs of health care reforms seldom ask what's happened to the monies needed not only for such reforms but also for a democratic society's future and well-being as embodied in a flourishing, egalitarian higher education system. We would do well to consider by comparison the kind of monies available in selected areas of Wall Street and the military sector.

Extremely wealthy investors contribute millions and billions of dollars to hedge fund managers, who transmit these monies electronically around the world in seconds. People criticizing America's salary culture tend to focus on the huge corporate and banking CEO salaries; and within the context of average wages, these CEO salaries certainly are brutally outsized. Yet, compared to the massive kinds of monies being invested and acquired by extremely rich people and by unregulated "too big to fail" banks, CEO salaries are, as economists like Paul Krugman have observed, merely sideshows.

Trillions of dollars are being circulated electronically to make *more* money. It is fair to point out here that the already-wealthy have reaped more than one trillion dollars in tax cuts provided to their class by former President Bush. The basic issue is that wealth has been structured in our country in such a way that vast sums of money acutely needed and *deserved* for social, public needs have been privatized. This complex, devious activity has evolved and been ramified in too many ways to describe here, but a crucial factor to mention has been the regressive taxation which, legislated by Congress in recent decades, provided huge tax breaks and subsidies to big corporations and generous interest rates to the big banks.

Thus, enormous sums of money that should be accessible for America's infrastructure—schools, medical health programs and facilities, aid programs to the poor and cultural venues—are pouring into corporation, defense industry, bank and private investor coffers. The most egregious manifestation of this horrific privatization of public monies was the 2008 financial meltdown in which the individuals and financial institutions that devised and profited from deregulated financial dealings were bailed out at enormous public expense but without public consent. This was surely one of the most heinous thefts of public wealth in history.

One institution using massive amounts of public monies with very little critical media attention or evaluation is the Pentagon. A 2010 *Mother Jones* ongoing report entitled "Shock and Audit: the Hidden Defense Budget" suggests that the Pentagon budget is monstrously large. After being informed that cost overruns for current major weapons programs now are $296 billion, the report observes that the 2009 budget President Barack Obama requested is almost $534 billion and that the 2010 Pentagon budget was $680 billion. Those two annual sums would combined amount to $1,214 trillion. But that's not all. There is the immense expense of some 725 American military posts spread around the world and the more then 900 bases on our own soil [see review of Chalmers Johnson's *The Sorrows of Empire*, Ch. 27].

As for the cost of a mere selection of warplanes, each (already constructed) F-22 amounted to $350 million (a grand total of approximately $65 billion for 78 of them). The F-22 and the F-35 (the Joint Strike Fighter) were reported in *Time* (August 27, 2009) as being merely two of the top ten most expensive American war planes.

Finally, as if to fantasize about more ways to spend American taxpayers' money, the Pentagon harbors a high-placed senior officer named Michele A. Flournoy with the formidable title of Under Secretary of Defense for Policy whose job in effect is to conceive and plan new wars. The golden era of peace that was supposed to follow the demise of the Cold War continues to be undermined by Washington's endless lust for wars and the Pentagon's endless demand for more and newer ordnance.

No one can demonstrate that national security demands the expenditure of the mountains of money only partly indicated above. It is well known that the U. S. defense budget is larger than that of all other nations' war budgets *combined*. Thus, in some essential respects, it would appear that the fundamental interests of the state and the public are polarized. The public is forced to lose its monies through regressive taxation, enormous government-expedited bank bailouts and fear-mongering about terrorism to justify expanding the military budget. This results in the public need—and the public itself—being sacrificed to a centralized policy of imperial power and what the Department of Defense has termed global "full-spectrum-dominance."

So how does the amount of money being spent in just these major categories—the military and the financial corporations—relate to student college costs? Monies going through hedge funds, corporation-taxable monies going instead to off-shore tax havens, monies supporting our two most recent unnecessary and illegal wars ($3 trillion over the next decade, according to Nobel-Prize-winning economist Joseph Stieglitz), the enormous ordnance and global military base costs and the huge medical care expense for our wounded soldiers—just a moderate portion of this would allow all qualifying young people to attend college free, rather than go to college via military service in Iraq and Afghanistan. Writing in *The Progressive* (2010), the journalist and political science professor Adolph Reed, Jr. urges that education is a right, not a privilege, and that free college education would cost about $80 billion, which he claims is much less than the 2008 bank bailouts. It is also less than ten percent of the current Pentagon budget. What better defense against external (or internal) threat can a democratic society possess than a deeply and widely educated citizenry?

In the 1950s the University of California, Berkeley, and other state universities throughout the country, comprised a wonderful exemplification of democracy in a crucial area of our society's promise of an egalitarian future. We are now betraying that promise through a rigidly class-oriented structure of higher education costs and access. If education is not once again democratized as it was for several decades after World War II, the ideal of the United States as an an open society of opportunity and advancement for all will be doomed. Monies unjustly and unwisely arrogated by America's financial and military sectors must be returned to essential civilian needs, among which higher education is crucial.

"Attending College Must Be Free Again (For the Country's Own Good)" by Donald Gutierrez—*Progressive Populist*, September 2009; *The Humanist Society of New Mexico*, September 2009; *Rio Grande Tribune*, February 3, 2010.

30

Prep Schools and America's Ruling Class

We are the rich; we own America; we got it God knows how,
but we intend to keep it if we can by throwing all the
tremendous weight of our support, our influence, our money,
our political connections, our purchased senators.... and our
public-speaking demagogues, into the scale against any
legislation, any political platform, any presidential campaign
that threatens the integrity of our estate. (millionaire Frederick
T. Martin, *Passing of the Idle Rich*, 1911)

In an article entitled "The Strange Fate of the American Boarding School,"
David B. Hicks, former Rector of St. Paul's School in Concord, New
Hampshire, says:

> The elitist mission of the boarding school was meant to
> reflect John Adams' realistic view of the human condition.
> Why, he asked, should we reject good birth in humans as a
> basis for assigning potential worth when we accept this as the
> first principle of animal husbandry and bet our money on it at
> the track. Besides, the wellborn and the wealthy, whether or
> not we like it, exercise a disproportionate influence on society,
> and this is all the more reason to attend carefully to their
> nurture and education. (*The American Scholar*, 527)

This quotation harbors a number of assumptions and presumptions,
but the cardinal one strikes me as being this: Because the wellborn and the
wealthy exercise extreme influence over society, it is important to "attend

carefully to their nurture and education." One can take issue with that outlook. If the wellborn and wealthy have an extreme impact on or control over society, their education should not be carefully monitored; their wealth and power should be *curtailed*.

Now, Hicks' idealistic view of the role of elite boarding schools is that they have traditionally attempted to make the young Masters-to-be selfless, high-minded, public-spirited:

> At Groton and other schools the students were provided
> with a considerable amount of corrective salutary deprivation.
> At St. Paul's and Groton the boys roomed together in barren
> little cubicles.... Historically, one did not send one's son to a
> school like Groton to secure a place in society. The place was
> already secure. One sent a boy to Groton to save him from the
> selfishness and softness of his secure place. (528)

Some fine individuals have undoubtedly emerged from Choate, St. Paul's, Hill, Groton and other prep schools, but then some fine individuals have emerged as well from slum schools and lower- and middle-class dysfunctional families. The latter however did not have a high place in society already secured, and the very great majority of them never would. In any event, idealizing a private, privileged and very expensive middle and high school education—based as it is on the British upper-class "public" (i.e., private) school system—as a way of making the best of an unjust class structure, is certainly not a happy idea. (Traditionally, let us recall, the English public school was partly intended to indoctrinate some of its youth into running the empire.) The unexamined assumption behind both Hicks' thesis and the prep school concept itself is that this class system embodies a fundamental, unalterable reality, one of those "natural laws" that, like it or not, we must all live with—or under.

But the occurrence of revolutions refutes this presumption. And though some revolutions have led to social catastrophe, many French people still celebrate the French Revolution as others do the bloodless British nationalizing of segments of industry after World War II. Further, how many Americans since the American War of Independence (i.e., revolution) have disapproved of that event? The pungent sentiment of the 17th century aristocrat and famed letter writer Madame de Sevigne that the lower and middle classes were excrement dramatically highlighted the accelerating corruption and inhumanity of this overprivileged and pampered class. America's "aristocrats"—royal solely through the lengthy possession of money and what (and who) money could buy—benefit enormously from the myth of American democracy. This myth obscures their wealth and their domination of society, and lends credence to the Horatio Alger fantasy that *anyone* can make it if only he tries hard enough. Thus, everyone who has become wealthy or powerful deserves it; this often is accompanied by the sentiment that everyone who hasn't *couldn't*.

The Horatio Alger ideal is of course the romance of America's Open Society, a society whose resources are supposedly available to anyone and everyone. Yet it is widely known by now that almost half of our society's financial resources are privately owned by approximately one percent of the population and that until recently large groups of people (women, African Americans, males under 21 drafted for war) could not vote. Further, millions of others who could vote but possess virtually no power financially or politically don't expect voting to help their circumstances or feel that anyone running for office would be interested in helping them. Worse, the Republican party and its operatives have been going out of their way to disenfranchise such people by, for example, setting up excessively narrow identification criteria.

Hicks rather disingenuously erects the fact of the class inequality represented by prep schools into an ideal:

> If by their very existence these schools seemed to undermine the notion of equality, they did provide an antidote to the vast leveling and conformist forces of democracy. They stood in some instances for truths much deeper than the egalitarian myth—to wit, that all men and women strive for superiority, not equality. It is, of course, in this striving within the rules for higher purposes…that American citizens are educated and ennobled and their democratic institutions preserved.

The Rector of St. Paul's surely must know that prep schools don't stand for "all men and women" striving for superiority. These elite schools do have some Minority and scholarship students. One recalls what their fate very possibly resembled from George Orwell's memorable and acrid essay about English prep schools "Such, Such Were the Joys!" Nevertheless, most preppies are from upper-class families who in some cases—St. Andrews, for one—dump them there to get them off their hands.

These youngsters are bred with the ideal that *their class*, not "all men and women," will strive for superiority. Usually, there is no overt or crude indoctrination; it is just quietly assumed by all parties involved that these youths will one day rule American society. It is almost virtually inhaled by these kids in their special and exclusive little world that they will master and control the very society that expels so much verbal air insisting that America is the freest nation in the world, the least class-structured and the most resonant with individualism, liberty and opportunity.

Hicks implies that, as we are stuck with an upper class (and thus a class structure), we should make the best of it and try to produce future rulers who are noble, selfless and public-spirited (John Kerry's self-idealization, for example). This is not a fatuous position; it seems at first to make good sense—make the best of an imperfect, unalterable situation. One can ask, though, whether it really is unalterable. Of course America has a class structure. It is a class order perhaps the harder to change because some Americans aren't aware of one, some don't like it but feel it can't be changed while others who benefit from it understandably like it. Paul Fussell, in his humorous yet sobering book *Class*, states the issue of class in America with insight and rigor:

> I do wish the word *caste* were domesticated in the United States because it nicely conveys the actual rigidity of class lines here, the difficulty of moving either upward or downward—out of the place where you were nurtured. (12)

Fussell notwithstanding, social class has, as argued earlier, shown fluidity (as well as rigidity) over the decades and centuries. What we take for a fixed, even concrete, entity—class *structure*, which sounds like (and can be) a social tower of cement—is surprisingly accessible to slippage, shifting, collapses, leveling-outs, revolutions. Revolutions represent a change in class structure so complete and rapid that one begins to see how artificial and impermanent class is in some respects (though of course some revolutions just put another class on top so that the phenomena of class can be fluid but also readily solidified).

All this is by way of suggesting that the American upper-class culture of wealth and excessive privilege that breeds prep schools and the high-level economic and political dominance they usually can lead to is not engraved in stone handed down from Above. One justly opposes a tiny class so massively empowered that in owning or controlling almost half the nation's wealth—as well as its mass media, banks, major law firms, corporations, politicians—it virtually owns the country (not to mention *other* countries). Not fire-breathing radicalism but a serious dedication to genuine political and economic participative democracy demands that no class should be so omnipotent that it can half suffocate American society and prevent distribution of the substantial wealth that really belongs to the public at large. As Saint Jerome said sixteen centuries ago, "Opulence is always the result of theft."

If, as Ferdinand Lundberg claims, preppies go on to Harvard-Princeton-Yale and end up on Wall Street as investment bankers, corporation power lawyers, CEOs and so on, they are by and large serving their own interest rather than living up to the altruistic public service that Hicks exhibits as the prep school ideal. And if, as Paul Blumberg states, "The educational system has been effectively appropriated by the upper strata and transformed into an instrument which tends to reproduce the class structure and transmit inequality" (Fussell, 154), then the role of the prep school in all of our American class/caste structuring becomes (and has been) sizable and pernicious. This is especially so if one accepts C. Wright Mills' perception that "Harvard or Yale or Princeton is not enough. It is really exclusive prep schools that count" (from Fussell, 162) or Fussell's own claims that "unless one has gone to Hotchkiss, Groton, Hill, St. Mark's, Andover, Exeter or Milton the whole Ivy college act is likely to be a waste" (162).

It is relevant here to mention the American upper-class social club, as it embodies little known but highly concentrated power and influence on the highest levels of government, business and finance. It is also part of a continuity of caste traceable back to prep schools and of course to the upper-class ethos that creates and supports the prep-school-Ivy-League-college-exclusive-Club tradition. According to Lundberg, "[The elite] class does mark itself off through the system of the private clubs, which in the East are so exclusive that neither the Pope nor most Presidents of the United States could qualify for membership." Nor, according to Fussell, could movie stars in the elite clubs in Los Angeles. But these, observes Lundberg, are only social aspects of the clubs. Their most repercussive impact on society, which Lundberg regards as immense if scarcely visible to the general public, is economic and political:

> The clubs are the scene, at least in the preliminary stages, of some of the biggest deals in the Capitalistic world... they are the places where attitudes are shaped towards proposed national policies. Once a consensus has been reached, the clubs serve to hand down a general "party line" to members who carry it to the world in their various functional capacities. (744)

So stated, these ideas at first sound paranoiac, and Lundberg does qualify his thesis somewhat by acknowledging, for instance, that not all club members toe the line. But considering that, for example, membership of the New York top-drawer Links Club consists almost entirely of corporation executives, bank presidents, upper-echelon Pentagon brass, elite college presidents and top political figures, Lundberg's culminating judgment strikes one as ominously true: "If its [the Links and other elite clubs'] membership does not exactly run the county it has much to say about its course. Here are what the Russian and Chinese Press morosely refer to as America's 'ruling circles'" (346-47).

Lundberg has observed, "Few children of the rich attend public schools" (338), and also that private-school ties are far more significant than even Ivy League ones. In this light, John F. Kennedy's famed Inaugural Address mot, "Ask not what your country can do for you; ask what you can do for your country," takes on a strikingly different meaning when we learn that if you substitute "school" for "country" in the above sentiment, you will behold the slogan of the prep school—Choate—that Kennedy attended. And, in a profound way, the high privilege of Choate strives most successfully in the national arena, for most Americans are continually if indirectly serving some of the well-heeled graduates of prep schools like Choate who have gone on to "serve" as corporation, banking, high-finance and defense industry heads and in other high-level areas of power that dominate American society.

At any rate, we free masses may derive confused comfort from thinking that we live in an equalitarian, even-surfaced society where anyone can become a multimillionaire by either going to the Right School or by being greedy and uncaring enough to make it big no matter at whose expense. But it must have been in some other universe millions of light years from ours that Walt Whitman said, "By God! I will accept nothing which all cannot have their counterpart of on the same terms." In the same vein, socialist labor leader Eugene V. Debs said, "Years ago I began to recognize my kinship with all living beings....I said then, and I say now, that while there is a lower class I am in it, while there is a criminal element, I am of it, while there is a soul in prison, I am not free!"

"Prep Schools and America's Ruling Class" by Donald Gutierrez—*Justice Xpress*, Summer 2004, v. 12, no. 3; *Progressive Populist*, January 2008.

31
Review: Terrence Des Pres, *The Survivor: An Anatomy of Life in the Death Camps*

> *This, finally, is the attitude survivors take: they might make it,*
> *they probably won't, but they will not stop "trying."*
> Terrence Des Pres, *The Survivors*

In 1975, Terrence Des Pres published an extraordinary book entitled *The Survivor: An Anatomy of Life in the Death Camps.* Born in Illinois in 1939, Des Pres, an American academic, had not been in the Nazi concentrations camps, and these facts make his book all the more impressive. Des Pres writes about the camps and the sensibility of the inmates with such sensitivity, profundity and empathy that his account has struck some as more authoritative and wise than even the highly regarded work of Bruno Bettelheim. Indeed, Bettelheim, for some the dean of Nazi concentration camp studies, is taken to task by the younger Des Pres on a camp issue central to both writers. Bettelheim, in his *The Informed Heart: Autonomy in a Mass Age,* has claimed that concentration camp victims regressed in activity, became childish, helpless, excessively passive. Des Pres, however, claims that, on the contrary, concentration camp victims manifested control (as far, of course, as the circumstances of extremity would permit), altruism, cooperation and a sophisticated awareness of one another. He further asserts that such traits not only contributed to survival, but were essential to it.

"Bettelheim," Des Pres writes, "says that the inmates behaved like 'incompetent children,' identified with the SS, 'became a shapeless mass,' 'lacked autonomy'" (Des Pres, 85). Des Pres refutes this with his own claims that the inmates were organized and even used their organization to run a black market.

If Des Pres is right, it would explain the extraordinary phenomenon of people surviving hellish conditions. One saturnine aspect, Des Pres says, is this: "The first condition of extremity is that there is no escape, no place to go except the grave" (6). What seems like a horrible contradiction—mutual aid for survival in opposition to what is likely a hopeless entrapment—becomes one of the defining conditions of the Belsens and Dachaus (Nazi death camps) of history. It might explain why "almost all survivors say 'we' rather than 'I'" (29); indeed, it belies the idea so dear to capitalism that competition is the heart's blood of social-economic life. What that "we" suggests is that cooperation or mutual aid helped human beings to survive some of the most brutal man-made conditions ever devised and imposed.

One of the subtler yet most deadly of these brutalities was the annihilation of structured time. Des Pres observes:

> Structured time, the blessing of a foundation for measure and purposive action, is one of civilization's great gifts. But in extremity the forms of time dissolve, the rhythms of change and motion are lost. Days pass, seasons, years pass and the fixer [the inmate] has no idea how long his ordeal will go on. (11)

Under extreme pressures of pain, fear, boredom, hopelessness, something can crack in one's character, in one's most elemental self. Day after day, month after month, year after year of squalid gray surroundings, excessive cruelty and brutality, poor and little food, harsh weather, the continuous threat of violent death—all this would be unbearable for many. Further, as Des Pres puts it,

> The death of time destroys the sense of growth and purpose, and thereby undermines faith in the possibility that any good can come from merely staying alive. This too the survivor must face and withstand. (12)

One must learn, Des Pres continues, two extremely difficult things in the concentration camp—not to despair and to sustain one's moral sense and dignity. To mention such virtues under the extremity of camp conditions is to explore—is to be forced for *survival* to explore—a *via negativa*. How much room the average person in a Western industrialized society has for suffering is hard to gauge. She or he typically assumes that two days to two weeks without heat or electricity (not to mention TVs, computers, cellphones, supermarkets, etc.) would be insufferable. This, in turn, would suggest that such an individual has not encountered extreme deprivation.

It takes a gifted spirit indeed to begin to see such deprivations as, if not desirable, at least endurable. The range of the endurable is far subtler and more elastic than most citizens of open societies realize or will admit. But that crucial range got tested every day in the Buchenwalds and Siberias of the 20th century. According to Des Pres, one crucial mode of making the darkness of the unendurable bearable, even glint, is to learn to think "we" rather than "I."

Bearing witness is a cardinal way of saying or feeling "we." Again, Des Pres puts it memorably: "The will to bear witness issues as a typical and in some sense necessary response to extremity. Confronting radical evil, men and women instinctively feel the desire to call, to warn, to communicate their shock." He continues, "'Horror' arises and in its presence men and women are seized by an involuntary outburst of feeling which is very much like a scream.... And in this crude cry the will to be in witness is born" (34).

A fascinating aspect of the resistance to the brutalities and horrors of concentration camp existence was its evocation of habits and practices closely resembling some of the central values of philosophical anarchism. Des Pres calls it "mutual aid" (which also happens to be the title of one of Russian prince-anarchist Peter Kropotkin's seminal books): "Nobody survived without help. Life in the camps was savage, and yet there was also a web of mutual aid and encouragement, to which all books by survivors testify" (38). This contention, if true, further detracts from Bettelheim's inmate-child interpretation. The key word for camp survival is camaraderie —care, concern, giving and receiving exercised in the barbed wired, shit-streaked context of a Dachau (or a Gulag). This meant more than passing social amenities—it was the very fabric of life warmth and affection that kept camp victims from going mad, succumbing to despair or committing suicide.

What were some of the horrors and brutalities of concentration camp life? Words like "horrors" and "brutalities" are far too general to convey the realities that they enclose and conceal. Only by witnessing the specificity of the horrors, degradations and pain can one see how invaluable the mutual aid was, what it cost, and the depth of resistance from which it sprang.

What we must now confront in reading eyewitness accounts quoted in *Survivor* might not be easy to contemplate, but contemplating is one thing, undergoing it another. The shock we feel at what these victims endured and some survived should be underscored by realizing that human beings no more evil or silly or corrupt or blameworthy than ourselves were coerced into these ineffably horrible experiences. As Des Pres relates:

> Defilement caused a desperation bordering on madness, as when a group of prisoners were forced "to drink out of the toilet bowls. The men could not bring themselves to obey this devilish order; they only pretended to drink. But the block-fuehrers had reckoned on that; they forced the men's heads deep into the bowls until their faces were covered with excrement. At this the victims almost went out of their minds—that was why their screams had sounded so demented." (Szalet, p. 42, quoted in *Survivor*, 73-74)

But the horror of such degradation was not an occasional "dunking": "Prisoners in the Nazi camps were virtually drowning in their own waste, and in fact death by excrement was common" (64) due to some unwary camp prisoners being thrown into long and deep latrine pits by the SS.

> Victims sometimes were forbidden to go to the toilet. The fecal smell in the barracks could literally floor one. Typhus at Belsen-Bergen made diarrhea uncontrollable. It flooded the bottom cages, dripping through the cracks into the faces of the women lying in the cages below, and mixed with blood, pus, and urine formed a slimy, fetid mud on the floor of the barracks." (Perl, 171, quoted in *Survivor*, 58)

Des Pres entitles the chapter on this material "Excremental Assault," an apt encapsulation of the relentless defilement of the body designed to degrade the mind and annihilate the soul. Debasement was achieved through total or brutal deprivation of dignity, the root dignity to keep oneself clean, to keep the ever-threatening contexts of filth and besmirchment— whether internal or impinging externally—at arm's length, under control. One needn't go into the psychological implications of such coerced defilement to realize that being so physically violated by our bodily wastes not only assails our dignity, it challenges our most basic identity and self-acceptance. Someone else is forcing us into a pit of degradation and abnegation of the self that we spend a lifetime avoiding.

Yet some survived these and other camp horrors: "These shit-smeared bodies," Des Pres claims (9), "were the accurate image of how much mutilation the human spirit can bear, despite shame, loathing, the trauma of violent recoil, and still keep the sense of something inwardly inviolate. 'Only our feverish eyes,' said one survivor of the sewers, 'still showed that we were living human beings'" (Friedman, 289, in *Survivor*, 86).

A horrifying idea about the Nazi concentration camps suggested by George Steiner (Steiner, 53-54, in *Survivor*, 201) is that "They are the deliberate enactment of a long, precise imaging of Hell." The camps, says Steiner, were intended to reproduce hell on earth. If so, they represented the institutionalization and implementation of the diabolic in human life and society. Des Pres sees something terrifying here. He hopes Steiner is wrong because, "if man eventually and necessarily realizes his deep imaginings in fact—then the end will come, the bombs will fall, the myths of the World's End, imagined for millennia, will arrive in actuality" (212).

What perhaps horrifies people most deeply about the Nazi concentration camps (or the Soviet Gulags or Pol Pot's Cambodia or the Serbian camp atrocities or the brutal American-run Bagram Air Base detentions) is their underlying nihilism. People willing to enact or actuate absolute evil *could* destroy the world, a realization we have lived with for over sixty years now. But whereas nuclear-weapons-rattling or industrial pollution are almost globally dispersed and centrifugal in their energy and menace, the concentration camps terrorize precisely by their centripetal energy, by their demonic concentration. In a post-Holocaust example, it was reported that Serb captors castrated a Croat son right in front of his father (*The New Yorker*, December 1992).

There may be Heaven or Nirvana or Paradise, but—the camps convey—there definitely is Hell, and *WE ARE IT*. Heaven might not seem very real in the midst of such hells; yet the latter implies the former, and bits of it could be found, as mentioned earlier, in instances of mutual aid among inmates.

Des Pres suggests that helping was invaluable both ways: "The survivors' experience is evidence that the need to help is as basic as the need *for* help, a fact which points to the radically social nature of life in extremity and explains an unexpected but very widespread activity among survivors" (160). Gift-giving was one form of such help. Inmates frequently exchanged little gifts, which, says Des Pres, not only sustained morale but sometimes literally helped keep others alive. The help, the aid, also occurred in camp hospitals, often, of course, places of grave danger and horror for inmates. One instance will suffice: "In every concentration camp where the political prisoners attained any degree of ascendancy, they turned the prison hospital...into a rescue station for countless prisoners" (Kogon in *Survivor*, 141). "And all these practices were carried through," Des Pres concludes crucially, "day in and day out, by men and women who knew they would be shot if caught" (139).

What made this radical helpfulness all the more remarkable was its being offered by people who could not, did not dare to, look to the past or to the future for hope or relief. Inmates in any concentration camp learn that if they dwell on the past, homesickness will destroy their fight to survive.[1]

The failure to control despair or self-pity could lead to one's destruction in one way or another. As for the future, the camps did all they could to convey that there was no future beyond experiencing the camp again in endless tomorrows terminated only by death. One lived, to quote De Pres's use of a survivor's words, "on a short-term basis, from day to day, hour to hour, even minute by minute" (220).

Perhaps this depiction of a realized hell on earth is far more effective and insidious than the traditional religious accounts, which attempt (sadistically enough) to eternalize pain and torment. Rather, the camps forced prisoners to live for and somehow through the moment. Yet, ironically, accepting that grim moment, hour, day, week, month, or year—those who could—made this human hell bearable, just barely.

---

1. This is a central idea in Jacobo Timerman's *Prisoner without a Name, Cell without a Number*, an extraordinarily moving account of one individual's incarceration and torture in Argentina in the 1970s.

"Review: Terrence Des Pres, *The Survivor: An Anatomy of Life in the Death Camps*" by Donald Gutierrez—*The Mustang*, March 4, 1994.

32

The New Electrical Meanspiritedness in America

An alarming trend in American prisons is the use of electrical devices on prisoners. This usage constitutes a serious erosion of what some regard as essential ethical restraint on prison authorities from imposing cruelty on convicts. In a long 1997 article in the *New York Review of Books* entitled "Cruel and Unusual Punishment," William F. Schulz, executive director of Amnesty International, USA, discussed the increasing use of such devices as stun belts, stun guns, shock batons and electric shields by law enforcement officials to control prisoners. To say that these relatively new devices are effective puts it mildly. According to Schulz:

> Stun belts deliver 50,000 volt shocks to the left kidney which fan out from there through blood channels and nerve pathways. Shocks can be administered by guards from a distance of up to 300 feet simply by the push of a button. An 8-second application of shock inevitably knocks a person to the ground and may induce urination, defecation or unconsciousness.

The Federal Bureau of Prisons, claiming these electrical devices did not inflict permanent damage, began to use stun guns in 1984 in medium- and high-security prisons, Schulz tells us. Many state and county officials have since bought them as well; these devices are "now commonly used in sheriffs' offices and prison-guard stations across the country." Further, at least forty American companies make shock devices, many sold internationally.

If there is little mystery about the use electrical devices are put to by nations with repressive regimes, it is highly relevant to consider whether these devices would be misused by American prison authorities. Schulz tests this possibility by considering the much-publicized electric shock tests of Yale psychologist Stanley Milgram. Professor Milgram wanted to see if volunteer subjects would be willing to administer shocks to a victim if urged to do so by an authority figure. It was discovered that a high percentage of people would indeed do so even though the victim pleaded with them to stop or went unconscious. Schulz relates this finding to the authoritarian prison structure within which guards work. The likelihood of guards using (or over-using) electrical devices increases if a power-ridden or sadistic superior urges or suggests it. This doesn't preclude the impulse of guards driven by their personal sense of power, cruelty, boredom or fear to send some currents out on their own.

As Schultz reports, another of Milgram's observations can be related to the penal use of electrical devices: "Milgram also found that the more physically remote the victim from the subject, the greater the likelihood the subject would administer shock to a dangerous level." One of the ominous features of electrical devices like stun guns is that shocks can be administered repeatedly, the final restraint on the "administrator" being his or her discretion. But as these shocks can be delivered up to one hundred yards away from the "shockee," one could think, as Schulz does, that discretion could or would be diminished by distance.

This factor of distance is also present in the practice of American companies selling these implements abroad. These companies are selling to nations that routinely resort to torture either by their security forces or in their prisons. Further, according to an Amnesty International 1996 Annual Report, hundreds of political prisoners in Mexico were tortured by these electrical devices, which are capable of inducing agonizing pain. Eighteen other nations were also cited for using these instruments.

One of the "shocks" in reading Schulz's piece is his evidence that in 1994 the U.S. Commerce Department licensed the selling of such equipment to regimes known for torture administered by the state. In the example Schulz cites, the department (our department, financed by our tax monies) approved of "police helmets/handcuffs/electrical shields used for torture" amounting in cost to $60,000. Furthermore, in two years in the early 1990s, the Commerce Department issued 2,100 licenses for this type of "equipment" to 106 nations at a price of well over $117,000,000. And our

Commerce Department can sell, and has sold, thumbscrews, blackjacks and electric devices to NATO nations with no restrictions on the re-exporting of these instruments to other countries.

American manufacturers, according to Schulz, are not likely to call such devices "implements of torture." Being labeled as "crime control" equipment masks their capacity for savage misuse. George Orwell cried out for truthful language in his famous essay, "Politics and the English Language":

> Millions of peasants are robbed of their farms and sent trudging along the roads with no more than they can carry: this is called "transfer of populations or rectification of frontiers." People are imprisoned for years without trial, or shot in the back of the neck or sent to die of scurvy in Arctic lumber camps: this is called "elimination of unreliable elements". Such phraseology is needed if one wants to name things without calling up mental pictures of them. (*A Collection of Essays*, 1945 pp. 166-67)[1]

Not calling up mental pictures of what electrical devices do to the human body and mind is what a dishonest euphemism like "crime control" devices tries to achieve. According to the Eighth Amendment of the American Constitution, states David Rudovsky in *The Rights of Prisoners*, "prisoners have an absolute right to be free from cruel and unusual punishment..." He continues, "Historically, courts have considered whether l-the punishment shocks the general conscience of a civilized society, 2-whether the punishment is unnecessarily cruel and 3-whether the punishment goes beyond legitimate penal aims" (1-2).

One is struck by the problematic relativity and flexibility of these criteria. In Colonial America and England, execution by decapitation and disembowelment were routine, though today they would be regarded in both countries as abominable. Overcrowding in prisons and inmates sexually abusing other inmates could (and should) be regarded as "cruel and unusual punishment" but their widespread and enduring occurrence in American prisons implies that such barbarism is acceptable to the general public.

While a Washington, D.C. court stated that sixteen months of solitary confinement as punishment for work stoppage was excessive, "numerous courts have held certain periods of isolation not to constitute cruel and unusual punishment, and some have held that isolation may be indefinite"

(Rudovsky, 5). That last clause should give us pause. Here we behold judges upholding the penal practice of indefinite placement in the "Hole." Rudovsky describes conditions of solitary confinement in some prisons where a convict gets one "full" meal every seventy-two hours and in others, a shower every eleven days; and in one prison a convict resides in an unlit cell measuring 5 x 7 feet with a hole in the floor for his body wastes, the flushing of which is controlled by a guard outside. The current defense minister of South Africa, Brigadier General Rocky Williams, who underwent solitary confinement for over a year as well as periodic and sustained beatings by his captors during the Apartheid regime, regards solitary as the cruelest torture of all.

In New Mexico in 1996 there was a move by Governor Gary Johnson to deny convicts in state prisons not only TV but air-conditioning. Later, he tried to eliminate reduced time for good behavior. Such deprivations would supposedly save the public money and remind convicts that prison is not supposed to be comfortable. More likely, they would lead to more inmate unrest, rioting and thus greater cost and danger to the public. Georgia's reversion to implementing the Chain Gang takes us back to the pre-twentieth century modes of penal servitude and other forms of excessive cruelty towards malefactors.

All these examples of privation and torment reveal that the courts exercise a conception of "cruel and unusual punishment" ranging from reasonably humane standards to virtually unremitting cruelty. This flexibility of tolerance suggests that at least some American courts would readily rule favorably on the habitual use of electric devices in prisons and possibly elsewhere—in courts, arrests, penal transitions and so on. Thus it should be stressed here that injuries sustained from the electric devices mentioned above can even be life-threatening: Schulz reports that a Texas Corrections officer died after testing an electric shield on himself.

The more that any society makes black and white judgments between the innocent and the guilty and, worse, targets certain groups or races as prone to commit evil or break the law, the more likely it would sanction what we would call "cruel and unusual punishment" for convicts: They deserve it, especially if they are poor. The literal use in prisons of electrical devices is also symbolic of the way people with too much power treat those with little or no power (not of course that all convicts are powerless or that helpless people are convicts). The apparent willingness to adopt these devices widely in American prisons reflects the Georgia Chain-Gang mindset among some prison authorities and judges and the excessive and unrealistic alienation between prisoners and the general public. This also suggests yet another dimension of the new meanspiritedness in America towards the down-and-out. The intensifying penal cruelty is especially disturbing in view of how more and more convicts seem to be not—or not just—innately evil individuals but victims of substantial social, economic and racist flaws integral to American society at large.

---

1. This issue of euphemistic language masking unspeakable truths seems as relevant as ever. For example, massive aerial bombing has been referred to as "pacification." During the Gulf War of the early 1990s, the term "collateral damage" covered the Iraqi civilians killed by relentless U. S. bombing, possibly numbering in the tens of thousands, according to Ramsey Clark in *The Fire This Time: U.S. War Crimes in the Gulf.*

"The New Electrical Meanspiritedness in America" by Donald Gutierrez— *Common Sense*, November 1998; *The Catholic Worker*, June 1999.

33
Review: Christian Parenti, *Lockdown America: Police and Prisons in an Age of Crisis*

> At a police commission meeting following the operation, a train of furious and sobbing African American victims recounted how police officers slapped and kicked them, stepped on their necks, and pressed pistol and shotgun muzzles to their heads as other officers ransacked their homes. Among those held at gunpoint were city employees and grandmothers. (Christian Parenti, *Lockdown America*, 126)

Bosnia? Rwanda? Nazi Germany? No. San Francisco, 1998, a police drug raid on a housing cooperative. In *Lockdown America: Police and Prisons in an Age of Crisis*, Christian Parenti suggests through many such accounts an emerging police state. Another venue: Jackson Hole, Wyoming, 1996. The sheriff and Border Patrol, looking for illegal immigrants, "swept through town, snatching Latino workers from the kitchens of 25 restaurants, routing them from their homes, and literally grabbing them as they rode by on bicycles" (152). Fifty of these residents turned out to be legal, while the rest were taken off for detainment in cow-manured trucks. More and more in such raids, police are outfitted in "combat boots, camo' battle dress, body armor, hoods, masks, goggles and kevlar helmets—armed with chemical sprays and H and K [Heckler and Koch sub-machine] MP54s...." (111) not to mention tear gas, pepper spray, metal clubs, dogs, and helicopters with night scopes and powerful beams.

Parenti's book divides into three interrelated sections: The first, "Crisis," explains the political and economic tensions that led in the late

1960s to the issues described in Section II, "Police" concerning the extraordinary police empowerment and militarization beginning in the late 1960s under Lyndon Johnson's LEAA (Law Enforcement Assistance Administration) and recommencing under Reagan and going strong today, which has culminated in the enormous prison-building industry and brutalization of two million incarcerated Americans as described in Section III, "Prison."

The crisis arose from the social uprisings of the 1960s, the growing economic and thus political power for working people, the enlarging social programs, and, most important, shrinking profits for the plutocracy following the post-war boom years. The lower orders thus needed "disciplining." The Federal Reserve raised interest rates, which put hundreds of thousands out of work, a process abetted by corporations moving their plants abroad. These actions, among others, left two large groups marginalized—the homeless and a "social dynamite" class, young males of "color." Because big business moved back into the center of cities, where they established "theme parks" consisting of banks, insurance companies and real estate, the two groups had to be contained. The homeless were swept away from upscaled city areas; and the "social dynamite"—severed from work, victims of racism, and regarded as a social menace—were headed towards prison.

Controlling these strata resulted in the "broken window" theory: police getting tough on petty crimes would also discourage serious, violent crime. Consequently, jaywalkers, subway-fare-evaders, truant school boys were being booked and even jailed. And when a youth brandished a gun in Fresno, SWAT (Special Weapons and Tactics) teams assembled as if they were attacking a Columbian drug lord.

Three ominous aspects of this "zero tolerance" policy are the growth of SWAT Teams, the militarizing of the equipment and mentality of American police and the political implications of increasingly sophisticated communications technology available to police and numerous other legal agencies. SWATs, begun in 1966, are now active in "thousands of small and medium sized towns" (112), and are customary in everyday policing. SWAT actions, evidence shows, lead to more police violence. With increased police militarization, civilians become foes to be vanquished, even destroyed. More sinister is the implication that if minor-offense criminals are in the nationally centralized databases established by police, there is no clear line concerning who goes in the database, given that "criminal" can be a relative concept. (During the 1994 massacre of Tutsis in Rwanda, the Hutus considered all Tutsis criminal.)

If capitalism, as Parenti claims, creates a surplus class without work and needs to keep the lower classes intimidated and paralyzed with Gestapo tactics driven by racism and big business avarice for profits, then the final threat to alienated classes is the Big House. "Prison" is an appalling section of *Lockdown America* and a ringing indictment of an American public led to think that prisoners deserve all they get behind bars. It underlines the savagely vengeful nature of modern American penology, the shocking growth rate of public and private prisons and the pivotal role of rape and convict gangs in prison administrative control. The growth of prisons in the mid- to late-1990s was facilitated by new criminal justice statutes—a thousand more in California alone—while conservative courts made warrantless searches and harsher police interrogations possible.

These factors and others led to a huge expansion of the number of Americans being jailed, though roughly two-thirds are nonviolent offenders. New prisoners at maximum-security prisons are routinely beaten by guards on arrival. Far worse is the incidence of rape in male and female prisons. Most young male prisoners are raped by inmates within the first 48 hours of incarceration. "Roughly 200,000 male inmates in America are raped every year, and many of them are raped daily" (185). Weaker prisoners are traded around like prostitutes and forced to become the "wives" of stronger inmates, succumbing to their every whim, to avoid general sexual exploitation. Prison guards not only tolerate this sexual slavery, they sometimes expedite it, handing over recalcitrant young prisoners to huge, brutal inmates called "Booty Bandits." The latter beat, torture and repeatedly rape their charges, in the process turning them into "punks."

According to Parenti, inmate rape is accepted by prison authorities because it directs hatred and fear among inmates, instead of towards guards. Rape thus serves as a mode of prisoner control, as does tolerating, even encouraging, racism among the four major prison gangs. These gangs control the rape, drug business and other forms of repression and power in prisons, but by their acute divisiveness they serve the purpose of carceral control. The widespread rape in women's prison is performed mainly by guards.

The question (not raised by Parenti) arises whether the public, conned into believing that the more prisons and prisoners the better, realizes that prison experience often signifies torture, mayhem and even violent death. One form of torture in prison is to be put in Special Security Units, isolated tiny cells in which one is stuck 23 hours a day with a bi-weekly shower, no human contact, no work and no educational facilities. Supposedly only for superpredators, SSUs also confine political activists and jailhouse lawyers. Parenti unifies the "Police" and "Prison" sections in an acute summary of current prison sociology,

> Mayhem in prison is parlayed into empire building. The more "deviance" the big house excretes, the more the guards and administrators need new prisons, new SSUs, more gang investigators, closer cooperation with other agencies, better computers, new tracking software, better guns, more tear gas, more body armor....Thus corrections bureaucracies grow. (209)

Parenti also presents convincing evidence that the private prison industry is inefficient and brutal.

His recommendations: "We need less .... policing, less incarceration, shorter sentences, less surveillance, fewer laws governing individual behaviors" (242). Parenti also recommends decriminalizing drugs (which has been a major factor in increased imprisonment for almost two decades, since the "War on Drugs") and providing more decent work.

Lockdown America is momentous because it intimates a growing totalitarian society. Parenti might have developed this intimation by elaborating how the police state could spread to encompass much of society. Nevertheless, he is movingly compassionate, angry and persuasive in his depiction of criminal-justice brutalization and paralysis of the lower classes. Could their fate soon be that of the middle class? Those huge police computer databases could enlarge to control not just the "superfluous" classes but any class or group that strikes those whom Gore Vidal calls "America's rulers" as a threat to their power and wealth. And, in view of the increasing vilification by the authorities of government critics, who knows how far the gates of America's increasing prisons will swing open to include not only someone you know but someone close to you. Parenti's book is a crucial wake-up call.

"Review: Christian Parenti, *Lockdown America: Police and Prisons in an Age of Crisis*" by Donald Gutierrez—*Common Sense*, April 2000; *North Coast Xpress*, April 2002.

34
Review: Randall Robinson, *Quitting America: The Departure of a Black Man from His Native Land*

Randall Robinson's *Quitting America: The Departure of a Black Man from His Native Land* is not only one Black American's justification for leaving his country for good. It is also a powerful and eloquent indictment of the Western world's disastrous impact on people of color for centuries:

> From Columbus forward, I know of no sustained contact with Western whites that black and brown peoples and their cultures have survived undevastated, anywhere. From the northernmost point in North America to the bottom of South America, Western whites have over time undermined every indigenous culture that they have encountered .... From Inca to Inuit, from African to Aborigine, little else do the world's far-flung dark peoples have in common beyond a shared victimhood at the hand of Western whites. (134-35)

This statement is hardly surprising coming from the man who has demanded reparations from the United States government for the enslavement of African Americans. However, Robinson backs it up in a variety of ways, such as indicating the extreme imbalance of wealth in the United States favoring Whites, the eradication of the historical memory of African Americans through slavery, (White) America's arrogance, "unrelenting self-adoration" (17) and immunity to self criticism and its "We're Number One!" mania. This last stricture Robinson presses with his customary acuteness:

> I think that when Americans say that America is the
> greatest country in the world, they mean only that it is the
> richest and most powerful....I don't think they can mean that
> Americans are the happiest people in the world...the most
> well-adjusted...or the most moral. (8)

Robinson hammers at this point by focusing on the darker side of
America's elephantine ego: "Could it be that the cultivated obsession of
firstness that makes America a rich and powerful country also makes it a sick
society under homicidal siege to the enlarging ranks of its alienated and
forgotten?" (24). This view is elaborated along another, ominous facet late
in the book:

> [O]wing to its size and power, America overpraises itself
> without fear, or even thought, of rebuttal which, in any case,
> it would not be inclined to notice. Thus, America has rendered
> itself all but constitutionally unable to learn anything about
> anything from anybody. (226)

America, thus, is blind with arrogance and power. Reversing the usual
White House opportunistic paranoia that the world is a dangerous place, he
implies that the main danger resides in the American government and in
associated institutions like the Pentagon and the defense industries.

Robinson structures his case by comparing the United States with St.
Kitts, the tiny Caribbean country he is adopting. In St. Kitts, people are far
safer, carefree and trusting. Kidnapping is unknown there, prisoners do
public work almost unguarded, merchants don't worry about customer bills.
Kittians enjoy the basic amenities of life in contrast, Robinson claims, to
Americans. Robinson observes, however, that American entrepreneurs are
investing there, which spells trouble for his new country.

Robinson stresses the profound danger of the extreme power America
has possessed since the fall of the Soviet Union, of "all decisions of world
consequence...now [being] made...by Washington for Washington" (85).
He wisely considers it disturbing that so much power should be located
anywhere. His implied point here, a motif in his book, is that such power
is—and has been—used not to spread democracy but to advance the
interests of a White elite. A crucial aspect of this view concerns ongoing
racial tensions: "No matter how many go-along-to-get-along blacks land

seats in the President's cabinet, America will always be a society of antagonistically opposed racial awareness" (83).

One of Robinson's major indictments of America concerns its obliteration of the racial memory of African Americans. In one of the most memorable passages in *Quitting America*, he insists:

> All people *need* history, a story, a memory, that gives them past and future.... Memory provides us the rich fuel of self-esteem. Foresight, born of memory, provides us direction and a purpose for living.... No worse crime can be committed against any people than to strip from them their memory of themselves. (134)

The idea of alienation became a fashionable subject for discussion among American intellectuals in the 1940s and 1950s. According to Robinson, however, it has been a flesh-and-blood experience for a countless number of American Blacks for centuries, trapping them in an existence deprived of psychological, social and spiritual continuity.

The climax of Robinson's jeremiad against White America occurs in a history he presents of America's treatment of Haiti. Asserting that he "had always belonged to the black world and not necessarily to America," Robinson significantly broadens his racial identity by associating the interests of American Blacks with the experience of brutalization, enslavement and genocide of Caribbean peoples from Columbus on. He further deepens this identification by presenting Haiti as an exemplar of successful Black resistance to European might and ages-long American political, military and commercial pressure. The latter includes a global embargo that America hit Haiti with in the early 19th century and that lasted until 1862.

According to Robinson, Haiti stood forth as the one nation in the American hemisphere that could not only gain its independence against overwhelmingly powerful Napoleonic France but threatened to undermine Black slavery in the United States. Robinson extends this line of argument in a spirited and persuasive defense of his friend President Aristide and his administration.

In the process of defending Aristide's Haiti and Aristide, Robinson unleashes a formidable critique of the kind of Washington-supported rebels who, like the Duvaliers earlier, brutalized Haitians. This condemnation includes other crucial participants like Emmanuel "Toto" Constant, who overthrew the Aristide government with the help of American ordnance supplied through the Dominican Republic. Constant, a proven major practioner of genocide of Haitians and a CIA-financed terrorist walking the streets of New York a free man, was the head of FRAPH, which Robinson describes as a "paramilitary band of armed thugs operating at the [Haitian] army's behest" (203).

FRAPH, Robinson claims, was responsible for the machete-slaughtering of Haitians during a Washington-backed coup in the early 1990s. (During this period, Robinson went on a long hunger strike to protest President Bill Clinton returning Haitians to certain and savage death at the hands of FRAPH). Rebel chiefs like Lucien de Chamblaine and Guy Phillippe were colleagues of Constant.

Quitting America ends with an angry condemnation:

> America. America....Hypocrite immemorial. My heart left long ago. At long last, I have followed it....how could I, in good conscience, remain for a country that has never ever, at home or abroad, been *for* me or *for* mine? I can remember in my forty years of social activism no occasion where American policy was instinctually consistent with America's stated creed of freedom. (212)

An eminent activist against America's history of racist dehumanization, Robinson has every right to leave America for a new life elsewhere. One wishes him and his family well in St. Kitts.

"Review: Randall Robinson, *Quitting America: the Departure of a Black Man from His Native Land*" by Donald Gutierrez—*Sun Monthly*, April 2005.

35

American-British Ethnic Cleansing in the Chagos Islands: The Tragedy of the Diego Garcian People

In his acceptance speech for the 2005 Nobel Prize for Literature, British playwright Harold Pinter made a crucial observation: while the hideous crimes of Joseph Stalin's regime are very well known, those of American imperialism are virtually unknown in the West (and certainly unknown, one might add, by many Americans). One heartbreaking example of this serious ignorance is America's (i.e., Washington's) and England's (i.e., London's) crimes against the inhabitants of the tiny island of Diego Garcia. We have infrequently heard reports of American bombers taking off from the island to bomb democracy on Afghanistan and Iraq but virtually nothing about the American detainee-torture cell also located there.

But what and where *is* Diego Garcia? Who lived there before it became an American base? How did the United States acquire and transform it into their fourth biggest expeditionary base in the world?

Diego Garcia is the main island in the Chagos archipelago, located in the middle of the Indian Ocean. For well over two hundred years it was inhabited by Creoles, who were brought by the French from Madagascar and Mozambique as slaves late in the eighteenth century. The Chagos Islands were seized from France in 1815 by England, the Chagossians thereby becoming British citizens entitled to all the rights accompanying that status. Nevertheless, in the late 1960s, the Diego Garcians (or Chagossians), numbering about 2,000, were forcibly removed from their island—which had been to them a very habitable paradise for generations—by the British to render a deal: London would lease the island to the United.States (i.e., the

Pentagon) for fifty years plus a twenty year automatic extension in exchange for a $14 million reduction on a Polaris nuclear submarine.

To push this deal through required a number of extremely secretive, illegal, criminal and morally outrageous offenses against the Diego Garcians. Among others, it involved ignoring and obliterating the British-citizenship rights of this people by expelling them from Diego Garcia with a ruthlessness reminiscent of Nazi ethnic cleansing. The Diego Garcians, who loved their dogs dearly, helplessly beheld them either gassed or burned alive by American troops already ashore building airstrips, rec centers, a swimming pool, a bar and barbecue facilities for themselves. The treatment accorded their dogs was apparently intended to suggest to these islanders that their fate would be similar if they did not cooperate with the British.

The Diego Garcians were moved by ship under conditions akin to those imposed on African slaves: men were corralled in the bridge, women and children stuck in the hold with a cargo of fertilizer (bird shit) for a bed, while, thanks to Sir Bruce Greatbatch, then Her Majesty's British governor of the Seychelles, horses were provided the most comfortable quarters on the ship for a five-day sea journey of 2,500 miles. According to one report, the horses were fed during the trip; the Diego Garcians were not.

The Chagos islanders were literally dumped in Mauritius, a British colony where they were unwanted and unemployable due to an already great overpopulation and scarcity of work. Treated like tramps, they remain there to this day, living in abject misery and extreme need, some dying of wretched poverty or even of sadness for loss of their island home.

When boldly confronting very high-placed officials in London and Washington, the well-informed Australian investigative journalist and documentary filmmaker John Pilger (to whose admirable book *Freedom Next Time: Resisting the Empire* this essay is much indebted) is told outrageous lie after lie about the plight of the Chagossians. It was claimed that these people had been paid for their removal, that they never lived in Diego Garcia, that the island was uninhabitable and thus unsafe for their return, that the Diego Garcians were temporary contract workers, that the Cold War necessity for a base surrounding the Soviet Union was more important than the fate of merely 2000 "natives" (that excuse from arrogant, authoritarian former CIA director and secretary of defense James Schlesinger) and so on. This monstrous, elaborate crime, covertly implemented by very high-ranking British and American statesmen against the Chagossians, was kept secret by Presidents Lyndon Johnson and Richard Nixon. Neither the British

Parliament nor Congress was informed about the "deal."

And even after the British High Court in 2003 repudiated a 1965 ordinance to expel the people of Diego Garcia and the Chagos Islands, when a few of the latter returned to their native land *with passports*, they were nevertheless told by a British sea patrol to leave the tiny island instantly. While this was happening, as Pilger with sharp irony remarks, "A hundred yards along the beach, a colony of Yachties and sailors, most of them not British, played volleyball on the beach. No one disturbed them" (52).

Not far from this sand playground for "Free World" athletes on one of the Chagos Islands, Muslim detainees at Diego Garcia's Camp Justice were likely being administered various kinds of "justice" via methods such as waterboarding, approved by the administration of President George W. Bush and his secretary of defense, Donald Rumsfeld.

Chagossian heaven had become Rumsfeldian hell, but at least the British government had gotten an American nuclear sub relatively cheap. Further, a beautiful island that had for many generations perfectly suited the modest subsistence needs of an indigenous people, had, as one senior American official demanded, been "swept and sanitized" of its inhabitants. Why? Pilger states, to accommodate "four thousand service personnel and support contractors, two of the largest bomber runways in the world, anchorages for thirty ships, two nuclear berths, space weapons tracking domes, shopping malls, nightclubs, a golf course, tennis courts, swimming pools and more" (45).

Meanwhile, the original Diego Garcia people continue to languish in Mauritius in their decades-long poverty and agony despite attempts on their part to secure legal justice.[1] Bereft of their stolen island and home, they are the victims of a crime against humanity that almost no one even knows about.

In a savagely ironic update, it was reported in the American press (*Albuquerque Journal*, Feb. 22, 2008) that the British were furious over Washington having lied to them about the United States using British airspace or land (i.e., Diego Garcia island) for rendition-torture flights or purposes. An American State Department official, Sean McCormack, the *Journal* states, "took pains to note that the United States had not violated any obligation it had towards Britain in using Diego Garcia for the flights at the time they occurred." Only in 2008 did the two countries begin to work out a "mutual understanding" about using the island for renditions.

Well, there are pains and pains. There is the pain of McCormack dissembling the Bush Administration's gross dishonesty towards its closest ally as an "administrative error," the much greater pain experienced by detainee suspects at the hands of possibly both foreign *and* American torturers on Diego Garcia and elsewhere, and the incomparably deeper and ongoing pain of the Diego Garcian people, whose history of horrific mistreatment is totally buried under this flap between the two major powers who conspired to destroy this little nation for their own imperial ends.

---

1. In 2006, the British High Court again held that the Chagossians had a legal right of return to their land, but matters are still pending.

"American-British Ethnic Cleansing in the Chagos Islands: the Tragedy of the Diego Garcian People" by Donald Gutierrez—*Progressive Populist*, April 2010; *Humanist Society of New Mexico*, January 2008; *Common Sense*, May 2008.

36
Leveling the Hierarchy

For a supposedly democratic, egalitarian society, the United States is extraordinarily hierarchical. According to Paul Fussell's *Class*, for example, America's civil service is divided into eighteen grades, from messenger at the bottom to high-level administrators. Granted, some hierarchy is unavoidable, even a good thing. Valuable, experienced workers usually deserve higher status and pay than younger or less experienced workers; they have earned it through years of service and increasing expertise.

Too often, however, such status becomes a means of rigidifying class and status. The whole employer/employee system embodies an enormous undermining of democratic, libertarian values. Walmart, as Barbara Ehrenreich points out in *Nickeled and Dimed*, tries to conceal this basic inequality by coercing its employees to regard themselves as employee "Associates," as if each $7.00 an hour worker owned part of the business. But it is clear that in every Walmart, Walgreens, Kmart, and other big box store that one enters, the "grunts" performing the basic services are overseen by managers (often male), the latter in turn taking orders from higher-ups. Someone may have to organize and run an enterprise, but that essential ordering has lent itself to excessively hierarchic stratification that seriously violates America's vaunted libertarian ethos.

Though probably few question the caste character of military hierarchy, its influence on rigidifying the class structure of civil society is considerable. Indeed, in the United States, military hierarchy as a model of organization has since World War II substantially influenced the authority structure of American institutions. This tendency is so pervasive that even civilian organizations as idealistically free of power structures as universities are markedly hierarchic. Janitors and dormitory cleaning women (usually minorities) and department office typists occupy the bottom, presidents and regents the top, while undergraduates are not much higher in status than janitors.

Corporations, hospitals, civil service all share in the hierarchic gradation. Professionals, physicians or employers are usually addressed as "doctor" or "mister" while the secretarial or clinical staff (usually women) are addressed by their first names, a differentiation matched by significant differences in salary. There is a pretense of democratic address in the ubiquitous first-naming in the business and medical worlds of customers and patients respectively. One notices, though, that it's one way: "John," says secretary "Betty" to a 65-year-old patient, "your appointment with Dr. Jones is on July 1." There is also a vertical "relationship" between mass-media celebrities and their fans, who, by idealizing their gods and goddesses, debase themselves. Such debasement is intensified by a society that pays CEOs and superstar pro athletes hundreds of times as much money as the average person earns.

What is most pernicious about American political, social and economic hierarchy is the extreme power it gives to people at or near the top such as CEOs of mega-corporations, the president and key senior senators, Pentagon generals and admirals, presidents of investment banks, health insurance presidents, defense industry CEOs and owners of major print and other communications media. These individuals command enormous power and/or wealth, and the average American who thinks she or he can walk into the grand offices of these personages and criticize or even discuss policy harmful to the general public's interest will be lucky not to be thrown out the front door.

These moguls in their chauffeured Lincoln Continentals, their multimillion dollar Long Island or Connecticut retreats, their lavish penthouses, their Lear Jets, their interlocking corporate board-of-directorships and regentships on boards of prestigious universities, their memberships in the Knickerbocker and Petroleum Clubs of the world, their revolving-door connection with Washington, their policy-writing chairs in the inner sanctum of key congressional committees—these magnates constitute the most serious undermining of American democracy because of the quantity and quality of their institutional connections and influence. They make more money in an hour than most Americans earn in a year. This is our modern aristocracy.

These individuals will always imperil democracy, as long as vertical power structures are tolerated by the public or are supported by a tax structure unfair to wage earners. Moreover, economic equalitarianism will continue to be undermined by so-called government incentives that provide subsidies, tax breaks and repeated tax cuts to business, industrial and war department institutions. Most of them think they fully deserve their power, wealth and complex connections in the stratospheric world of finance, industry and mass media that allows them to go on possessing approximately fifty percent of America's wealth. More to the point is that their institutionalized attitude, wealth and influence over society mock the democratic ideals propagandized through school, mass media and politicians.

Enforcing social and economic equality is impossible and would be absurd. People will always possess differing abilities, skills, ambitions and goals, and a genuinely democratic society can and should accommodate these differences. But the disparity gap between not only the rich and the poor in America but between the rich and the shrinking middle class has obviously grown so wide and deep that the country has once again become a pronounced plutocracy. As is well known, the post-WWII economy and progressive-tax system did a great deal to elevate low-income people and their children to the middle class. This period, lasting roughly three decades, is the closest the country ever got to a genuine economic democracy—the kind of democracy that counts most, because all the other forms of democracy depend on it. Since 1980, however, middle-class income has stagnated; and, more recently, millions of Americans have lost their jobs and homes because of decisions made in corporate boardrooms and Washington. All this represents an economic, political and psychological catastrophe, as it means the disappearance of the very class crucially stabilizing to a democracy.

What clearly is resulting is a top-bottom social structure that makes even the concept of a hierarchy sound like a good thing by comparison—at least in the latter, there were several classes with some proximity between them and thus the possibility of ascension. What is emerging now is division into just *two* classes, one small and extremely wealthy and powerful, the vast rest increasingly poor and desperate. The United States has of course always been a class society. Women, Blacks, Indians and propertyless Whites were denied voting rights by our Founding Fathers. Going to Yale places one in quite another universe than attending Arizona State U. One's car, clothes, choice of restaurant, speech, residential area and home all designate class and even caste. Americans of different classes can hardly converse and usually prefer to avoid one another as much as possible.

So the problem of hierarchy goes deeper than widespread gradation of classes. It goes deep enough to be an ongoing crisis many Americans are either unaware of or too apathetic or powerless to concern themselves with. As already mentioned, the crisis is that the economic, political and military leaders of the United States possess so much power that they are really our rulers and covertly think of themselves as such. They are so regarded abroad in third world nations, where Rockefellers and their ilk have the red rug literally rolled out for them.

Some might contend that a democratic ethos is sufficiently flexible and pervasive in America to absorb such extreme social and class differentiation. Supposedly, in the richest country in the world, there is enough wealth and opportunity to surmount such differentiation, thus rendering the basic needs and satisfactions of life and society widely available. However, the facts contradict this vaunted democratic breadth and flexibility. If, despite President Obama's health care program, many millions of Americans still lack adequate medical insurance in a society that demands it, if one out of every six children in the country either goes hungry or is part of a family living under the poverty line, if millions of senior citizens have to use a sizable part of their food funds for medical prescriptions, if one percent of the population possesses more wealth than nearly fifty percent of the rest, if minority children are being increasingly re-segregated educationally and thus encountering markedly substandard educational facilities (further disqualifying them from college), then we behold an American society stripped raw of actualized democratic values. What mostly remains of a democratic culture is the hypocritical, opportunistic libertarian rhetoric of politicians and corrupt mass-media publicists. And if the average American begins to smell a rat, there is always a war or war threat yanked down on the nation to distract us masses from the grossly inequitable distribution of our country's wealth and power.

The Land of the Free and the Home of the Brave encourages neither freedom nor bravery, because neither mean much in a society in which wealth and power have been monopolized by, and institutionally sanctioned for, an oligarchic plutocracy.

"Leveling the Hierarchy" by Donald Gutierrez—*Eldorado Sun*, 2005; *Progressive Populist*, 2009; *Humanist Society of New Mexico,* November 2009.

37
Review: John Pilger,
The New Rulers of the World

The pivotal thesis of John Pilger's *The New Rulers of the World* is that rich nations—especially the United States—dominate the world commercially through "overwhelming force." The misleading association of "free trade" with "democracy" conceals a new imperialism. Early on in *Rulers*, Pilger amplifies this central idea by asserting that the "new rulers" are implementing "terrorism" as the new Red Scare, "justifying a permanent war footing and paranoia, and construction of the greatest military machine ever" (10). But, Pilger argues, the most dangerous and destructive terrorism in the modern world is, and for decades has been, state terrorism.

Vigorously dismissing the rhetoric of liberation and democracy dished out by the "new rulers," he cites former Secretary of State Madeleine Albright's comment, "the price is worth it," regarding the deaths of 500,000 Iraqi children that resulted from Washington's sanctions policy against Iraq. In addition, Pilger instances U. S. General William Looney's declaration that, "They know we own their country...we dictate the way they live and talk." Pilger also quotes George Kennan, a U.S. diplomat and respected authority on the Cold War, who, commenting on America's possessing fifty percent of the world's wealth but around six percent of its population, stated in the late 1940s: "Our real job is to maintain this position of disparity....we should cease thinking about human rights, the raising of living standards and democratisation" (120).

In Pilger's outlook, these sentiments describe globalization, which he elaborates throughout *Rulers* as the global assault against the poor. Financial institutions like the International Monetary Fund and the World Bank represent the priorities of Washington and Wall Street. They do so in part through Structural Adjustment Programs (SAPs), "consisting of privatisation, indebtedness and the destruction of public services," that result in the impoverishment and misery of most people in the world. "When tariffs and food and fuel subsidies are eliminated under an IMF diktat," Pilger continues, "small farmers and the landless know they have been declared expendable" (122).

That these conditions result in farmers in Mexico, India and elsewhere committing suicide apparently doesn't bother World Bank officials. These magnates fly into the capitols of developing nations on a Monday, make SAP deals in posh hotels and fly out Wednesday carrying briefcases stuffed with deals worth billions. Leaders of countries that don't cooperate with the "Washington Consensus," whether it's Castro of Cuba, Allende of Chile, Saddam Hussein, or Sukarno of Indonesia, encounter American covert or overwhelming force. Pilger quotes Thomas Friedman, who has stated the arrangement with brutal succinctness, "The hidden hand in the market will never work without a hidden fist" (126)—the "hand" being McDonald's, Silicon Valley, and the like; the "fist," America's armed forces.

Rulers consists of an introduction and four substantial chapters. The first deals with the West's carving up of Indonesia, the second with the extreme inhumanity of the West's Gulf War I assault and sanctions on Iraq. Chapter Three broadens the scope of the first two chapters, with discussion of the West's plan and efforts to dominate the world. Chapter Four concerns the history of the racist genocide against the Aborigines by the White government and settlers of Australia.

Indonesia is perhaps the most dramatic case in point of the West's imperial "steel fist" bashing the weaker nations in the world. In the chapter "The Model Pupil," Pilger examines Indonesia as the West's exemplar of globalization. During a "regime change" that lasted 33 years, almost 70 million people in Indonesia lived in poverty. Women were sometimes forced to work in sweatshops for 36 hours straight. Pilger goes behind the display window to expose the extraordinarily violent change that occurred in 1965 when the United States and England helped the troops of General Suharto usurp the presidency of Sukarno. This usurpation initiated a genocide targeting Indonesian Communists and "suspects," and resulted in the murder—with the crucial help of Washington's telecommunication equipment and lists—of 500,000 to a million people.

According to a CIA report, "the massacres rank as one of the worst mass murders in the 20th century" (27). Sukarno was a popular leader but he didn't cooperate with the West's corporate interests. Equally shocking was the thunderous applause this genocidal "stabilization" evoked in the American media and among such statesmen as American Ambassador to Indonesia Marshall Green and famed journalists like James Reston, who described this event in the *New York Times* as "a gleam of light in Asia."

What followed this enormous Washington-backed massacre could also qualify as one of the most cold-blooded acts in modern history as super powers carved up Indonesia's economy like a roast turkey. Financial experts from the West met Suharto's people in Geneva a year following the bloodbath:

> They divided up into five different sections: mining in one room, services in another, light industry in another, banking and finance in another; and what Chase Manhattan did was sit with a delegation and hammer out policies that were going to be acceptable to them and other investors. You had these big corporation people going around the table, saying this is what we need, this, this and this, and they basically designed the legal infrastructure for investment in Indonesia. (Pilger, 41)

Real control of the Indonesian economy (and, thus, government) fell into the hands of the United States, Europe, Japan and Canada. At the beginning of the 21st century, Indonesia was indebted by over one-fourth of a trillion dollars, a debt that, as in other countries deliberately impoverished by the superpowers, will be paid for by the poor. Despite this involvement in genocide and gross economic exploitation, the United States and Canada continue training an Indonesian officer elite that is part of a military never punished for its 1965 mass murders.

This Indonesian saga of horror is just one of several found in *Rulers*. Pilger cites analogous cases of American and British use of "overwhelming force" in Iraq War I, Kosovo and elsewhere, exhibiting the same merciless disregard for civilians and civilian infrastructure that Suharto's troops exhibited in taking bank employees out of a bank during the "regime change" and beheading them.

A little light in this immense darkness is cast by the moral presence and anger of Pilger. In his follow-ups to these horrible events, he confronts various political personages with the kind of uncompromising questions one seldom witnesses in American journalists and interviewers. Pilger attempts to interview James Wolfensohn, then head of the World Bank, about Indonesia. Wolfensohn won't see him, so Pilger instead interviews a World Bank officer: "I asked him why, during thirty years, the World Bank had failed to say anything about a regime that was guilty of mass murder, in Indonesia and East Timor. 'I think we got a number of things wrong,' he replied 'and we have to understand that'" (44).

In the chapter "Paying the Price," an extended confrontation occurs between Pilger and James Rubin, assistant secretary of state under President Bill Clinton. Pilger not only asks tough questions but rigorously disputes Rubin's deliberate State Department obfuscation about whether Saddam or the United States was to blame for the high child mortality rate in Iraq during the sanctions period. The following exchange occurs:

> He [Rubin] retorted, "If you'd like to give a speech, we can switch chairs." [Pilger] "I don't think it becomes a senior State Department official to speak like that." [Rubin] "Let me hear your speech." [Pilger] "Why have you misrepresented the Unicef report?"

Pilger, who apparently does his homework thoroughly, queries Rubin about Albright's brutal response to the dead Iraqi children issue. When Rubin claims Albright's statement was out of context, Pilger hands Rubin the context, Albright's interview transcript.

These journalistic confrontations may seem like small victories against the vast backdrop of lies and murder committed by institutions of state and finance. However, as a journalist's struggle with powerful institutional individuals to pry the truth loose, they are crucially important. Probably few Americans are aware that a senior CIA officer named Ralph McGehee once described "the terror in Indonesia from 1965-66 as a 'model operation' for the American-run coup that got rid of Salvador Allende in Chile seven years later." Indonesia, according to McGehee, also served as the model for "Operation Phoenix" in which American-led death squads murdered at least 50,000 Vietnamese (50).

Throughout *Rulers*, Pilger especially punctures the government propaganda of the United States and England. As a major American justification for attacking nations like Iraq and Afghanistan has been their alleged connection with terrorists, Pilger at some length provides numerous instances of the United States harboring terrorists. He cites, among others, Guatemala's defense minister Hector Gramajo, El Salvador's general Jose Guillermo Garcia, Argentina's admiral Jorge Enrico and the Chilean death-squad soldier Armando Fernandez Larios, all individuals involved in state torture and murder, sometimes on a mass scale. Most of these major criminals and others like them have lived in comfort in areas like Florida.

According to Pilger, "What all these people have in common, apart from their history of terrorism, is that they were either working directly for the U.S. government or carrying out the dirty work of American policies." It is only a step from mentioning these Washington-backed terrorists to underlining the terrorist character of the formerly named School of the Americas: "Given that the evidence linking the school to continuing atrocities in Latin America is rather stronger than the evidence linking al-Qa'ida training camps to the attack on New York, what should we do about the 'evil-doers' in Fort Benning, Georgia?" (140-41).

Pilger's final chapter analyzes a First World's brutalization of the Third within the same country. "The Chosen Ones" elaborates White Australia's racist policies towards the Aborigines, from depriving them of land rights (by acting as if Australia was unoccupied until Europeans arrived) to policies of genocide. According to one authority, the Aborigines' population fell from 120,000 to 20,000 by 1920, with at least 10,000 killed outright. Pilger also deflates the myth among White Australians that that the government is pouring millions of dollars into Aborigine welfare to no avail, pointing out that Aborigines continue to be deprived of housing, access to education and hope.

Pilger is an outstanding journalist because he asserts the crucial questions and considerations few journalists want to pose, such as whether Saddam Hussein or American and British leaders and their sanctions killed more innocent Iraqis. The ultimate question he poses is whether the West's war on terrorism is really an elaborate hoax meant to disguise the state terrorism behind the new imperialism called globalization.

"Review: John Pilger, *The New Rulers of the World*" by Donald Gutierrez— *Progressive Populist*, February 2004; *Justice Xpress*, Spring 2004, v. 12, no. 2; *Eldorado Sun*, February 2004.

38
Systemic Greed: L. Dennis Kozlowski and Beyond

The 2001 trial of two Tyco International executives, Dennis Kozlowski and Mark Swartz exhibit big-time CEOs losing all self-control. According to the *Albuquerque Journal*, these two businessmen were indicted for stealing $130 million "by claiming unauthorized compensation and made another $430 million on their Tyco shares by lying about the conglomerate's condition from 1993 to 2002." The total amount allegedly stolen by Kozlowski and Swartz, then, came to $600 million. What makes this thievery egregious is that, by most standards, these corporate executives made enormous salaries in one year alone (2000)—Kozlowski, $137 million and Swartz, $54 million.

Their attorneys argued that the two men were legitimately rewarded for developing Tyco into a huge business and that their "pay and bonus recommendations were approved by an outside auditor." Further, the defense insisted, all these financial compensation transactions were done in the open: "All the people who were supposed to know about the compensation did know."

What appears glaringly apparent is that if all the "right" people knew about Kozlowski and Swartz's licit and allegedly illicit financial gains, then the flaw goes beyond two individuals; it is systemic. If an approval apparatus for pay increase was virtually in place that could either justify or overlook two executives already earning $137 million and $54 million acquiring $600 million *more*, something is rotten at the core of the operation. And even given the possibility that their managers might have been unaware of the stolen money, it is telling that, as a *New Yorker* article indicated, "No one at Tyco begrudged Kozlowski his salary."

Kozlowski's defense attorney claimed that Kozlowski worked hard for Tyco and deserved his pay. Of course one frequently hears that argument, not only from outrageously overpaid CEOs but from Business and Economics professors, their graduate students and the money media. Further, it is an argument central to those supporters of capitalism who feel that, at least in the so-called private sector, one's income and compensation system are a private matter and that, when it comes to making money, the sky's the limit. To paraphrase Ronald Reagan on the big wave of his first presidential election, America is a place where anyone should be able to become a millionaire.

If, however, every American, thus inspired, is out to make his or her million or billion, what happens to the social needs of the population at large, to those whose chief aim in life is something other than amassing money or who don't have the "correct" gender or racial credentials to get ahead or who don't think that making a lot of money is the noblest goal in life? And what kind of civic ethic is exhibited when making a fortune is trumpeted by a president of the United States as the cardinal ideal for a nation?

Kozlowski's salary and greed are hardly an exception. Grossly excessive pay for American CEOs has been the norm for several decades. Major American corporate CEOs get paid at a ratio of as much as 1000:1 compared to their company workers. This contrasts shockingly with the far smaller CEO-to-worker salary ratio in other advanced nations where a far larger portion of private or corporate wealth goes into essential social programs.

Many Americans, hearing of this extraordinary disparity between American CEO and worker salaries, simply shake their heads and go their way, some perhaps fantasizing about themselves making millions. They might feel that Kozlowski's grand larceny is part of an intricate system of financial operations that has absolutely no relation to their life or to the scope of their power or needs.

They are right to think that these CEOs and the business world they move within are hardly part of the landscape that the average person inhabits. Are they right, though, to feel that these criminal executives and their milieu are inaccessible? After all, Kozlowski and Swartz were on trial and deserved to be convicted—as they were; Kozlowski received an eight-and-a-half- to 24-year sentence, Swartz presumably less. Even so, one doubts that they would have ended up in the state pen along with "common" criminals, but that is another issue. Some would say, as the pundits said after Watergate, "The system works; justice prevails, after all."

The system works all right. Even though Kozlowski was sent to prison, the system will continue creating more Kozlowskis (and Swartzes) because, despite the media melodramatics of Enronism, the 1990s mantra that "Greed is Good" persists. No one might proclaim that creed anymore but it is sustained by the deep-seated dogma that private wealth, no matter how vast, is sacrosanct. It need not be shared with the general public regardless of how desperate and widespread the public needs may be or how much the public contributed to that wealth. The incredibly irresponsible tax cuts pushed by former President George W. Bush and vociferously defended by Republicans during the Democratic administration of Barack Obama—supposedly to encourage the rich to create more jobs for the masses—brutally underlines that outlook.

From the standpoint of the basic needs of society at large, the central issue should be how much of private wealth ought to be private. The courts and Congress have created a formidable bulwark of laws and legislation down the years supporting the idea that individualism and private economic activity justify the unbridled accumulation of wealth. This outlook has even fraudulently assumed the status of being essentially American and democratic in the crucial 1886 court decision (*Santa Clara Country* v. *Southern Pacific Railroad Co.*) that mistakenly and outrageously granted personhood to corporations. The *Citizens United* decision of 2010 (which should be called the *Corporations United* decision) massively enhances the power of Wall Street wealth in our time and endangers the viability of democracy in the United States to an unparalleled degree.

This dominant perspective has of course seen important counter-currents, such as Populism, Progressivism, the New Deal and the Civil Rights and Women's Liberation movements. A core ideal of these movements has been not only the more equitable distribution of a society's power but also of its wealth. The question remains, however, as to the extent to which the income of a J.P. Morgan or a Dennis Kolzowski should be private or accessible to a country's needs.

This question is not easily answered because it moves into intensely controversial ideological issues that go to the core of capitalism. For example, how much of the $137 million Koslowski was paid in 2000 should be put back into the public coffers? Doesn't this taxation, especially if it is large—but then, what is "large?"—move us into socialism, the state "devouring" Kozlowski's millions hard-earned by others? And if the government is helping corporations earn fortunes through subsidies, tax cuts and other lavish incentives, is this not socialism for the rich? But, if that is so, would not such socialism for the millions of Americans struggling to make ends meet obviously be far more just and ethical?

People either know or suspect that the rich manipulate the politicians, the courts and the media to defend concepts of private enterprise and privatized wealth. Indeed, with the enormous assistance of the Bush administration the wealthy, through unelected but extremely influential advisers and activists like Karl Rove and Grover Norquist and a conservative Congress, tried to privatize every privatizable institution in America. Furthermore, those who want a fairer distribution of the countless billions of privatized dollars that a few Americans have acquired down the years are up against deeply entrenched biases towards the sacralization of private riches. Yet anyone can see that when people like Kozlowski (not to mention "legit" CEOs like Disney's Michael Eisner or billionaire hedgefund managers) acquire excessive wealth, something is inane in our social order—the order is disordered to a point of criminal lunacy when a Kozlowski can make $137 million in one year.

"He earned all of it," his defense lawyer claimed. On the contrary, no one deserves that kind of money when millions of Americans lack adequate (or any) health insurance; one out of every five American children go hungry; some seniors have to choose between food and medication; water, soil and air quality in the country continue to deteriorate; mass unemployment is rising sharply; youths from lower income families can't afford to go to college; and the Defense budget enlarges cancerously year after year as the Pentagon and the president engage in war after war. The systemic context that partly explains Kozlowski's avarice can be seen in the *Forbes Magazine* statistic that the aggregate net worth of the 400 richest Americans is $955 billion (up 10 percent from 2002). The immorality of Kozlowski's purloined millions becomes less dramatic when viewed within the brutal reality of merely 400 Americans commanding nearly a trillion dollars. But even this staggering figure of upper-class wealth is minimized by the fact that Bush II's tax cuts to the rich amounted to over two trillion dollars—during an eight-year period when the country was waging two wars.

The capacity to make huge sums of money free of restraint has been extolled by others besides Reagan as the fundamental ideal of democracy. However, this ethos overlooks the bedrock truth that no one could make a fortune without the aid of the social infrastructure that made manufacturing, mining, railroading and, more recently, telecommunications possible. Millions of badly paid individuals over generations laid the tracks and wiring, dug the mines, built the dams and factories and plants and roads that created the means for massive wealth to pour into a relatively few pockets.

The courts and Congress were there to defend that narrowly channeled wealth by legal decisions and legislation protecting corporations and, particularly, its executives and major investors. As Richard L. Grossman puts it: "Judges and legislators have made it possible for business to keep decisions about money, production, work and ownership beyond the reach of democracy" (*Defying Corporations, Defining Democracy*, Dean Ritz, ed.). And, as Ralph Nader and William Taylor claim in *The Big Boys: Power and Position in American Business* (1986), "The 'support functions' of government are manifested on scores of subsidiary programs, tax expenditures, R&D transfers and protection from competition worth billions of dollars annually." They add, "The corporation has now become…an institution seeking limited liability for itself and unlimited privilege for its managers." Such is the setting for the emergence of the Kozlowskis of American corporate capitalism.

Kozlowski is said to have left a $5,000 tip at a restaurant, given his Nantucket home decorator a $5,000,000 budget and provided his second wife a $2,000,000 birthday party at a posh hotel in Sardinia. But then, all this was merely chump change to the CEO who along with Swartz robbed Tyco of almost two-thirds of a billion dollars. Perhaps no one can say with authority how much of both Kozlowski's legal income and illegal gain belonged to the country itself. But the Kozlowskis of corporate capitalism don't only represent rogue CEOs; these high-flying crooks also symbolize a critical blurring between personal and corporate accountability. Until such institutions as Congress, the Security and Exchange Commission or the courts fully accept their proper role as media of democratic expression and sanction, such accountability will never be adequately addressed. Brave and principled individuals like Brooksley Born, once head of the Commodity Futures Trading Commission (and described and affirmed at length in Robert Scheer's *The Great American Stickup*) tried to regulate derivatives in the years before the financial meltdown of 2007 but were brutally beaten down by powerful individuals in the financial world like Alan Greenspan, Robert Rubin and Security and Exchange Commissioner Arthur Levitt.

The larcenous scandal of Kozlowski is not only the disgrace of Tyco

International, it is the profound disgrace of an economic order that allows its top managers, investment bankers and entertainers to acquire multimillion dollar salaries while tens of millions of Americans lack adequate food, shelter, medical care and social services. This appalling injustice will never come to an end until enough Americans fully realize that the ownership and hoarding of billions of dollars by a very small number of corporations, banks and individuals is robbing them of *their* money and that it is also robbing them of economic democracy and a decent life.

"Systemic Greed: L. Dennis Kozlowski and Beyond" by Donald Gutierrez— *Common Sense*, December 2003; *El Tecolote*, December 2003; *Eldorado Sun*, December 2003.

39
American Presidents and Business Versus Community

The business of America is business.
President Calvin Coolidge

The well-known quotation above has almost assumed the status of sanctity in the minds of some (usually business) people, but it is an ill-balanced and pernicious idea. First, it suggests that the highest elected political figure in the country thinks that business is the primary, basic, most important activity of the nation. It also suggests that America's central elected official is not above the frenzy, ruthlessness and greed of the marketplace, but is in and for it. It overlooks the fact that probably the majority of Americans are not business people or are only indirectly involved with business—spouses of workers, civil servants, factory workers, field "hands," employees, most military personnel, teachers, manual laborers and so on. It suggests further that the President (not to mention Congress) regards a significant part of his role to be the encouragement of business and thus of business values and interests at the expense of promoting civic unity and community. Competition, profits, capital growth and the acquisition of foreign markets—all of these pursuits have had an enormous impact in the class-dividing of Americans as well as on the well- or ill-being of the inhabitants of countries vulnerable to formidable American market pressures.

Probably one justificatory ideal behind this sentiment is, as a high-placed corporation official put it in the 1950s, "What's good for GE is good for the country." That remark comes across in 2012 as savagely ironic amidst the devastating results of the country's economic collapse caused by a deregulated Wall Street and its consequent avarice as exhibited by incredibly inflated CEO raises and other payoffs. Yet even back in the supposedly more financially level 1950s, what was good for a corporation was hardly good for average adult factory or service employees (not to mention migrant workers or the masses of adolescent workers). Though they had a job and some job security, their salaries were hardly within shouting distance of their bosses' salaries. Often, the retort to the enormous income disparity is that these employees didn't have to bear the responsibilities, risks and stress of corporate management. Does that justify a CEO at the time making twenty times as much as a company worker? How about 39 times as much? That was a 2008 estimate reported by G. William Domhoff in *Who Rules America* (2010, 6th ed.). As of April 2010, according to Domhoff, 15 percent of American wealth was held by 80 percent of the population while over 80 percent was owned by 20 percent. And, the Institute for Policy Studies claims, American taxpayers subsidized the pay of corporate executives by more than $20 billion a year in 2008. Since then, the financial disparity between the very rich and the rest of the American population has only become more extreme.

Where do working people and exploitation by their bosses fit into Coolidge's blunt little aphorism? If business is concerned primarily with profits, and an employee's wages get in the way, who or what protects a decent wage for the employee? Employer benevolence? There are benevolent, humane employers oriented toward making a profit *and* treating their employees decently. But the rise of unions in the latter part of the 19th century hardly occurred in a vacuum; it resulted from an urgent need to protect the rights of workers from unscrupulous or merciless employers. Whatever the excesses of some unions—mob infiltration or control, union leaders exploiting their membership, unions placing unfair demands on companies—the fact remains that without unions the basic work, and thus living, conditions of millions of Americans would not have improved significantly.

When a president of the United States proclaims that the main concern of the country is business rather than community, he is showing his hand—and that hand is the influence and interest of Big Business on the thinking and values of the highest political figure in the nation. It is now common knowledge that Richard Nixon was selected and financed for a political career by top corporate executives in Southern California. The same can be claimed for Ronald Reagan in regard to the presidency, not to mention the support of George W. Bush by the corporate big guns in Texas and elsewhere.

Carmen Trotta, writing for *The Catholic Worker* (Aug-Sept. 1996), has made the arresting observation that presidents Ronald Reagan and George H. W. Bush, undermining popular revolutionary potential in Central America by stigmatizing it as a sign of communism, cleared the way for the maquiladora system:

> [T]he Reagan-Bush administration channeled over a billion dollars through the United States Agency for International Development to Central America and the Caribbean basin to set up industrial parks designed to subsidize and facilitate the movement of US. manufacturers away from the U.S. workers to the phenomenally cheap, union-free pool of the Third World.

(This practice of manufacturing in other countries with ensuing tax benefits came to be known by the Spanish term *maquiladora*, referring to millers charging a maquila for processing other people's grain.)

It is critical to note, however, that the Reagan-Bush administration (Bush Sr. was Reagan's vice president before he was elected president) is not the exception but the rule. Both Presidents Bill Clinton and Barack Obama have been deeply influenced by corporate interests. Even as liberal a president as Franklin Delano Roosevelt, who came from the wealthiest class in the United States, had close friends among big financiers and industrialists. Thomas Lamont, for example, a high-placed figure in J.P. Morgan and Co., connected Roosevelt with the U.S. Steel magnate Myron Taylor. Roosevelt used such connections often enough to help both industry and labor. The point here, however, is that men in industry, business and finance have close and very effective access to the president and thus exercise major influence on presidents in a way few other Americans ever could.

And that influence is alarming. The massive impact of PAC lobbying on Congress and of the more recent Super-Pacs on the public through media ads seriously undermines representative democracy in this country—it has almost destroyed democracy. Moreover, presidents often derive socially or culturally from the American upper class. Thus, "The Business of America is Business" manifests both capitalist and class interests; their mergence more than suggests plutocracy. But the business of America should not be business; it should be community.

There is community, some would say—the business community. To be sure, there is a community among, say, business owners in terms of identical or analogous interests or a proclivity to regard value in identical terms. This community shares interests in profits, in the significance of interest rates, government subsidies and tax deductions, keeping employee costs down, outsourcing American jobs and so on. But by these very terms the public, as consumer, is usually not part of this community. Moreover, the individuals at the apex of the business world, the CEOs, live in a gilded world of their own, in their youth going to prep schools and prestigious colleges, intermarrying, interconnecting on numerous high-powered boards and very exclusive social clubs, having their mansions and neighborhoods rigorously patrolled and protected by police, and even being buried on private burial grounds. The powerful people in finance, industry and banking comprise such a tight community and are so inexorably exclusive as to be more properly called a dominant caste rather than a community.

A genuine community includes or attempts to include everyone— again, not because of their financial prowess or material acquisition but through the indissoluble reality of their basic humanness and the resulting sense of their organic interdependence. Such a community is pivoted on the ineradicable and determinative fact of one's humanness.

"Humanness" may seem a vague and broad criterion for community; but, conversely, the term suggests the force of its appropriateness. One's human status to solicit one's right to community transcends the more specific, traditional and excluding criteria like race, class, income, gender or education, all of which delimit a community. This sort of delimiting results in numerous subcommunities warring with each other, some so powerful (such as the corporate or financial community) as to dominate or even destroy others.

Here one might observe that in modern mass industrial societies there are irresistible forces moving individuals and groups into collectives. Rather than such groupings empowering people, it often makes them more vulnerable to centralized control economically, politically, psychologically. That very atomization, that mass relation as a form of social organization which is vulnerable to authoritarian control, is the opposite of true community. People in community relate as subjects, not as objects. They fiercely resist dehumanization by any abstracted central force like the nation or the state—or, as is finally becoming clear, by Wall Street. They are "subjected" only in the accessibility of their human dependence on and interrelatedness with others. And the others are not arbitrarily high-placed "authorities," but individuals more or less as dependent and vulnerable and, one can hope, as compassionate and accessible as they. Indeed, the way power and its concentration are defused and minimized is by this mutual accessibility and dependency, what the sociologist Philip Slater and other communitarians have called "interdependence." *Representative* democracy, supposedly unavoidable in our heavily populated modern societies, is better kept under control when "vested interests" are at least partly restricted by the empowerment of community relatedness.

This idea of interdependence may not seem very American in a country once flaunting (and now haunted by) such legendary culture heroes of rugged independence as Teddy Roosevelt, Horatio Alger and John Wayne. But interdependence is a necessity in developing methods of mutual aid such as cancer-support groups and crucial safety-net programs (i. e., Social Security, Medicare and Medicaid). The metaphor of society as a social *body* means that *everyone* is living, and thus deserves inclusion in regard to the basic needs of life—food, shelter, education, work and play.

A society primarily oriented towards business interests and the idolization of profits—especially high and quick profits—is bound to be ruthless in the pursuit of those goals and thus likely to need restraints imposed by some disinterested medium or agency. Theoretically, that restraint is the role of the government, and once in a while the government has provided restraints in the form of antitrust laws, the crucial Glass-Steagal Act (repealed in 1999), occasional protection of workers through improving working conditions, wages, health coverage and other benefits. But all too often, government has failed to protect wage earners and working people against business, especially against Big Business, with all its ramifications of power, influence and presence in the halls of Congress and on very exclusionary bodies like the United States Chamber of Commerce and the Business Roundtable. But then, "The business of America is business." As long as that deadly motto is believed and sustained by the most powerful economic forces in American society, there will never be community in the United States to a significant extent—not in the sense of everyone counting, everyone included.

1. The attempt since 2010 of right wing governors under corporate influence, such as Walker of Wisconsin, Kasich of Michigan, Ritchie of New Jersey and Scott of Georgia, to destroy unions through outlawing collective bargaining suggests how the Wall Street ideology of suppressing unions, fundamental worker rights and thus the viability of a middle class remains powerful and virulent.

"American Presidents and Business Versus Community" by Donald Gutierrez—*Desert Exposure*, September 1996; *Common Sense*, December 1996.

PART IV

POWER OF THE PEN

ICONOCLASTS TO THE RESCUE

40
Review: Howard Zinn, *The Zinn Reader: Writings on Disobedience and Democracy*

Howard Zinn, who died in 2010, was one of America's great activist historians. His famous *A People's History of the United States* highlighted "people" because it told the story of the millions of individuals whose experience and worth seldom get mentioned in traditional history books—the enslaved Black people, the unheralded Chinese and Irish people who built the railroads, the people who worked the mines until Black Lung disease or mine collapses killed them, the ethnically-cleansed Native American peoples, the women and children and people of color brutalized by an America ruled by White men of property.

Now we have *The Zinn Reader: Writings on Disobedience and Democracy*, a more than 700-page supplement to Zinn's numerous books that further accentuates his status as a superb iconoclastic historian and polemicist. *Reader* offers a broad and varied collection of his work—essays, articles, lectures, speeches—from the 1960s to nearly the end of Zinn's life. The book is organized under such topics as Race, Class, War, Law, History, and Means and Ends that orient the collection around many of Zinn's chief concerns. Further, each piece has a useful short introduction explaining the circumstances under which it was originally published.

One of these introductions vividly illustrates the character of Zinn's mindset:

> I wrote this piece, *which would not have found publication
> in the press* [emphasis added] to argue against the principle
> of retaliation. I am always furious at the killing of innocent
> people for some political cause, but I wanted to broaden the
> definition of terrorism to include governments, which are
> guilty of terrorism far more often, and on an infinitely larger
> scale, than a band of revolutionaries or nationalists.
> (Introduction to "Terrorism Over Tripoli")

That quotation offers an insight virtually never mentioned in the media
and especially not by governments—that governments create far more
terrorism (including state torture) than "insurgents," radical Islamic
terrorists and the like.[1] It is indeed that vein of iconoclasm in Zinn's
thinking that sets him apart from many historians and journalists. Zinn
further empowers his observations and moral passion with a persuasive
conviction that objectivity in writing history or journalism is a deception
masking an ideology. All this (and more) Zinn gets across in lucid prose as
free of academic jargon as it is authentically personal and personable; the
style, as they used to say, is the man.

Zinn's thrust as a "subjective" historian is to present—he would say,
select—the Other history that traditionally gets left out of the books . We all
went through school constantly hearing about the presidents and generals
and captains of industry, the great industrial and technological and
transportation achievements that, we were told, made America great.
However, claims Zinn, "we were not told of the human cost of this great
industrial progress." He goes on to give voice to the voiceless, the people
who did the savagely hard infrastructural labor, and he also reminds us of
the many millions who continue to live in poverty and misery in the world's
richest nation.

Choosing the top pieces in *Reader* is hard because there are many fine
ones. Among the outstanding in the "Race" section is "Abolitionists,
Freedom Riders and the Tactics of Agitation"; in "Class," the heartbreaking
description of "The Ludlow Massacre," in which coal miners and their
families faced the overwhelming and murderous firepower of unified
company and government forces; in "War," "Just and Unjust Wars," in
which Zinn comes to feel there *are* no "just" wars (partly his reaction to
being a World War II bombardier); and the lengthy, seminal essay "Law and

Justice," in the "Law" section, in which Zinn broaches the antithetical relation of law and justice in America. The large "History" section starts off appropriately with Zinn's "dark" Columbus, a strikingly different personage from the traditionally represented explorer. The final section, "Means and Ends," climaxes in a notably affirmative review essay on philosophical anarchism based on Herbert Read's pro-anarchist book *Anarchy and Order*.

Reader can also be profitably approached by tracing some of its major themes and ideas, though space demands choosing only a few key topics here, one being civil disobedience. Tellingly, the subtitle of *Reader* is "Democracy and Disobedience." Without disobedience, Zinn contends, America would not have had the powerful antislavery movements, the courageous Civil Rights and Women's Rights movements, the defiantly individualized action of people like Daniel Ellsberg, Rosa Parks, the Berrigan brothers, Big Bill Haywood, freedom-bus-rider Jim Peck and so many others less well known. The problem in America, says Zinn, is not civil disobedience but, "civil *obedience*. . . . our problem is that people are obedient while the jails are full of petty thieves, and all the while the grand thieves are running the country" (438). Without civil disobedience, Zinn argues, it is hard to possess or sustain democracy.

For Zinn, the issue of civil obedience versus disobedience comes down to law versus justice. Is it wrong to break the law? *Which* law, he asks. "I'm not against all law" (44). When the law violates justice, and, for example, allows Dow Chemical to manufacture Agent Orange for use abroad in America's wars in Vietnam, Iraq and elsewhere, then the principle of justice far outweighs that of law and compels civil disobedience.

Another pivotal theme in *Reader* is American imperialism. Time after time, Zinn reminds us that the United States has carried out ethnic cleansing (Native Americans) and annexation or control of another nation's territory (Mexico, the Philippines, Puerto Rico, Iraq); and the United States has exerted enormous financial control through gunship/bayonet intervention by the Marines (Haiti, Dominican Republic, Nicaragua), and later in the 20th century, after World War II, in military bases established globally. Moreover, American soldiers killed in Vietnam, Iraq, Afghanistan didn't die "for their country," they died for their *government*. "They will die for Bush and Cheney and Rumsfeld." They will die, Zinn continues, for "the greed of the oil cartels, for the expansion of the American empire, for the political ambitions of the President" (716-17). What Zinn's reading of American imperialism suggests is that this country must account for a great deal of evil perpetrated abroad.

Zinn's last words in *Reader* are warmly encouraging to activist citizenship: "You don't have to do something heroic, just something, because all of these somethings, at certain points in history, come together, and make the world better" (735).

A flaw in *Reader* is that it lacks an index. Considering the wide range of allusions in this book, an index would have been invaluable.

Certainly *The Zinn Reader*, with its stunning compassion for the millions of innocent people murdered by American wars of "intervention," the millions brutalized and killed by work for which they got very little pay and no credit whatsoever and the millions whose story has seldom if ever been told, embodies a marvelous gathering of writings by this superbly compassionate historian and social critic. Zinn has made so-called left radical ideas seem so humane and natural and right as arguably to move social-political discourse out of the tiresome Left-Right gamut and into another, purer sphere of moral contemplation and action. This is no minor feat.

---

1. See the Gareau review in Ch. 5 for elaboration of this point.

"Review: Howard Zinn, *The Zinn Reader: Writings on Disobedience and Democracy*" by Donald Gutierrez—*Progressive Populist*, May 2010.

41

The Humanities: "Finite Perfections"

For the last decade or so, alarm has been expressed about the state of American education. What alarmed me on reading a "Report" a few years back was that Science and Mathematics alone constituted education for the author of the report. The essay discussed the woeful inadequacies of American education exclusively in terms of those two subjects. Not a word was mentioned about the state or value of the Humanities in our schools or in society at large. This attitude cannot be dismissed as one individual's opinion, because it is shared by people of considerable power and influence in America, such as a former president of Intel, and, for that matter, former president George W. Bush whose administration can be credited for reducing learning largely to test-taking.

The article represents a position that I feel is widely supported through America's political and educational hierarchies. The humanities are all very well, but, according to this outlook, the meat and potatoes of education are science and math, because they best help us to get ahead in our high-tech world and to fit into cubicles in places like Intel. They are thus practical subjects, understandably significant in a corporate-dominated society more and more inclined to view colleges primarily as (very expensive) vocational schools. Succeeding in that society might, however, be part of the trouble. Perhaps that rapidly developing, fast-lane world in which the Intels and the Exxons and the BPs and Goldman Sachses reign supreme should be slowed down, scrutinized for where it is taking us, and at what human cost.

Of course science and math are important in themselves. They have exhibited some of the most brilliant reaches of the human mind and deserve to be cherished. But those areas of knowledge and culture are incomplete by themselves in fleshing out the world of learning, let alone wisdom, and that's where the humanities come in. There is an esthetic, ethical, philosophical and psychological dimension to the humanities that certainly occupies important ground of its own. For one thing, the humanities—the arts, literature, philosophy, history—might harbor crucial lessons for us about not necessarily going along with our high-speed, global-economy, high-tech culture, which is primarily oriented towards commercial global hegemony.

The humanities are essential not only to education but to society and civilization. Art—poetry, drama, fiction, film, painting, music—can arrest time, progress, the national obsession with profit, competition; it can even ease depression and offer the sublime dimensions of psychic "depth" and the creative imagination. The humanities stimulate contemplation, meditation, critical analysis, exaltation, exploration and refinement of emotion—esteemable qualities indeed. The California poet and man of letters Kenneth Rexroth goes so far as to say that "Civilization endures as long as somewhere they [contemplatives] can hold life in total vision. When it [a core of transcendental calm] is lost sight of, society perishes" (*Bird in the Bush: Obvious Essays*).

The humanities are felt by some to be impractical, even obnoxiously pretentious. Further, some humanities academics get too involved in research specializations that have little or no connection with the potential educable interests of the public. Humanities professors should feel an obligation—and some do—to shape, at least to some extent, their knowledge of and insight into their discipline into a compelling vision of existence and society accessible and inspiring to non-specialists.

Surely there is a crucial need to popularize and broaden the experiences, revelations and perceptions of great art and of historical and philosophical thought. This is especially so in a country as dominated by commercial, business interests as the United States. The frenzied absorption in money-making and the infinite power created through major corporate control of monies amount to what Norman Mailer once called America's commercial totalitarianism.

Those who love or teach the humanities might feel that they don't need to make a case for the humanities; its supreme worth is obvious. But if so, it is obvious to only a relatively small portion of society. There has been and is a pernicious social or class dimension to the humanities, especially in the

Fine Arts, that makes philistinic disapproval or hostility understandable. As a concert pianist recently put it, young people regard Classical Music as "elitist," the preserve of the rich or highly cultivated. Moreover, some codes of masculinity in America still regard the arts as mainly a woman's—or womanly—domain. And some performing artists have claimed that taking Bach into the inner cities is a waste of time.

However, there is no convincing reason why a poem by the great 8th century Chinese poet Tu Fu, a Navajo or Persian rug, a Mozart piano trio or a Giotto fresco would not excite or inspire a lower-class Native American or Black or Hispanic child as much as an upper-class White child. The arts—from William Byrd to Miles Davis, Phidias and Lady Murasaki to Yeats and Clyfford Still—can be accessible and exciting to anyone. The only class that need apply is the aristocracy of receptivity and taste.

Some of the most profound and enjoyable experiences of literature and music occur in one's youth. A young person can read Dostoyevsky or Jane Austen, Ibsen, the Brontes, or D. H. Lawrence's *Sons and Lovers* or see a Shakespeare—Moliere, Shaw—drama performed, or read some of Plato's *Dialogues*, or plunge into Edward Gibbon's majestic *Decline and Fall of the Roman Empire*. Even if one doesn't fully understand them, the youthful encounter with the subtly evolving, numinously fictional, theatrical, philosophic, historical world of these great authors is so deeply interwoven into the emotional and subverbal consciousness of one's being, that the resultant imprint becomes an essential aspect of one's deepest sense of self. Who, for example, can forget the incredible, vibrant feeling of opening vistas experienced on first hearing the heroic strain in the first movement of Beethoven's "Eroica" Symphony, or the thrill-dread of the first sentence of Kafka's novel *The Trial*—"Someone must have betrayed Joseph K., for, without having done anything wrong, he was arrested one fine morning"—or the rapturous poignancy of Keats's "Ode to a Nightingale"?

Lewis Thomas suggests the fundamental reality of the humanities as analogous to the genetic residence in our cells occupied by language: "If language is at the core of our social existence, holding us together, housing us in meaning, it may be also safe to say that art and music are functions of the same universal, genetically determined mechanism" (*The Lives of a Cell: Notes of a Biology Watcher*). How much more basic to life can the humanities get than *that*?

To regard the sciences and math as the sole or primary substance of education is to manifest a standard of learning that not only impoverishes both school and general public education but minimizes and even obliterates the moral and esthetic imagination. To be deficient in moral and esthetic imagination is to be seriously deficient in our humanity. This deficiency makes individuals vulnerable to the forces in post-industrial, time-stressed mass societies that engender mechanization, psychic and social uniformity and self-alienation. The quantification of experience and societal repressiveness are more readily resisted by the individuating vitality and revolution in sensibility offered by the arts.

Lastly, let a mathematician have his say: "Art heightens the sense of humanity. It gives an elation to feeling which is supernatural. A million sunsets will not spur on men towards civilization. It requires Art to evoke into consciousness the finite perfections which lie ready for human achievement" (Alfred North Whitehead, *Adventure of Ideas*). We need these "finite perfections" of the humanities as much as anything else as we attempt to absorb and confront the 21st century in the most crucial terms, that is, humanly, humanely, humanistically.

"The Humanities: 'Finite Perfections'" by Donald Gutierrez, 2012.

42
Why Read Good Fiction?

I live in New Mexico, and have two granddaughters who live out in California. So I don't see them often and was wondering recently whether they are getting exposed to good fiction. That consideration led me to think about whether such exposure really made any difference, whether reading Cervantes or the Brontes or Balzac or Dreiser or James or Conrad or Lawrence or Lady Murasaki really mattered, and, if it does, why or how it matters.

Why indeed read Melville, Fielding, Jane Austen, Mark Twain as a youth, let alone as an adult? Does it make one a better person? "Better" of course has a moral ring to it. Art has been viewed by literary theorists and idealists as making one better by organizing one's sensory, emotional and intellectual faculties, thus giving sensible, even at times exalted, shape to life experience. Thus, art could make one a more coherent person.

That might be true, but it sounds overly idealistic. In our contemporary world, so discontinuous, sporadic, aggressive and violent, can fiction really make much difference? Despite war, crime, pollution hazards and critical overpopulation globally, people—even without having read Proust or Faulkner or Ford Madox Ford or Doris Lessing—seem to order their senses and lives not only to survive but to secure some decent measure of stability, pleasure and even joy.

But reading good fiction might add to these positives as well as enrich leisure. As everyone knows, post-industrial societies today are, for a number of reasons, triggered by speed, pressure and stress. Geared to this intense, automated energy are sensationalism in entertainment (increased violence in sports and movies), excessive consumerism, more productivity and high-profit demands, and ingenious progress in high-tech culture. All these developments have a profound impact on human sensibility, and by and large it is not for the good, as it corrodes elements of human nature—such as tranquillity—vital to human culture and even to sanity. Patience is necessary because it helps us to deal with stress but also because it is essential to learning, enjoyment and experience. It is also essential to reading good fiction. Put conversely, reading good fiction develops or *can* develop patience. One might want to know what happens to a character getting entrapped in a perilous situation (job, marriage, foreign country, wilderness), but the very nature of significant fiction virtually enforces our capacity to wait for an event or process in fiction to evolve.

Further, even when we know what will happen to a character (Dreiser's Hurstwood, Hardy's Tess, Flaubert's Madame Bovary), we go back time and again to watch and experience the enchanting intercession of character and fate. This sort of reader tolerance or even engrossment ideally trains one to live life at a slower or more "human" pace. "Haste makes waste" is a profound adage for our hyped-up, time-devouring society, as is "give time time." Reading *Don Quixote, The Tale of Genji, Robinson Crusoe, The Good Soldier, Sons and Lovers* (let alone *Remembrance of Things Past* or *War and Peace*), forces us—better, persuades, entices us—to accept a great novelist's rendering of life rhythms, and though this is "art" and thus in a sense artificial, if it is great or even good art it is also *truer* than life.

The life rhythms found in good fiction could teach us something about the rhythms and patterns we might try to evolve around our own life and the social interaction surrounding it, whether we're talking about the pacing of a conversation with a friend, buying a home or car, or dealing with the workload on a job. Patience has lot to do with time and one's sense—and one's society's sense—of time. Though reading Thomas Mann or Balzac or George Eliot might *not* grace us with recognizing the eternal within the moment, it just *might* do so—at least, while we're reading—and perhaps beyond the reading!

Interpreting life, the world and experience through fiction—surely this can be dangerously distorting. Life is not like *that*, we sometimes hear, usually from people with a naive sense of the reality fiction exhibits, or of how it exhibits reality. Of course fiction is usually more ordered than life, more patterned and selective. Yet to say that life's raggedness and disorder disprove the availability, even ideal, of fiction as an example of what life is and can be is like saying that virtue is impractical because there's so much evil in the world. One pursues one's insights into the boundaries of the possible, into instances of the desirable and wonderful, the repulsive and horrible, where one can. If fiction offers such instances, and does so compellingly, evocatively, numinously, one does well to go with it.

Just as important, fiction familiarizes us with the World, the Flesh and the Devil. We learn not only what the world has been like, or could have been like, but what it is or could be in the present or the future. Granted, what we experience on the written page and in the "actual" situation are not the same, but we also know by now that reality is sinuous, ambiguous, often enough even seemingly *unreal* so that our imagining of a place or situation can feel *really* real or more real than being there in the flesh, and thus what is actual or authentic becomes problematic.

Fiction can create or shape reality, rather than only entertainingly reflect it, and thus affect the kind of impact readers have on their surroundings. "Poetry makes nothing happen," said W.H. Auden in a famous poem, but the word "happen" is ambiguous. It might not affect overtly a corporation's ethics or a nation's decision to go to war, yet who is to say whether it might not affect some individual's outlook or mental fiber—an individual who someday in a position of power might cast a determinative vote or exert key influence for something humane, decent, sane on a crucial occasion? It is hardly arresting to say that great fiction is more real than ordinary life, but it might be worth observing that either fiction or life experience is as real as the person involved in them.

Another important aspect of reading *good* fiction is that it can subtilize our mind (I stress *good* because cheap fiction can do the opposite—coarsen thought or feeling). The great and good novelists do instruct us—if usually indirectly—how to perceive and evaluate life in the round. I don't mean by this that one learns only from novels dealing in depth with characters (that would, for example, leave out much of Dickens). I do mean that Stendahl's *The Red and the Black* or Mann's *Dr. Faustus* or Ralph Ellison's *Invisible Man* offer us Life, the World, Places, People, Society High and Low and the labyrinths of interior experience with such fullness or vigor or color or penetration or completeness or deliberate, haunting incompleteness that we as a result assimilate, willy-nilly, substantial portions of life's options, variations, potentialities, dangers and blessings.

As the British man-of-letters Cyril Connolly once put it about literature generally, what does literature do best and uniquely? I think it is this: More than any other art, it incites or encourages us to help make a world or segments of a world in our own mind. The reader obviously does not write the fiction but his involvement in it is critical to its imaginative potential being realized. All the arts stimulate the imagination one way or another, but none elaborates places, crowds, scenes, individuals, and the senses and the mind through the brick-by-brick use of language that fiction exhibits, erecting realms of thought, feeling, site and action through the great needle's eye of words, words, words. What could be less stimulating to the senses than words (compared to painting, sculpture, music), yet what medium in skilled hands can be more dynamic than the all-absorbing "second" worlds of literature, which can seem and be more real than the "first" world?

And if fiction can create other people, settings, patterns of events than those in our daily world, it can also exhibit more desirable or terrible worlds. The terrible ones are not quite so terrible because we can put them away any time we feel like it, yet we can be second-remove witnesses of terror and horror that it would be unbearable to experience ourselves (although, at its worst, this becomes voyeuristic involvement in sensationalism). *1984* warned us before then of itself, and educated the world about the perils of totally socializing human communities. It did not prevent Rwanda or Pol Pot's Cambodia or America's Middle-East-detainee torture practices, but Orwell's novel emerged from a pattern of political, institutional traditions and experience foreign to these more recent social catastrophes. *1984* could not have terminated the governments of the Soviet Union, Mao's China or any other totalitarian society. Fiction seldom has that sort of direct force or effect and should not be expected to (though Flaubert once said that if enough people had read his novel *Sentimental Education*, the Franco-Prussian War would not have occurred). Yet fiction does work on individuals in a way that could have political consequences, quietly, subtly, yet accumulatively, issuing in political act, movement, change.

The terrifying world of fiction, then, can also be a desirable one not only because we can escape from it, but because of our own surreptitious engrossment by it. We might be grieved by Pip's illusions or torments in *Great Expectations*, but we also "enjoy" them—not out of sadistic response, but because the sophisticated attitudes one can bring to or develop from reading good fiction stimulate this complex indirection in our reading.

Fiction of course is just that—it is something that is and isn't happening. It isn't really happening because it *is* fictional, made up, artificial. But it *is* happening, because of the craft, the inspirited imagination and the empowered sense of reality with which it is conceived. This "doubleness" of fiction comprises no little of its Utopist character. Ultimately fiction *is* a kind of Utopia (or, as in Margaret Atwood's novel *The Handmaid's Tale*, a dystopia), offering attractive or horrible alternatives to ours, the latter itself even attractive exactly because it is *not* ours—or not *yet*, which could put us on guard. Yet fiction offers the ideal and safe opportunity for appreciating what we have or trying to make it better, to make of life a "work" analogous to fictional art. One could do much worse than educate oneself on good fiction. It might not explain how to work a computer or do a valve job on a car engine or make money (or it *might*), but in one way or another it shows—more than tells—how to *live* (and not live), and that is enough.

"Why Read Good Fiction?" by Donald Gutierrez—*Humanist Society of New Mexico*, February 2010.

"The Man He Killed"
by Thomas Hardy

Had he and I but met
By some old ancient inn
We should have sat us down to wet
Right many a nipperkin!

But ranged as infantry
And staring face to face
I shot at him as he at me,
And killed him in his place.

I shot him dead—because—
Because he was my foe
Just so: my foe of course he was;
That's clear enough; although

He thought he'd list, perhaps
Off-hand like—just as I—
Was out of work—had sold his traps—
No other reason why.

Yes! Quaint and curious war is!
You shoot a fellow down
You'd treat if met where any bar is
Or help to half a crown.

43
Spirit Versus Spirit:
Meditation on a War Poem by Thomas Hardy

Thinking about Hardy's poem, "The Man He Killed," published in 1902 around the time of the Boer War, might make us begin to ask where one's most fundamental loyalties or values reside. We at first take it (and leave it) as facile anti-war verse: all men are brothers; given the proper chance enemy soldiers could be friends. Had they met near a tavern in time of peace, they would have treated each other to a bottle of ale, perhaps even sung a song or two together. But at war, they would kill each other without hesitation.

Tim O'Brien's *If I Die in a Combat Zone*, a book about the Vietnam War and his army experiences, indicates why the will to kill would be automatic:

> [Drill Sergeant] Blyton.... gives us our lesson in the bayonet. Left elbow locked, left hand on wood just below weapon's sights... lunge with left leg, slice up with the steel. Again and again we thrust into mid-air imagined bellies, sometimes towards throats. "Dinks are little shits," Blyton yells out. "If you want their guts, you gotta go low. Crouch and dig.... Soldiers! Tell me! What is the spirit of the bayonet?" He screams the question.... "Drill Sergeant—the spirit of the bayonet is to kill! To kill!" (51)

Aside from the gross racism in this passage, there is a suggestive unifying of two symbolic entities usually considered the very opposite: spirit and (versus) bayonet. A bayonet has a "spirit" by its capacity to kill the enemy (friend) by a savage, quick, eviscerating twist. This bayoneting (or shooting) of a man who could be a friend in peacetime suggests that in some crucial respects war is basically insane, at least from the standpoint of an individualistic ethic.

Hardy's soldier says this foe/friend contradiction is "quaint and curious," but the excessive mildness of these terms, considering the context of the poem, delivers an irony of harsh understatement. The collectivist war values are deemed by society (but especially by its leaders) to be not only dominant but exclusive in time of war. Yet, Hardy's poem suggests a significant space for an individuated response possibly sharply opposed to war and to social conformity in regard to a war.

The leaders who start and administer wars try to develop a moral, political or emotional rationale for starting, continuing or finishing the war (Saving the World for Democracy, Preventing the Spread of Communism, Halting Saddam's—or Iran's—Tyranny and Nuclear Potential, but often these rationales—or rationalizations—are meant more for the folks at home than for the troops. Before long the latter come to realize that the only meaningful goal of the war is to end it or at least to not get killed or mutilated. When the realization develops that some soldiers are intended by their commanding officers to be sacrificed to gain some distant strategic or even tactical objective, i. e., that they are regarded as cannon fodder, the war outlook of combat soldiers readily becomes cynical if not nihilistic.

The troops also come to realize something else—often unavoidably: "In the Second World War the American military learned…that men will inevitably go mad in battle and that no appeal to patriotism, manliness or loyalty to the group will ultimately matter" (Paul Fussell, *Wartime*, 282). The high PTSD rate—and often grim consequences in civilian life—of American servicemen and veterans since the Vietnam War and through the Iraq and the Afghanistan wars provides further evidence of Fussell's alarming claim.

One reason why the enemy/friend in Hardy's poem is part enemy is that the poem's speaker in real life often has another friend not alluded to in the poem—his combat buddy. One doesn't have to be an expert on combat motivation to know that intense camaraderie is the prime binding element in a basic fighting unit; the squad is a soldier's immediate "family." With its support and loyalty, or lack thereof, during combat, the soldier likely either lives or dies. When one's unit buddy is killed or horribly wounded, a part of one's self is maimed.

The consequent rage towards the enemy responsible (whether literally or symbolically) is massive. One remembers all too many scenes from the Vietnam War in TV coverage, movies like "Platoon" or books: Vietnamese villagers of all ages being dragged out of their huts by their hair or feet, their heads bashed in by weeping, riflebutting American soldiers, their homes—mere huts—totally destroyed.

Hardy's poem effectively simplifies the situation by omitting the squad buddy, or by turning him into the "foe" and then changing him back again into the buddy. The key difference is that this buddy is also the enemy (though of course men in the same squad sometimes become enemies too, and officers considered incompetent pose dangers to survival). The violent wrenching of reality embodied by the image of one's deadly war enemy also potentially being one's good friend should seriously diminish the grounds on which war is justified. That it does not evidences the authoritarian power possessed by a monarchy, a plutocracy, the patriarchy, a tyrannical regime or an oligarchy posing as a representative democracy (as in America) to wheedle or bully its populace into accepting a basically unnecessary or even thoroughly immoral war. A closer look at "The Man He Killed" reveals a sly sophistication in a poet whom some socially conservative American literary critics, such as the academic "New Critics," once considered little better than a "rural" (i. e., simple-minded) poet.

The poem is narrated in the first person by the British (and Everyman) soldier himself. Hardy uses this dramatic point-of-view technique to allow us to see the soldier groping his way from darkness to light, the gray light produced by a grim realization surrounded by irony. The entire poem is a retrospection. The soldier has already thought out the "curious" war situation in interpersonal terms and almost resolves it in the final stanza.

Right off the bat Hardy's soldier says that he and his war foe might have liked each other in peaceful circumstances. Meeting in a tavern, they would have had "right many a nipperkin" (or half-pint of ale), but in the context of war, positioned in opposite trenches, they would—and did—shoot at each other. They also would have known what the spirit of the bayonet is: each, come trench warfare, would have unhesitatingly tried to disembowel the other.

The poem's speaker is quicker, and lives, and then lives to come to terms with his act of—of what? Defending his country? Defending British imperialism? Saving his own life? Murdering with the approval of the State?

"I killed him because," (hesitation, looking for justification), because he was the Enemy. Then doubts arise. The foe, now becoming the "foe," probably enlisted out of a whim ("Offhand like") because, "just as I," he was unemployed and at loose ends.

The society that both soldiers fight and risk their lives for did not provide them work. Thus, one often is economically (if not legally) forced to risk possibly making the "ultimate sacrifice"—as writers like Ford Madox Ford, Robert Graves and George Orwell bitterly pointed out long ago—while some civilians were profiting off the war. (Recent examples might be former Vice President Dick Cheney, Wall Street, General Electric and other CEOs.) One is reminded of fantasies front-line soldiers had of turning their weapons on the civilians at home and particularly on those who had initiated and profited from the war and sent them into it. Put another way, war has been described as a revenge of old men against young men. Turned around, son/soldiers could feel deadly revenge towards the symbolic fathers who, safe at home and likely prospering, concocted the war.

The fourth stanza of Hardy's poem is electrifying when its deeper meaning surfaces. The "foe" probably enlisted because he was out of work, as perhaps did Hardy's soldier ("No other reason why"). Enemy stereotyping—the savage Boers or Huns—doesn't figure in the combat motivation at this stage. Hardy's possibly unemployed soldier had no other reason to enlist. The state's war slogans had apparently not impressed him. He joined the army because survival requires food and shelter. War breaks out, he's caught in it, and, thanks to the Sergeant Blytons of the world, his killing or survival instincts are better than his "foe's" (now his foe, again). Thus, he kills (murders?) the man he would treat like a brother had they met under friendlier circumstances.

Hardy, or his soldier-narrator, actually ignores the physical horror of war, in part because he is concerned with the psychological horror of its simple yet profound irony. Chances are good, especially during World War I, that the two foes could have ended up in hand-to-hand combat, each trying to kill the other in the most efficient way possible. In these dire situations the most efficient means would perhaps be the most brutal. Bayoneting through the throat, belly or groin seems more likely than a surgical stab or gun shot through the heart.

Fussell is disturbingly informative on the surreal, demonic nature of combat injury:

> What annoyed the troops....[about the public] was its
> innocence about the bizarre damage suffered by the human
> body in modern war. The troops could not contemplate without
> anger the lack of public knowledge of the Graves Registration
> Corps with its space for indicating "Members Missing." You
> would expect front line soldiers to be struck and hurt by
> bullets and shell fragments, but such is the popular insulation
> from the facts that you would not expect them to be hurt,
> sometimes killed by being struck by parts of their friends'
> bodies violently detached. If you asked a wounded soldier or
> marine what hit him, you'd hardly be ready for the answer. My
> buddy's head, or his sergeant's heel or his hand, or a Japanese
> leg, complete with shoe and puttees. (270)

The usually suppressed reality in this quotation leads to Fussell's
sinister generalization later, in a chapter correctly entitled "The Real War
Will Never Get into the Books":

> In war it is not just the weak soldiers, or the sensitive ones,
> or the highly imaginative or cowardly ones who will break
> down. Inevitably all will break down if in combat long enough.
> "Long enough" is now defined as between 200 and 240 days.
> As medical observers have reported, there is no such thing as
> getting used to combat.... Each moment of combat imposes a
> strain so great that men will break down in direct relation to
> the intensity and duration of their experience. Thus—and this
> is unequivocal—psychiatric casualties are as inevitable as
> gunshot and shrapnel wounds in war. (281)

I present this reality-of-war dimension first to underline the overt
irony in Hardy's poem. The man who he would buy drinks for, perhaps
become good friends with in peacetime, would in war embody the foe he
would do anything to destroy in the rage and terror of combat. Hardy's
soldier kills his foe/friend ultimately at the dictate of the State. Hardy's
poem doesn't include societal coercion—the Draft—but it is part of the
scenario implied by the poem. Although Hardy's soldier enlisted, sooner or
later he would have otherwise been drafted. Being a lower-class out-of-work
person suggests that the narrator is a marginal figure economically forced
into enlisting. Further, the foe/friend relationship of Hardy's speaker and his
enemy suggests a friend/foe relationship between a soldier and his own

society, particularly the power centers of that society or what libertarian-anarchist social theorists from Peter Kropotkin to Kirkpatrick Sale have called "the state." As the French-Jewish writer Simone Weil once pointed out, an enlisted man's real enemy could well be his own officers and the authorities empowering both that military hierarchy (the Pentagon and the White House, say) and the war itself.

Thus, the military is ideal for a society that has no place in civilian life for such people as Hardy's soldiers. That the rulers of Edwardian England, the era in which the poem was published, had their own geopolitical and egotistic reasons for wanting to engage in war is suggestive about the possible fate of unemployed classes and races in our time and nation. The reader of "The Man He Killed" possibly knows, as Hardy did, that there was a British Empire out there, and that it had to be defended from those savage imperialist Dutch (or, twelve years later, Germans)—or, many generations later, Middle Eastern "insurgent" Muslims.

Hardy's soldier might not realize why his society wants a war and wants him in it, but he does sense the vivid and profound irony of having to kill his foe/friend; it's "quaint and curious." Though the poem's understatement is strong, is it strong or suggestive enough to lead this soldier to the "separate peace" of Frederic Henry in Ernest Hemingway's *A Farewell to Arms*? Perhaps not. But the irony might cause the reader to wonder, should another war come and he or she (and "she" is now definitely all the way in it, including combat) enlists or is drafted, whether she or he will obey the spirit of the Bayonet. Or will she or he obey another spirit—the spirit of peace, compassion and resistance to the state's lust for wars—that directs one either to go underground or to go to jail as a Conscientious Objector. That latter spirit might suggest pulling down the criminal leaders—the high-placed political chiefs, the military brass, the corporation war-profiteers who start or want wars in the first place. For be sure of it: There will be more wars, and they will be justified by slick lies concocted by the state and sent out by the "embedded" and corporatized media, forcing us or our children or theirs to choose between the two Spirits.

"Spirit Versus Spirit: Meditation on a War Poem by Thomas Hardy" by Donald Gutierrez—*Common Sense*, October 1997; *Humanist Society of New Mexico*, May 2010; *The Mustang*, v. 103, Issue 16, July 1997.

44
Maker/Worker/Profit-Maker:
B. Traven's "Assembly Line"

Creativity is one of the basic needs and satisfactions of a good life. The ancient Greek word for poet was "poietes" or maker. In a sense, then, almost every human being is a potential artist, one who can make something beautiful or do something well, or make "beauty" by giving meaning or value to some aspect of his or her life.

The nature of modern industrial technology—its modes of operation, organization and distribution—has made creativity through wage work difficult if not impossible. Although modern industrialists can produce goods in huge quantities and at low prices, both product and producer-worker suffer. The product suffers because much of the mass of goods turned out is superfluous and inferior in quality; factory workers suffer because industrial societies have traditionally dehumanized them by assigning piece work, which is only a small part of a creative process. Factory workers do not have the overview of "their" work that a "maker" would have. As a result, they are deprived of meaning and, thus, of beauty in a basic life experience.

A vivid example of how the quality of our work determines the quality of our lives can be found in a short story entitled "Assembly Line" by B. Traven, author of *The Treasure of the Sierra Madre* and the less known but stunning novel *The Death Ship*. Traven skillfully compares the life of a small village in Mexico to the metropolitan pressures of New York City, and dramatizes two opposed ideas about the value and purpose of work.

"Assembly Line" revolves around a discussion between an American businessman named Winthrop and a Mexican-Indian basket maker concerning the possibility of mass production of the latter's baskets. It is an allegory of the Capitalist and the Artist, of mass man versus primitive individualist, of city versus village culture.

Winthrop, aware of the beauty of the baskets, and hearing how cheaply they are sold by the Indian (fifty centavos, or four cents each), realizes that he has chanced upon a potential gold mine. Described by the narrator as a "dynamic promoter," Winthrop pretends that the baskets have "no real use whatever." However, he soon returns to New York where he bargains with a candy merchant about creating a massive marketing plan for the baskets.

Thus, the Indian appears to get enmeshed in an extensive economic scheme, in which, as manufacturer (or, more accurately, wage-laborer), he would be the production part of a marketing system. Winthrop and the candy merchant would be profiteering middleman and retailer respectively. (It is virtually taken for granted that the fourth and most important constituent of this scheme, the consumer, would be overcharged for the finished product.) There is no question about who would do most of the work on this "assembly line": "Each basket cost him [the Indian] between 20 and 30 hours of constant work, not counting the time spent gathering bast and fibers, preparing them, making dyes and coloring the bast."

The uniquely creative aspect of the Indian's work emerges early in the story:

> It was clearly seen from the small baskets he made that at heart he was an artist. Each basket looked as if covered all over with the most beautiful sometimes fantastic ornaments, flowers, butterflies, birds, antelopes, tigers, and a score of other animals of the wild. Yet, the most amazing thing was that these decorations, all of them symphonies of color, were not painted on the baskets but were instead actually part of the baskets themselves.

The fact that the Indian actually finds his materials in his natural environment and transforms them into works of art radically distinguishes his work from that of many working people in a commercialized industrial society. Despite making hundreds of baskets during his life, no two of them are alike in design. The satisfaction arising from the creation of beautiful objects is deep and lasting enough to make the poverty and hardship of his daily life bearable.

Winthrop tells the Indian to calculate a mass-production rate for baskets according to this formula: (a) 100 baskets at fifty centavos, (b) 1,000 baskets at...? By capitalist standards everyone, including Winthrop, expects a lower rate per basket because of the higher quantity of the sale. Producing a large number of commodities usually lowers the cost per item—but also it often leads to a reduction of their quality and of the worker's creative involvement in the work.

The Indian, however, arrives at a very different formula. For him, the more baskets he makes, the more expensive each one is. The increasing value of each succeeding basket is a measure of his increasing artistic skill; further, it recognizes the increased difficulty of producing more and more, but still esthetically successful, artwork. The artist's formula, then, controverts the capitalist's: one recognizes the value of individual expression, while the other recognizes the value of mass consumption.

In response to the Indian's formula, Winthrop suggests that because gathering materials for a basket takes so much time, the Indian either persuade his village relatives to cultivate his field for the corn and beans essential to his survival, or even to help gather materials for the baskets and help make them. The Indian responds with a shrewd question: if his "relatives" help him in mass-producing baskets, who would tend *their* fields and cattle? Untended, the price of staples like corn and beans would rise so high that no one in the community could afford them, and all would starve. Even the price of baskets, concludes the Indian, would have to go up.

What Traven describes is a cooperative agrarian society which manages to survive by not practicing the extreme division and specialization of labor associated with industrial mass societies. It ekes out a living, creating just enough flexibility to permit one of its members to make works of art, though with no profits for the artist and at great cost of time and effort to him. Although Traven's village is no artist's paradise, following Winthrop's scheme for increased output would not only separate the artist from his art (transforming art-baskets into commodities), but also destroy the whole structure of a simple, cohesive society.

Thus, two types of societies are opposed: one is devoted to creative work, and one is devoted to making a lot of money. The first makes work meaningful and society beautiful, and the second creates unlimited goods for potentially high profits (too often hoarded by a few), but at the cost of making work meaningless and destroying humane values. People existing in a Winthrop society learn to endure their senseless work, and the discontent that arises from it, by accepting the idea/value of the production and purchasing of more and more goods.

In the end, the Indian tells Winthrop why his plan would not work:

> I've got to make these canastitas [his baskets] my own way and with my song in them and with bits of my soul woven into them. If I were to make them in great numbers there would no longer be my soul in each. Each would look like the other with no difference whatever and such a thing would slowly eat up my soul. Each has to be another song which I hear in the morning when the sun rises and when the birds begin to chirp and the butterflies come and sit down on my baskets so that I may see a new beauty.

A potential victim of universal human greed, Traven's Indian survives and continues to enjoy a creative fulfillment. Such an end must be possible and more widely available if modern society is to become fully human and beautiful.

"Maker/Worker/Profit-Maker: B. Traven's 'Assembly Line'" by Donald Gutierrez —*Common Sense*, May 1998; *The Horsefly*, April 18, 2000; *Desert Exposure*, September 1999.

45
Competition, Cooperation and "Us" Versus "Them"

Many Americans are conditioned through their upbringing, their institutions and the mass media to think that free enterprise embodies America's greatness. And, it follows, what makes free enterprise great is competition and the profit system. Now I wish to propose something contrary: that de-emphasizing the competitive principle and stimulating the principle of cooperation might make America a more just, equitable and happy society. One can already hear the uproar on that one, "No competition? Why, it's the life blood of Capitalism, the motor of business dynamics! It sharpens the edge, embodies and ignites Purpose! And think of competitive sports and all the excitement they bring to millions!" (not to mention the millions they bring to a very few).

There is some truth in these outcries. Competition can make blood run faster, put a fire under the rockets of aspiration. Sports can create enormous excitement, expectation, joy—as well as misery, gambling losses and depression. But one should not forget that competition also means winning at someone else's (or group's or nation's) expense, which more often than we like to think is not such a good thing. There are instances in commercial sports in which both teams compete so magnificently that the announcers justly claim that it's a shame one of the teams has to lose. One can extend that situation well beyond the sports arena. It is sometimes bad—even tragic—when one side has to lose disastrously, whether it is a business, a country at war or a competitor in a contest. The problem is that competition can stimulate a savagery towards others that seriously discredits it as an ideal.

Worse, in the business world it can lead (and has led) to its own dissolution in the form of monopolization. When one company or corporation corners the market or forms a ring of companies to control the market, this negates the very customer choice and selectivity that competition is supposed to offer. In spite of anti-trust laws, this sort of heavy-handed anti-competitive ruthlessness has figured as a recurrent feature of American high-stakes capitalism ever since the 1860s. According to Ferdinand Lundberg's *The Rich and the Super-Rich*, these virtually criminal activities, seldom punished legally, do no good for any community other than the business community. Rather, they seem to spring from the dynamics of competition running its natural course, which stresses not only beating the competitors but dominating if not destroying them.

Furthermore, competition can result in the basic and often deeply dehumanizing divisiveness in human culture and social experience of Us-versus-Them. Although fun and not entirely harmful in sports, competition is often negative, hostile and even belligerent in many other areas of society, setting up "enemy" camps based on international politics (France vs. England, America vs. Russia, Rome vs. Carthage), race or racism, gender, class, religions (Muslims vs. Christians) and so on.

Granted, there is a deep-rooted, tribal gratification many of us feel in siding with one person or group against another, even though another part of us at times senses something ill-balanced or even corrupt about this all-too-human activity. It can come as a shock to discover, under the pressure of special circumstances, that some species of Them are not only human, but likable—even lovable, as Romeo and Juliet knew all too well. Such a shock might occur when we have an exchange of touch with one of Them, and feel the same warmth of blood flow in their fingers that we experience with one of Us. How disturbing and revealing that sensation can be. Indeed, it leads to a potentially revolutionary insight in Thomas Moore's lovely book *Soulmates* (1994): "Wherever we leave the realm of soul, where opposites melt into each other, the divisions tend to appear, often in the form of power and control."

"The realm of soul, where opposites melt into each other" is, I contend, the realm of cooperation where there is little Us-versus-Them. There we are mostly so Us that the fundamental alienation loses much of its force. Of course, as human beings we will probably always feel some orientation towards For and Against; however, these orientations can be modified, humanized, civilized. A competitive society might lose some fire and excitement by restraining the competitive impulse in its institutions or public entertainment, but much would be gained by diminishing the "Them" distinction in society and in our minds. For instance, there could be a reduction of wars and genocide and less racial or gender prejudice, class or national division, less alienation from work, and less friction between colleagues, between workers, between employee and employer.

A beautiful thing about people helping one another in the fundamental—and even minor—needs and activities of life and society is the deep and sometimes enduring glow of satisfaction it gives us. More important, cooperative enterprises can lead to a habit and even to an institutionalization of helping each other. Interdependence then takes on a strong affirmative cast rather than seeming—incorrectly—like a lack of "rugged individualism." Granted, it can be exhilarating when one's teammates or family members or work companions win in some activity or situation, but, as this remains cooperation within a competitive context, it is exhilaration at someone else's expense. On the other hand, a successful marriage or string quartet or community self-help project possesses little or no competitive dimension and, thus, probably no losers. Virtually everyone wins, although "winning," given the nature of the cooperative experience, becomes a meaningless idea. Perhaps it is best put in Moore's diction: The group has achieved soul; it has made a great moment, attained a breakthrough into significant relating.

One major way to de-emphasize the competitive drive is to stop glorifying the profit motive. Attend to its tight grip on one notorious fellow:

> Good morning to the day; and next my gold!
> Open the shrine that I may see my saint.
> [Mosca opens the curtain, revealing Volpone's treasure].
> Hail the world's soul, and mine!
> (Ben Jonson, *Volpone* I, i)[1]

The promoters of the profit motive urge that society, and especially the world of commerce, cannot function efficiently or inspirationally without it; they claim it brings out the best in people. But look at what it did to Jonson's Renaissance "Venetian"/Englishman/Everyman Capitalist. "Gold" enslaved him; it became his saint and he saw it all too correctly as the "world's soul." *Soul!* Money can mean bread, provide the staff of life, but something has gone dangerously awry when it is regarded as sacred. One is outraged at the convicted felon-financier Ivan Boesky's motto "Greed is Good" because, aside from the radical perversion suggested by that sentiment, it also sounds close to "Greed is God." That is Volpone's fix and the virtual motto of corporate Capitalism.

> Yet I glory
> More in the cunning purchase of my wealth
> Than in the glad possession...
> (*Volpone* I, i)

This sentiment is more sinister than Volpone idolizing wealth, because it suggests a kind of utter moral recklessness of financial accumulation. It justifies "the more gained the better," especially if it is done dishonestly ("cunning purchase"), through delusion, deceit, bribery, perhaps even coercion—whatever it takes. The thrill of acquiring more money has recently been medically claimed to affect the same area of the brain that is stimulated by cocaine—the more one gets of either, the more one wants, and the more one wants to get it by "cunning purchase."[2] There are too many Volpones around. Goldman Sachs's CEO Lloyd Blankfein and Citigroup's Sanford Weill come to mind, and do so in no small measure because capitalism tends to incite an accumulative, endless profit-seeking lust (perhaps analogous to Stalin's or Mao's totalitarianism inciting a lust for endless political power).

The serious problem about the ideal and pursuit of the profit motive, especially in the concentrated form of the large corporation, is that there is something uncontrollable about it. Sooner or later it smashes through everything—ethical limits, environmental health, worker safety and employment, community responsibility and, ultimately, life and the earth itself. Greed and ruthlessness are certainly major forces in propelling the profit motive far beyond the boundaries of societal coherence and health, let alone basic decency.

Perhaps greed is also aroused by accepting uncritically the dangerous aspect of the American Dream that anyone can become a millionaire if she or he tries hard or unscrupulously enough. Not only is this ideal an illusion, it is also an unworthy, vulgar and extraordinarily self-indulgent goal. People should consider finding something more noble or creative or humane or magnanimous to do with their life energies than striving to "make a mint," "make a killing," (who's getting "killed"? perhaps millions of people losing their jobs and homes) or identifying one's personhood with the six or seven digits in one's annual salary.

Whatever the motivation for unrestrained profit-making, a point comes when the lust for profits and the well-being of a society forcefully move in opposite directions. The most recent and sensational example of this is the ongoing corporate lay-offs of many thousands of employees while simultaneously paying top executives six- to seven-digit bonuses. The options alone would appreciate to sums far surpassing the outrageous salary raises should these CEOs and their officers bring in profits for the stockholders and, particularly, the tiny controlling minority among the latter. A forgotten and more concentrated example of big corporation brutality was General Motors' destruction in the early 1980s of Detroit's Poletown, a community formerly inhabited mainly by thousands of poor people. In its place was built the Roger Smith GM headquarters, its construction costs coming largely out of city taxes.

But the profit motive problem is far more systemic than CEO Roger Smith's despicable callousness towards a neighborhood of defenseless individuals. The dynamic of the profit motive is not just to make enough to live comfortably (though "comfortably" is, of course, relative). The primal thrust of the profit motive is to make money so as to make more money and to acquire power so as to acquire more power. Money and power in this context become fused absolutes. The danger to society of economic absolutes not countered by any socially protective dimension (such as the pro-regulation Glass-Steagall Act of 1933), is that, unappeasable, they destroy the crucial social and psychological fabric of human interdependence and compassion. Absolutes, whether economic, political or religious, leave little or no room for change, creativity, limits, the needs of others and the intimate climates of the soul.

The profit motive is inherently corrupt, even if it doesn't corrupt everyone who engages it. And if those corrupted are the big "wheelers-and-dealers," then the impact on society is all the more pernicious and profound. Sixteen centuries ago, St. Jerome said, "All riches come from iniquity and unless one has lost, another cannot gain" (*Letter to Chromatius*). He continued even more severely: "Opulence is always the result of theft. If not committed by the actual possessor then by his predecessor." So much for the unquestioned legitimacy of inheritance here in Christian America, upon which so many huge American fortunes have been founded—estate taxes notwithstanding—and vastly enlarged.

In view of the immense mergings and consolidations going on in the business and financial worlds today in order to accumulate more profit, influence and power, it is clear that financial concentration is and will be a major barrier to the values of cooperation, and thus an alienating force in society for some time to come. The profit motive as a form of competition does not produce the healthy, balanced rivalry that is supposedly the healthy lungs of a democratic open society. It leads rather to what Norman Mailer once called commercial totalitarianism. Contrary to the claims that the profit motive improves our standard of living, it actually debases our quality of life through stress, illness, dependence on drugs and liquor, hostility, homicide and, sooner or later, wars.

By opening the social and economic channels of modem society to the energies, inspiration and communal binding of the cooperative principle, competition as expressed by the drive to make a lot of money can be effectively rerouted. Competition may never be eliminated and probably shouldn't be, but there is enormous room yet for cooperation and its powers to rejuvenate and humanize the basic social organization and ideals of our society.

---

1. From the collection *Elizabethan and Stuart Plays*, Baskervill et. al.
2. *Inside Job*, (2010). Documentary film, director Charles Ferguson.

"Competition, Cooperation and 'Us' Versus 'Them'" by Donald Gutierrez—*Desert Exposure*, February 1999.

46
Review: Jack Loeffler
Adventures With Ed: A Portrait of Abbey

Adventures With Ed: A Portrait of Abbey, as its author Jack Loeffler points out, is not a biography of his close friend Edward Abbey, but a "biographical memoir." This is a meaningful distinction because it allows Loeffler more flexibility in relating his impressions and memories of his many years hiking, river-running and sharing ideas and hundreds of campfires with the famous, controversial author and eco-activist. Loeffler's title is suggestive because, as he frequently shows, being Abbey's best friend was an adventure in more ways than one. It could lead to extraordinary travel and hiking experiences; vivid exchanges while driving, hiking or camping; sharing of ideas and emotions (twice leading to fisticuffs); and a horsing-around, "Old Buddy," beer-drinking camaraderie that appears to have been inspiriting and sometimes hilarious to both men but can occasionally make for tedious reading.

 Adventures is divided into two parts. The first, more biographical than the second, ends in 1970. The second part, comprising almost two-thirds of the book, covers the period from 1970 to Abbey's death in 1989. It includes large sections describing the trips to areas like Comb Ridge, Utah, Big Bend National Park, Texas, Sonoran Desert in Mexico, hikes and exchanges of ideas between Abbey and Loeffler, as well as important quotes from Abbey's journals, lectures and work. The date 1970 marks both the death from leukemia of Abbey's third wife, Judy Pepper, and Abbey's intense awareness of the death threat to wilderness areas. Loeffler aptly describes the building and presence of the Glen Canyon Dam in Utah as the "symbol of the prevailing cultural paradigm of turning habitat into money" (105). The dam created Lake Powell and destroyed, through flooding, what Abbey and others regarded as one of the most beautiful stretches of wilderness in the world.

Adventures brings Abbey fully alive as an individual, an iconoclastic thinker and prankster, and a key inspirer to environmental activism. One shortcoming in *Adventures*, however, is an insufficiently critical attitude towards its subject. Though Loeffler frequently mentions Abbey's rampant promiscuity and even quotes Abbey's own despairing sense of and puzzlement by it, he doesn't analyze or censure it. Probably the memoir character of the book and the author's relation to Abbey are factors here—one doesn't want to belabor in print the flaws of one's best friend. (Loeffler does mention Abbey's habit of throwing empty beer bottles out on highways while driving—this by an environmentalist.) Abbey himself admits that, though he hates cruelty, he was cruel to his wives. The reader naturally would like to hear more about that, not out of morbid curiosity but out of interest in this character flaw in a man whose life energy was devoted to valiantly fighting against extreme government and corporation cruelty to the natural environment.

Abbey's attitude towards illegal immigrations (especially Mexican) has created controversy. Loeffler claims several times that Abbey was not a racist, citing, for example, Abbey's support of the compassionate Tucson Sanctuary Movement and his having Mexican friends. Abbey doesn't strike me as a racist either, but he sounds like one in his essay "Immigration and Liberal Taboos" (in *One Life at a Time, Please*, 1988) where he remarks that (apparently) Mexicans are a "morally-genetically impoverished people" (43). One of the engaging qualities about *Adventures* is the way Loeffler frequently stands up to Abbey, reminding the latter when he complains about the alleged welfare "freeloading" of minorities that Abbey is buying beer with *his* welfare checks.

Nevertheless, Abbey's general outspokenness was part and parcel of his strength and character. It was not only his speaking his mind that was (and is) important but his speaking out in ways that were invaluably audacious and liberating to others. Loeffler does indicate several times Abbey's justly grave concern about the world's catastrophically excessive population growth and its relation to the immigration problem in America and to the perilous deterioration of the urban and natural environment. Still, Loeffler could have probed the contentious issue of Abbey's stand on immigration more than he does.

In reading Abbey's books, one encounters a high-spirited, comedic, iconoclastic and morally wrathful mind and personality. This comes across continually and vividly in *Adventures*. As editor of a University of New Mexico student literary magazine, Abbey put the following mot on its masthead: "Man will not be free until the last king is strangled with the entrails of the last priest!—signed, Louisa May Alcott" (36). The quote, actually from Voltaire (as Loeffler indicates), was considered in poor taste by some. Whether in poor taste or a good idea, that stunt was a presage of more to come from libertarian Abbey.

"Alcott's" provocation suggests one of the major elements in *Adventures*, Abbey's anarchism, a position hardly surprising, considering Abbey's fierce sense of independence and his strong attachment to ideals of self-reliance, autonomy and anti-authoritarianism. Early in the book, Loeffler states that Abbey "would come to be regarded by some as the most important anarchist thinker in America during the last half of the twentieth century" (41). Abbey possessed a sophisticated sense and knowledge of anarchism, having written a master's thesis at UNM on the history of 19th century anarchism. Sensibly, he knew that achieving an anarchist society completely would be unlikely, as it "requires that all men and women be utterly responsible in their self direction" (56).

What is outstanding about Abbey's anarchism, as Loeffler underscores, is its originality. Abbey was one of the key minds in 20th century America to integrate traditional anarchist concepts with radical environmentalist activism, or eco-anarchism. As Loeffler puts it, "He [Abbey] was trekking beyond anarchist tradition by perceiving that the land itself was bound by the long arm of centralized government and had therefore lost its freedom to exist as wildlife habitat" (86). Another valuable aspect of Abbey's anarchism and work is his typically American satiric jocularity and his personae of "good-old-boy," curmudgeon and hell-raising desert rat. These are qualities not readily found in the writings or personality of anarchists like William Godwin, Errico Malatesta, Emma Goldman or Sir Herbert Read. They embody a protective toughness against the massive power, humorlessness and violence of his institutional adversaries.

Abbey's eco-anarchism leads to one of the most stunning passage in *Adventures*. Earlier in the book, one reads about a visionary experience Abbey once underwent in Death Valley: "Everything was alive. Even the rocks. I was part of it" (242). This experience culminates intellectually in a lecture he gave at St. Johns College in Santa Fe where he argues that wilderness is "worth saving for its own sake" (127). What comes next is an extraordinary passage of monistic thinking, which follows his persuasive polemic against human overpopulating:

> Rocks have rights.... Is it not possible that rocks, hills and mountains, and the great physical body of the Earth itself may enjoy a sentience, a form of consciousness which we humans cannot perceive only because of the vastly different time scales involved? For example, the mind of a mountain may be as powerful and profound as that of Buddha, Plato, Spinoza, Whitehead and Einstein. Say that a mountain takes 5,000,000 of our human ... years to produce a single thought. But what a grand thought that single thought must be. (127)

This is not lunacy. The idea, better, the *sense* of the earth as a living, sentient being not only goes back to the pre-Socratic Greek philosophers but often resides in the sensibility of poets, artists and creative people generally. D. H. Lawrence, whom Abbey regarded as a "bad" writer (along with Aeschylus, Sophocles, Dante and others), also harbored monistic tendencies in his work, as these necessarily brief quotes from one of his last travel books, *Etruscan Places*, indicates: "The cosmos was alive, like a vast creature. The whole thing breathed and stirred....The cosmos was one.... but it was made up of creatures. And the greatest creature was earth, with its soul of inner fire" (Loeffler, 49).

Lawrence's monistic sense of the earth, though awesomely vitalist, is not blended with a libertarian ethic and polity, as was Abbey's. Abbey had a philosophic, even spiritual, base to his eco-anarchism, which reveals the depth and intensity of his dedication to protecting the earth from corporate and government predators, a position to which Loeffler is also devoted.

Elaborating his ideas on anarchism, Abbey felt that the best way to defend wilderness against corporate rapacity (aided by Washington) was through the keystone anarchist concept of decentralization. As Loeffler puts it: "Decentralization could lead to a more balanced communal way of life with minimal impact on the environment, especially if human populations were gradually reduced through natural attrition to an optimum rather than a maximum level. In this way, human community could evolve socially and economically to accommodate the needs of the land and the larger biotic community" (128).

An ethical concern in anarchist theory is the issue of violence. (Peter Kropotkin, for example, at first supported, then later in life, opposed it). The average person's notion of anarchism is solitary men with heavy black moustaches and large, black hats hurling bombs. If that were an accurate definition, America, England and other powers would be colossal anarchists—moustache or no moustache. Abbey addressed this problem in his master's thesis: "Violence in itself is an evil, granted; but unless one takes up a pacifist position...all those who are concerned with good and evil ...may someday find themselves confronted with that critical situation in which all moral alternatives have been eliminated..." (Loeffler, 57). The alternatives that Abbey offers come down to these: people either offering passive submission or exerting violent response to unquestionable wrong.

Abbey's stand on violence seems not to have changed over the years. In a journal entry written perhaps around the time he wrote *The Monkey Wrench Gang* (1975), he suggested that a time comes when one has to leave the workplace and "meet the enemy face to face" (Loeffler, 175). Abbey apparently did his share of yanking surveyor markers and burning billboards but his closest approximation to the violence labeled by German anarchist Johann Most as the "propaganda of the deed" was writing *Gang*, which the brilliant anarchist literary scholar Kingsley Widmer has called an "intended handbook of troublemaking." Intended or not, that novel certainly helped ignite the radical activism of organizations like Earth First!

Both Abbey and Earth First! felt that violence committed by eco-activists to protect the earth from the developers was ethically justified—so long as no one was injured by it. The real violence, they felt, was committed by the construction of dams like Glen Canyon and by the mega-corporation poisoning and savaging of earth, air and water. This position is hardly outdated, considering the deregulatory policies towards the environment instituted by the administration of George W. Bush and its love affair with the energy and extractive industries.

As for the literary quality of *Gang* itself, Loeffler quotes Abbey as worrying that all his major characters in the novel sound alike, indeed, sound like him (accurate criticism both, surely). But that raises the question of whether fiction is best as fine writing investigating the labyrinths of mind and character or as compelling narrative embodying important social or activist values. The novel can be a magically deep well or an electrifying spark to activism. Would one throw out Upton Sinclair's *The Jungle* because it is not Henry James' *The Golden Bowl* (or vice versa)? Abbey felt the novel should not reflect but reshape reality. Good and bad fiction have been written out of both esthetics.

One of the most moving episodes in *Adventures* concerns Abbey's dying, death and his early attitudes towards dying. Abbey emphatically did not want to die in a hospital assaulted by its barrage of artificial life-sustainers that undercut one's dignity. He wanted instead "A Re-union with the elements of Earth and sky" (76). (There's that Abbey monism again.) Loeffler and Abbey promised each other that whoever died first, the other would assure him an appropriate kind of death. Not only is this promise kept by Loeffler, Abbey's last wife, Clarke, and others, but is done so in a manner faithful to the early commitment of the two close friends. Abbey had fantasized about having a "useful" death, such as taking out Glen Canyon Dam in a boat filled with dynamite. Instead, he was appropriately buried in a desert area in Arizona.

Although Loefflers's book is enriched by photographs spanning Abbey's life and a sizable index, unfortunately it lacks drawings of the jaunts made by Abbey and Loeffler and of Abbey's favorite haunts in Arizona and southern Utah. *Adventures* will not only be of great interest to Abbey fans but provides a generally attractive and intimate introduction to the man and his passions and ideas. At the beginning of *Gang*, Abbey quotes Walt Whitman: "Resist much, Obey little." No one could have urged the acute relevance of that libertarian maxim amid the increasingly authoritarian/plutocratic rule of Washington/Wall Street more forcefully than Edward Abbey. *Adventures* gets that message across effectively.

"Review: Jack Loeffler, *Adventures With Ed: A Portrait of Abbey*" by Donald Gutierrez—*Sun Monthly*, February 2002; *Desert Exposure*, April 2002; *Eldorado Sun*, February 2007.

47

Industrialization, Nature and Human Nature
in the Work of D.H. Lawrence

Few modern novelists have taken the threat of industrialization to human integrity with such passionate seriousness as did D.H. Lawrence. His substantial body of work on this fundamental contemporary issue points up one reason, among many, why Lawrence is one of the great writers of the 20th century.

Lawrence has long been famous as an imaginative writer about instinctual experience and its relation to consciousness, character, and conduct. Only more recently have readers realized that Lawrence is basically a writer obsessed with the nature of being. He regarded sexuality as the key dimension for such a perspective; to him it symbolized deeper strata of human nature that suggested crucial significance about the character and quality of existence. In long and short fiction, essays, poems, and even literary criticism, he probed the interrelatedness of life, love, and death with remarkable force and insight

Lawrence, moreover, broadened his intimate explorations of inner life by relating his fiction to modem industrial culture. His first important novel, *Sons and Lovers* (1913), dramatizes the breakdown of the family in ways that also embody a major symptom of the disintegration of 20th-century industrial societies. As is well known today, in acting out the patterns of dysfunctional families, the young encounter problems with intimate relating that make it difficult to achieve a fulfilling, stable relationship in love and marriage. Himself such a victim, Lawrence barely escaped with his life and gifts from his possessive mother and unjustly hated father, and came away with a messianic drive to save everyone else. "Salvador Mundi" is Lawrence's persona in his greatest novel, *Women in Love* (1920), and though the name is partly derisive in that novel, it indicates aptly that Lawrence felt his role as a literary artist was "savior of the world." Though an outrageous ambition, it was, in a large way, his. And it is crucial for understanding the range of Lawrence's scope as a literary artist that here again "world" means the world of work, of companies and machinery and miners and coal dust and time-clock, not just sex or a social subset or two.

Lawrence's sense of modern crisis was one the era compelled, for the First World War occurred during his young manhood and deeply scarified his sense of reality. In an age prone to mechanizing social experience and thus threatening to deaden much private experience, Lawrence explored (and sometimes preached) the transcendent value of personal, interior reality. However, his attitude toward industrialization was usually negative to the point of anathema.

In two major works from his early middle period, *Twilight in Italy* (1916, later reprinted as *D. H. Lawrence and Italy*) and *Women in Love*, Lawrence reveals the bent of industrial society to mechanize and thus erode the forms of social culture within which, it is implied, significant being coheres:

> It is as if the whole social form were breaking down, and the human element swarmed within the disintegration, like maggots in cheese. The roads, the railways are built, the mines and quarries are excavated, but the whole organism of life ... is slowly crumbling and caving in.... So that it seems as though we should be left at last with a great system of roads and railways and industries, and a world of utter chaos seething upon these fabrications." (*D. H. Lawrence and Italy*)

Lawrence's last words in *Twilight in Italy* (1916), a book as much about the evolution and state of the modern psyche as it is about Italy, lament the industrial rigidification and consequent corruption of early 20th-century sensibility: "In Milan...I saw that here the life was still vivid, here the process of disintegration was vigorous, and centered in a multiplicity of mechanical activities that engage the human mind as well as the body. But always there was the same purpose stinking in it all,...the perfect mechanizing of human life."

Lawrence's work integrates radical criticism of the mechanizing and dehumanizing impact of the modern social order with intense, sensitive, and metaphorical representations of the instinctual life and relations of individuals either doomed by that order or trying to free themselves from it. In a poem from his *Last Poems* (1932) called "What Then Is Evil?" Lawrence relates the industrial mechanization symbolized in the wheel to the mind moving mechanistically in circles:

> When the mind makes a wheel which turns on the hub of the
>   ego
> and the will, the living dynamo, gives the motion and the
>   speed
> and the wheel of the conscious self spins on in absolution,
> ... absolute, absolved from the sun and the earth and the
>   moon,
> absolute consciousness, absolved from strife and kisses
> absolute self awareness, absolved from the meddling of
>   creation
> absolute freedom, absolved from the great necessities of being
> then we see evil, pure evil
> and we see it only in man
> and his machines.
>
>   (*The Collected Poems of D. H. Lawrence*)

When humanity severs itself from the organic rhythms and "great necessities" of passion and nature, when the human will strives for the absolute in the form of an industrial and technological mastery of nature, then such egotistic over-reaching results in a "perfection" Lawrence acutely views as pure evil. It is an insight that is formidably relevant to the economic culture of our time.

The sociologist Philip Slater, in his book *Earthwalk* (1974), has generalized in analogous terms about a modern humanity out of touch with the realities and organic processes of nature: "The kind of growth Western culture has experienced over the past 300 years would be considered a sign of gross malfunction in any other context. Healthy growth is paced differently—it does not absorb or destroy everything living around it."

Slater's sense of the modern individual's perversion of ego and will seems strikingly dramatized in the social and personal conduct of the major industrial magnate in Lawrence's *Women in Love*, Gerald Crich, when Slater says: "The attempt to control and master the environment thus automatically pollutes it, for it decreases that aspect of the environment that renews, refreshes, surprises and delights us," or "control and pleasure cannot coexist, for they destroy each other."

The personality of Gerald Crich has more than a little to do with the character of the mining system he imposes on his mine operations and miners:

> There were two opposites, his will and the resistant matter of the earth. And between these he could establish the very expression of his will, the incarnation of his power, a great perfect machine, a system, an activity of pure order, pure mechanical repetition. (*Women in Love*)

The narrator goes on to project Gerald as a deity in his "perfection" of industry as an expression of absolute will over both nature (the earth, coal) and human nature. Gerald thought of "his" miners as one does a knife: "does it cut well? Nothing else mattered.... Suddenly, he had conceived the pure instrumentality of mankind."

Carrying out such a conception kills something in both humanity (the miners) and the earth, and its expression is "pure" because it is so ruthlessly indifferent to the radical assault being waged against the nature and human nature within Gerald's reach. This modernized, "perfect" system, we are told, is what the miners really wanted:

> They were exalted by belonging to this great and superhuman system ... this participation in a great and perfect system that subjected life to pure mathematical principles ... was a sort of freedom, the sort they really wanted. It was the first great step in undoing, the first great phase of chaos, the substitution of the mechanical principle for the organic. (*Women in Love*)

This "system" is "pure" because it is gauged to obliterate any human distinctness in a mode of industrialization so perfect that it robs even its maker, Gerald Crich, of further purpose. If humans can be turned into objects of utility ("knives") by Lawrence's magnate, the implicit attitude toward nature itself is more frightening still, for it reaches its logical (and technological) conclusion in fantasies of global annihilation that two dissolute lovers (one an "industrial" artist) share near the end of the novel.

One of the major concerns in *Lady Chatterley's Lover* (1928), Lawrence's last and most vehemently anti-industrial fiction, is again the gradual destruction of virgin land and of the men mining it by British coal-mining enterprises. This erosive process is elaborated at some length in the episode of Connie Chatterley's memorable car trip through a mining town halfway through the novel. Connie has already been stirred into new life by her developing love affair with the gamekeeper Mellors. Sexual rebirth sensitizes her to her socioeconomic milieu, reminding one of a passage in one of Lawrence's letters that should be better known: "I think societal instinct much deeper than sex instinct—and societal repression much more devastating." For the first time Connie really sees what industrialized surroundings have done to human beings born into a lower social niche than hers:

> The car ploughed uphill through the long squalid straggle of Tevershall, the blackened brick dwellings, the black slate roofs glistening their sharp edges, the mud black with coal dust, the pavements wet and black. It was as if dismalness had soaked through and through everything....When Connie saw the great lorries full of steel workers from Sheffield, weird, distorted, smallish beings like men, off for an excision to Matlock.... she thought: "Ah God, What has man done to man?" (*Lady Chatterley's Lover*)

Connie has a brief moment of hope: "Mellors has come out of all this!—Yes, but he was apart from it all as she was. Even in him there was no fellowship left. It was dead." Despite one critic's objection that Lawrence romanticized the lovers and projected all evil onto the socio-economic world, the insidious, blighting character of industrialism in *Chatterley* is movingly presented. It even appears before the narrative present of the novel in Clifford Chatterley's prior disfigurement by a war that itself symbolized concentrated and intensified industrialization taken to its most destructive extremes.

But *Chatterley* is also tentatively affirmative. Nature embodies—in the most literal sense of the word—the setting of the love affair. After one love sequence, Connie is described as being "like a forest, like the dark interlacing of the oak-wood, humming inaudibly with a myriad unfolding buds." And shortly after another pastoral interlude with Mellors, in which her experience of coitus is described as being "like the sea," and this as her being delivered (rather suddenly) into a new condition of womanhood, we witness this climax: "As she ran home [from Mellors' cottage] in the twilight the world seemed a dream; the trees in the park seemed bulging and surging at anchor on a tide, and the heave of the slope to the house was alive."

One beholds here a monistic mentality and cosmos at their most vibrant. Put more conventionally, Connie is projecting the overflowing spirits of her sexually and emotionally enhanced life upon her immediate world.

Thus, *Chatterley* divides into two major perspectives toward nature: the depiction of its obliteration by modern industrialization, and the implied sense of its salvation by uniting nature and human nature. The distance between these two perceptions in the novel—and it is considerable—measures the degree of optimism in Lawrence's outlook on humane survival in the age of extractive industries. All that seemed to him to remain was an apocalyptic, physical bond between the two lovers—their Pentecostal "little flame," as Mellors puts it. That flame or bond might not strike us today as enough, but at least it affirms both nature and human nature in as significant and testing a context of societal adversity as one is likely to find in modern fiction.

"Industrialization, Nature and Human Nature in the Work of D. H. Lawrence" by Donald Gutierrez—*Bloomsbury Review*, March 1997; *Humanist Society of New Mexico*, March 2011.

48
Poets, Poetry and Social Crises

In all people I see myself.
....Whoever degrades another degrades me.
Walt Whitman, "Song of Myself"

Not till people don't respond—
'What do you really do?'
when you tell them you're a poet
is there any hope for America!
Antler, *The Selected Poems*

...if way to the Better there be,
It exacts a full look at the Worst.
Thomas Hardy, "In Tenebris, II"

Poetry can be the most liberated and liberating, exalted and exalting expression of language in human culture, and the one closest to total integrity. It speaks when inspired from the heart or through a Muse or the gods or goddesses or from strong coffee or ale or the Jungian or even the Freudian Unconscious—what you will. Yet to achieve its final chiseled form in which every word, image and rhythm count, it also evolves out of the most intense consciousness the human mind can attain—never mind the overvalued brilliance of rocket scientists. When poetry achieves this finish, it has arrived at a kind of perfection and, paradoxically, naturalness that can be liberating and even exalting to the reader, releasing him or her from the exasperation, stresses and imperfections of everyday life. Even when poetry deals with a sad or horrifying subject, one ends up feeling not depressed or full of horror, but somehow favored, even graced by deeply sharing an overwhelming experience from which one also enjoys a protective distance.

Significant poetry possesses stature through an integrity of meaning and transformed experience which becomes obvious when one compares it with the daily lies and hypocrisies conveyed through the language of politics, mass media and commerce. Politicians every day talk out of both sides of their mouths, claiming to represent and stand up for Democracy, The American People, Free Trade, and The Free World while giving enormous preferential treatment to the big corporations and other insider power interests—at the extreme expense of "The American People" and supporting *any* thoroughly corrupt and brutal regime abroad that's anti-Communist or pro-American corporations.

The mass media essentially collaborates with the power centers, manipulating a deceptive rhetoric of responsibility to the public and dedication to truth and objective reporting while generally ignoring racial and gender prejudice, rotting infrastructures throughout the country, grossly increasing class inequity, enormous corporation welfare handouts, industrial and high-tech pollution and America's truly massive arms sales abroad. And everybody is familiar with the endless lies of exaggeration, seduction and deception in advertising, one of the major corrupting forces of language *and* values and thus of reality in the modern world. No glistening new automobile, no refrigerator, perfume or Rolex is going to bring home the lasting happiness—let alone wisdom—promised by Madison Avenue hucksters.

Yet in the process of adjusting to the constant verbal (and visual) barrage of commercial, social and political lies, we adapt to them by desensitizing ourselves to their slick, fraudulent language and imagery. It makes us less receptive than we could be to the force, the glory, the numinosity of the language of poetry when it is used with integrity, originality and what one might call passion of thought. Poets, artists and individuals with integrity are often the ones who say out loud that the Emperor is wearing no clothes. Though often noble or bold, such outspokenness and nonconformity exhibited by some poets, writers and artists can occasionally be annoying or disconcerting to others.

Indeed, I want to stay clear of over-idealizing poets as people. Kenneth Rexroth once said that ninety percent of the most horrible people in the world are poets. By "horrible" he perhaps meant "obnoxious" or "difficult" and he might have made this colorful remark during the period around 1956 or so when another poet—Robert Creeley, then known around the Bay Area as the one-eyed poet—took Rexroth's third wife, Marthe, away from him. Perhaps some poets tend to be high-strung, and that can at times make them seem difficult. But that quality is also part of the very sensitivity and integrity in their make-up that could educate society through the poet's visionary imagination, truth-telling and heightened awareness of areas of reality and hidden motivation that society ignores at its peril. In other words, while not discounting the tendency of some poets to hypersensitivity, narcissism or withdrawal from the common pursuits of society, one can also hold that when the poet is rising to the occasion either in his poetry or for some social crisis (like war), the integrity of his or her mind is something precious, something invaluable that society should be more receptive to.

The poet's honesty often refuses to tolerate what Rexroth, following D.H. Lawrence, has called "the Social Lie"—that is, a society that claims that the naked Emperor *isn't* naked. The poet's language of integrity, his/her free being in the audaciously honest, vigorous or creative handling of language and significant experience, potentially liberates *us*, just as a brave gesture in a frightening or oppressive situation encourages the community surrounding the heroic individual. Perhaps it goes without saying that America does not really accommodate poets, especially in its power centers, a point I will elaborate later in this chapter.

The emancipative truth or audacity of poetry can reside in its satiric sting. The sting can be made by a tiny jabber, but it can get our attention, as it does in little verse gem of Lawrence's:

"The Mosquito Knows"

The mosquito knows full well, small as he is
he's a beast of prey.
But after all
he only takes his bellyful,
he doesn't put my blood in the bank.

The San Francisco poet Robert Duncan in his book-length poem *Groundwork: Before the War* suggests how close to universal suffering the poet can be in these searing empathetic lines: "The poet turns in his sleep, the cries of the tortured and of those whose pain / survives after the burning / survives with him..."

Poetry can condemn an entire city, society or civilization, as the late 18th century English poet William Blake does in this short poem:

"London"

> I wander thro' each chart'd street,
> Near where the chart'd Thames does flow,
> And mark in every face I meet
> Marks of weakness, marks of woe.
>
> In every cry of every Man,
> In every Infant's cry of fear,
> In every voice, in every ban,
> The mind-forged manacles I hear.
>
> How the Chimney-sweeper's cry
> Every blackning Church appalls;
> And the hapless Soldier's sigh
> Runs in blood down Palace walls.
>
> But most thro' midnight streets I hear
> How the youthful Harlot's curse
> Blasts the new-born Infant's tear,
> And blights with plagues the Marriage hearse.

Blake's "London" embodies a massive condemnation of a late 18th century European city. The breadth of the condemnation is registered through the hammering repetition of certain key words running throughout the entire poem: "every" (repeated four times), "chart'd"—not only all London streets are "chart'd" but even the river Thames is, i.e., both human nature and nature are "chart'd"—that is, controlled, regimented, repressed.

Of course some degree of order is essential for civilized functioning in human societies. But, the poem suggests, ordering has gone far too far, become virtually insane, almost like a police state, resulting in "weakness" and "woe" everywhere one looks. The repression goes deeper, too, visible in the "cry" of adults and children, in their everyday talk, even in the marriage ceremony (the word "ban" in the poem). If one doubts this, the climactic eighth line drives the underlying point home: "The mind-forged manacles I hear." The imprisonment has been internalized. People have been overwhelmed by whatever is oppressive and rigidifying in the social-economic culture—the "chart'd" motif—and the life of freedom, spontaneity and joy has been handcuffed. People sigh, cry, curse. Blake's London almost feels like Auschwitz!

Blake was one of the first Romanticist libertarians in the ongoing fight against societal suppression, imprisonment or, as *today*, corruption of the elemental human energies. Of course one can say that the poem "London" is just one person's "opinion." Moreover, Blake doesn't offer statistics, footnotes, both sides of the argument, the authority of paraded erudition or compelling logic to prove his case that Londoners—that is, Europeans—are in misery and their institutions (like ours?) are oriented towards death. But then Blake is not making a "case." He is projecting a *vision* of societal repression, perversion and, ultimately, psycho-sexual paralysis (the reference in Blake's poem to the harlot and the newly married husband). This is quite similar to what the Old Testament prophets did in reviling the ancient cities of iniquity, or as Allen Ginsberg does in his long poem "Howl" and Kenneth Rexroth in his very wrathful long poem "Thou Shalt Not Kill," with their powerful lamentations and curses against mid-20th century America's self-alienation and its worship of materialism and war. One also thinks of the magnificent denunciation of usury in Ezra Pound's *Cantos* which begins "With usura [usury] hath no man a house of good stone," and continues with such memorable lines as:

> Usura rusteth the chisel
> It rusteth the craft and the craftsman
> It gnaweth the thread in the loom...
> Usura slayest the child in the womb
> It stayeth the young man's courting
> It...lyeth
> between the young bride and her bridegroom
> CONTRA NATURAM.

I hope, then, that what I've said so far suggests that poets bear a certain unique authority, the authority of sublime truth-telling, integrity of imagination and prophetic power. What I am now going to propose will seem controversial if not worse! Poets should have significant public input on crucial social issues.

Whenever Washington deliberates on a "police action," intervention or "surgical" bombing abroad, the media invites the generals, present or former Defense Secretaries, Henry Kissinger (a war criminal), Ollie North, CIA directors and others of their stripe to explain the crisis. All too often these dour, square-jawed pit-bulls justify the choice of violence based on the Hard Facts, the National Interest—or paranoid fear.

Now I submit that these are not necessarily the best or only people to inform the public about, let alone determine, whether or not to start or continue the war in Vietnam, invade Panama to snag Manuel Noriega (which resulted in perhaps as many as 2,000 innocent civilians being killed by American firepower), bomb Kosovo with deliberate non-surgical strikes, deal with the horrific Rwandan genocide (in which both France and the United States were seriously complicit), defend Taiwan by threatening mainland China with nuclear bombs—or, as Secretary of Defense Clinton asserted, "nuke" Iran if it attacked Israel.

Granted, on certain aspects of considering, say, a war action, the generals and Secretaries of State will be consulted whether peace activists like it or not; they represent the power structure in place and obviously cannot be ignored. I object, however, to their exclusive presence because they traditionally have virtually *all* the input, and thus give the public a very one-sided perspective of often very complex and sensitive international crises or situations. Thus, we're given a Donald Rumsfeld but not a Noam Chomsky, a Madeleine Albright but not a Diane di Prima or Anne Barrows, a Paul Wolfovitz or Henry Kissinger but not a Daniel Berrigan or a Jidi Krishnamurti (unfortunately long deceased). Further, because of their hyper-nationalistic mindset established by excessive identification with the state, these men and women representing the state frequently propose solutions to conflicts abroad that lack, to put it mildly, a key humane and humanitarian character.

So, enter the poet. Is he or she more humane or humanitarian than some president, admiral or secretary of defense? Not necessarily. As suggested earlier, poets, like the rest of humanity, have shortcomings. Some drink too much, abuse their spouses or companions, get into bar brawls, go mad. Going back some centuries, one recalls Dante's vindictive savagery in *The Divine Comedy* towards individuals he disapproved of. But by and large these are failings poets share with non-poets and don't concern what is most significant in the creative character of poets—the esthetic, ethical and visionary character of their work. These men and women possess an ordering of esthetic, emotional, moral and psychological sensitivity not only ideal for creating poetry but for responding deeply and originally to the *human* predicament and, thus, very possibly, to a given societal crisis.

One of the ethical outrages about the thinking that went into the decision to drop the atom bomb on Japan, as the British author and medical ethicist Jonathan Glover observes in his recent book *Humanity: A Moral History of the Twentieth Century*,[1] is precisely the lack of consideration of the personal, human consequences of the bomb's explosion—the crucial dimension of the horrible, gruesome forms of death and suffering that a nuclear bomb can—and did—inflict on the actual living, breathing, sweating bodies and anguished minds of human beings. Did Secretary of State John Foster Dulles consider this consequence when he threatened Communist China with nuclear attack in the 1950s, or John F. Kennedy, when, according to an October 2001 article by Fred Kaplan in *The Atlantic Monthly* titled "JFK's First Strike Plan," Kennedy seriously considered launching a surprise nuclear strike against the Soviet Union and its millions of individuals already brutalized by Stalin? According to Glover, many motives went into the thinking that dehumanized the Japanese sufficiently to allow American leaders—including the famous President of Harvard, John Bryant Conant, a chemist, ardent Cold War supporter, and inventor of a poison gas designed for use in warfare—to push for the Bomb being dropped. These include psychic distancing, fragmentation of responsibility, racist and animal stereotyping and vindictiveness. What seemed to be evaded or ignored in the mental process was the inevitability of hundreds of thousands of innocent civilians, totally vulnerable human beings, being exterminated in a nuclear bombing.

It is just this ignored but crucial consideration that the poet might well zero in on—and not only the poet literally, but the "poet" in the broader, figurative sense of anyone who has evolved in himself or herself an acutely humane and imaginative responsiveness to massive evil and suffering. This "poet" could be a grocery store manager or clerk, a shoe salesperson, a telephone line repairwoman, a multimillionaire, or even a retired general. (Ret. General Telford Taylor, the Chief Prosecuting Counsel in the Nuremburg Trials, later stated that if the same standards of justice were applied to the American presidents carrying out the Vietnam War as were applied to principal Japanese militarist General Yamashita at the end of

World War II, those Presidents also would have been hanged).

But I select an actual poet for this special role because he or she is more visible for social consultation and symbolic value—or would be if the types who generally run our government and war industries were either aware of or not utterly hostile to poets and their kind of essential sensitiveness and moral intelligence. Poets are "experts" in exploring and cultivating the center and subtle interconnections of consciousness and instinct that define the quintessence of the human—but also can, like the great novelists in their different way, numinously connect the personal with the social. Further, it is those very regions of blunted realization in our "practical" leaders that can be so terrifyingly possessed by the most destructive, nihilistic energies concealed behind a rhetoric of bland, meaningless generalities or sanctimonious platitudes.

In contrast, the magnanimous sensibility of a Walt Whitman can grace the human community when he declaims: "I am the mate and companion of people, all just as immortal and fathomless as myself. They'd not know how immortal, but I know..." Yes, Whitman did know, and poets *do* know that irreducible preciousness in individual human being and experience that the social engineering of our rulers' mentality ignores. When Pentagon brass describe the horrific deaths of Vietnamese, Central American, Chilean, Colombian, Yugoslavian, Palestinian, Grenadean, Iranian, Kurdish, Sudanese, Indonesian, East Timorese, Panamanian, or Iraqi and Afghanistan mothers, fathers, children and old people caused by extremely heavy American bombings or by American-supplied arms as "collateral damage," they are not considering the ghastliness of that phrase being applied to the brutal deaths of their *own* family members. America's 9/11 should have registered in full force the cruelty of that expression to the Pentagon generals and their Commander in Chief—but it looks like it did not and probably never will.

One objection to poetry and poets as a social force worth considering is that much poetry is too personal, too private. In a symposium essay entitled "The Writer in Our World," the literary scholar Terrence Des Pres attacks the idea of a personalist poetics:

> [P]oetry in the Emersonian tradition, the poetry of self-and-nature that Keats once called the "Egotistical Sublime, no longer speaks to us, no longer even makes sense. Further adventures of the self-delighted are not what's wanted. Rather

> a poetry that... stands up to the world in which it is written.
> Poetry that does not retreat into the inconsequence of self but
> rather confronts the burden of the terrible world and
> announces against the sort of political torment that all of us
> suffer or witness.

These words, coming from the author of the deeply moving book *The Survivor*, have force.[2] Though not himself a victim of the Nazi concentration camps, Des Pres' sense of that catastrophic experience is so profound and empathetic that one can well appreciate his cry for a poetry that "stands up to the world." He is a literary academic who, out of an acute awareness of the vast horror of the age, is pursuing the concept of the humanities into their basic connotations—human, humane, humanitarian.

Nevertheless, Des Pres' argument against "Emersonian" poetry will not do. Despite the holocaust, *why* does a poetry of self-and-nature no longer speak to us? Why, further, does Des Pres assume that all self-explorations are "self-delighted," that is, narcissistic or hedonistic? Some, including those of the "confessional" poets such as Sylvia Plath and Robert Lowell, are agonized and reflect a sizable courage to pursue and verbalize their guilt. Worst of all, why is the self "inconsequential?" After all, as *The Survivor* itself testifies, it is a sense of self, stimulated, to be sure, by the camaraderie and rough-hewn communalism among inmates in the Nazi camps, that helped those people survive. Partly reflecting the Judaic religious philosopher Martin Buber, Kenneth Rexroth would say that in a vital community one saw one's self in the Other, and vice versa. Without some sense of privately esteemed and thus empowered self, even if socially oriented or nurtured, few would have endured those camps. Also, one endured not only, as Des Pres put it so movingly, to bear witness to the hellish realities of the concentration camps but to experience again something of the indispensable microcosm of private sensibility. That "I" is what we all inhabit most fully or uniquely, and even if it cannot or should not be totally self-enclosed, it needs its own expression and elaboration so as to meet the Other and the world on terms that are interdependent, inter-reflective and thus crucially important for enriching personal identity. The power to stand up to the world must come partly from the Keatsian "garden" of private sensibility.

Another objection to my proposal to listen to poets on social crises is that their great sensitivity to beauty—and, thus, to ugliness—doesn't necessarily make them more ethically humane or sensitive. I think, though, that it usually *does* make poets more sensitive to good and evil. Furthermore, poets like Ginsberg and Rexroth engaged the evils of modern American society and the American state respectively in poems like "Howl" and Rexroth's extraordinary book-length travel poem *The Dragon and the Unicorn* at such depth and with such visionary fury and eloquence that some would say the *poem* is the best arena for a poet's persuasive impact on society. Some poets, however, were effective social activists during the Vietnam War, making speeches and reading anti-war poems on and off college campuses, writing statements and poems for print media and radio, participating in protest demonstrations and occupying other venues with a strong anti-war stand. Rexroth was also engaged for decades as a left wing activist and cultural educator in San Francisco and in helping Japanese-American friends and acquaintances avoid being sent off to American concentration camps. Major poets during the 20th century became quite public and active as protesters of conscience for social justice or for peace. Robert Lowell went to prison as a Catholic Conscientious Objector to protest the Second World War and publicly demonstrated against the Vietnam War, and Ginsberg, Robert Duncan and Denise Levertov were continuously vocal in combating societal malaise and evil in and committed by the United States and by other nations.

The real hindrance to major access to the general public by poets (as well as by seers, mystics, philosophic-spiritual anarchists, iconoclastic clergy) is that the very leaders who carry out the policies and programs often brutalizing other countries don't read serious poetry, let alone polemical poetry. These power people obviously don't take poets and seers seriously—nor does the corporate-dominated mass media. A lot of this negligence of the Voices in the Wilderness results from choices made by the media for spokesmen on crucial issues, and that power of choice exhibits a major obstacle not only for poets, philosophers, seers and mystics, but for independent historians and social critics like Howard Zinn, the late Edward Said, Noam Chomsky or the Portland Anarchist guru John Zerzan getting major-media access to the public. Even a medium like PBS, which has the word "public" in its title, is so controlled by corporate interests that any truly libertarian, audacious, radical view is rarely presented, and certainly not to the same degree that "centrist" viewpoints get aired.

Further, with attempts not many years back by the once-libertarian Pacifica Foundation to politically "centralize" its radio stations, the room for the integrity of the boldly imaginative, personal, authentic outlook central to poetic vision becomes even narrower. Norman Mailer, despite whatever has been obnoxious in his public style or personal life, understands the necessity of the literary person propelling himself into the limelight. A poet doesn't have to get physically removed from a prizefighter's room before a big bout or run for Mayor of New York City to acquire publicity, let alone try to get appointed Secretary of State. But he could try harder to make himself available to whatever media is accessible and form ongoing organizations more politically enterprising than P.E.N. to pressure the government and sensitize the public on crucial issues. Adrienne Rich, on justifiable ethical grounds, turned down a National Endowment for the Arts award in 1997 that would have been given by President Clinton. Perhaps instead she could have used the public character of the occasion to make her moral objection against the government—as the educator, libertarian Anarchist and poet Paul Goodman did in a blistering lecture-tirade against corporate arrogance and greed delivered to an astounded, then outraged National Association of Manufacturers conference on a memorable occasion in Washington D.C. back in the 1960s.

What needs to be taken seriously is the poet's prophetic role—his or her special gift to imagize and thus to imagine and censure a society's evils, sicknesses and crookedheartedness. The merging of the esthetic and the ethical can endow the poet with a special power to pierce the amoral realpolitik and ruthless self-interest that too often characterizes the outlook of public officials and large corporation executives. As observed earlier, poets don't achieve this power by employing the analytical strictures of the social critic or the often unavoidable compromising of the politician but by implementing the power of the poet's imagination to express either what has not been said before or what most people would not dare to say or be capable of putting so unforgettably into words.

The people running most governments and major commercial organizations of the world of course don't want any poets sticking their noses into concerns and problems that require a "practical" mind. That would be unthinkable to them. In fact, these types never think of poets or of poetry as having anything relevant to propose about the "real" world's problems and crises. This is a great loss, because a Marianne Moore, a William Carlos Williams, an Octavio Paz, a Gary Snyder (let alone a Walt Whitman or an Antler) could offer what is otherwise tragically missing in the policy planning of the American rulers. I refer to the intimate human touch and communication along both personal and societal dimensions, that sense of warm-blooded, intensely personal human reality one insuperably experiences in shaking hands with even a stranger or holding hands with a loved one. It is of course easy to sentimentalize that flesh contact; Hitler's, Stalin's, Mao's hands probably felt warm too (or did they?). Further, most politicians greatly enjoy—or appear to enjoy—shaking hands, the more hands the better. Poets don't usually run for office and aren't always warm or gregarious people. But the stress I would make here is the "warmth," that is, the intensity and authenticity of their imaginative re-creation, as artists of language, of significant or unusual human experience. As for actual human touch, it could remind us—and especially the very powerful above us—that actual physical warmth could not only represent human contact but the quintessential sign of the humane and thus something that should never be violated by the callous, murderous depersonalization of a state's foreign policy.

Poets, then, by their very nature register a heightened sensitivity to the human, whether in their sense of the profundity, subtlety or complexity of intimate human sensibility, or of the radiant potential of society as the Beloved Community of the saints, seers and mystics. All too many individuals in power lack this sense of and sensitivity to the human and the humane—and thus to the inhuman and inhumane as well. They, often to an extreme degree, are corrupted by having far more power and influence than any individual should have in a given national and international context (one cannot forget LBJ and Nixon-Kissinger planning bombing sites in, respectively, North Vietnam and Cambodia while having lunch). Many of these people, too, certainly in the United States, enter politics from professional and business areas—like banking, law, investment firms, large corporations—that are often utterly indifferent to humanistic values. At best they regard the humanities as ornaments to show off with on occasion, rather than understanding what they really are: part of the fiber of wisdom and inspiration essential to achieving the good society and the good life. Instead, as argued earlier in this collection, these powerful individuals are often strongly oriented towards magnifying power, wealth and control, and, more important, towards sustaining and enlarging the societal and global domination of the political, military and commercial institutions that they head. The humane voice, the sensitive connection, the Beloved Community is hardly their concern, and, when they do become aware of that voice, that connection, that community, they regard this—in colossal folly—as primarily a woman's domain or that of impractical idealists.

Consequently, I am making an issue about the poet and the "poet" having input on societal crises because to my mind that input represents an invaluable and much neglected ideal, and ideals must always be formulated and believed in. One could perhaps believe in the ideal value of the moral-esthetic imagination of the poet, and, crucially, of the poetic imagination that readers can develop. This imagination can, among other things, sensitize us to realize and respect the humanity of others. It can particularly make us aware of the humanity of opponents and especially the humanity of the often repressed and helpless civilian populations of enemy states, rather than give vent to the opportunistic paranoia of heads of state that restlessly look for, create and need (really *need*) enemies, rogue nations, evil empires.

Making that humane imagination a real force in the minds of a Nixon, an LBJ, a Reagan, a Clinton, a Bush Sr. or Jr. (let alone a Margaret Thatcher or a Tony Blair, the man who coined the memorably oxymoronic phrase "compassionate bombing") may seem virtually impossible. Perhaps it *is* impossible, but that type will not necessarily be in power forever. Life, society, the manifestations and handling of power are subject to change, flux, contingency. Anything can happen in the configurations that human societies and organizations can assume. Individuals, groups or even large movements could arise that are more oriented towards the humane. Consider, for example, the Progressive Caucus already existent in the Congressional House as well as the extraordinary demonstration of ethical energy and social conscience seen in the huge anti-globalization protest movements in Seattle, Washington D.C. and, most recently and sensationally, in the bold opposition to capitalist plutocracy of the international Occupy Movement.

Should such renewals occur and enlarge, the moral-esthetic imagination of the poet, that is, of the creative, bold, sensitive individual, could more and more permeate society through books, readings, media publicity or publicity conveyed by various public personalities, or, more broadly, through the leaders of enlarging grassroots movements. The special mentality of the poet and the integrative receptivity and social activism of the public reformer could perhaps join forces to create a more humane society. The poet and the activist leader will probably not exactly see eye to eye, for what they envisage is bound to be somewhat different. Yet both in their different ways perceive our current society as one in which power, wealth and callous ideological indifference to the country's social needs dominate—conditions all too often accompanied by vast social cruelty: millions of Americans lacking health insurance, or thrown out of work and homes, or incarcerated in bulging prisons. The fully humane individual—not necessarily just the poet, and certainly not all poets—would likely support the development of an institutional culture of radical compassion for all people everywhere and a more egalitarian distribution of the world's wealth and resources rather than one in which, say, an American CEO makes over 500 times as much money as his employee.

If we don't persist in identifying and then vigorously pursuing the ideal of the humane, we will go on groping through increasing darkness until the human race finally falls over some catastrophic precipice. Poetry, the arts, the seer, the fully humanized individual embody and provide us crucial light. We better use it before it is too late.

---

1. See Ch. 15 for Glover review.
2. See Ch. 31 for Des Pres review.

"Poets, Poetry and Social Crises" by Donald Gutierrez—*Eldorado Sun*, November 2008.

Afterword
The "Occupy Wall Street" Movement

We have come full circle to French philosopher David Rousset's statement that I quoted in my Introduction, "Normal men do not know that everything is possible." Indeed, everything is possible—in the worst sense that Rousset intended, though many choose not to face it—and in the best sense, though the powerful for whom the status quo is working try mightily to deprive us of that vision. My positive reversal of turning Rousset's negative into an affirmative is not only a statement of belief but a value and a fact proven by experience and history. One could contend further that the negative "everything" can actually *produce* the positive, beneficial "everything," as movingly exemplified by Terence des Pres in *Suvivor* (see Ch. 31).

The "Occupy Wall Street" Protest/Movement/Revolution indicates the heartwarming latter "everything." Devoured as the United States and much of the world has been for decades by Wall Street and its counterparts abroad, increasing masses of dispossessed people are the more recent embodiment of Rousset's terrifying maxim. For the middle class, unjustly kicked off jobs and out of their homes and health programs—losing virtually everything and joining the increasingly hard-pressed "working" class— "everything is possible" is now "the possible has become the actual." As for people in Iran, Afghanistan and other smaller, vulnerable nations on which Washington has bombed democracy, "everything is possible" has meant the literal obliteration of their society, not only jobs, homes and medical coverage, but their lives as well.

Now, however, thanks to the "Occupy" movement that has spread through the United States and worldwide, the humane, affirmative side of "everything" is emerging. While it is still hard to tell where exactly this development is going—whether it will assume the character of a mass movement, a political party (which seems unlikely) or something else—what looks undeniable is that it is almost global and appears permanent enough to represent a serious challenge to the financial-corporate-political powers that be. Antedated by the "Arab Spring," the OWS movement is conceptually identical in trying to restore a kind of social-economic-political democracy. Both the Mid-East peoples and the American protesters passionately want to destroy the vertical power structure dominating their societies.

Part of the permanent character of the OWS's affirmative "everything" is insuperably related to the negative "everything": The forces making life nearly unbearable for countless millions have, like a law of nature, led to an inevitable opposite. Individuals and groups are irrepressibly rising up against the money-power elites, and increasing their effectiveness by spreading their protests, plans, ideals and messages far and wide.

Undoubtedly the biggest social protest event since the anti-Vietnam War movement, what makes the "Occupy" protest movement potent and durable is due in large part to the numerous types of people who embody it—not only the young and the atrociously debt-plagued college students, but civil-service, union, middle-class business and clerical workers. In short, the movement is composed of varied and significant social, economic categories of people who have been dumped as so much garbage by utterly unscrupulous financial transactions aided by Congress and, more recently, by the Supreme Court's "Citizens United" (i.e., Corporations United) ruling.

Where will this increasingly widening, highly determined protest go? It is of course hard to predict, because when you have lost everything, the only survival way is to protest against and counter what is destroying you. An October 2011 report indicated that the movement has spread to 150 cities. A contributing factor is the support of unions, starting in New York. The types of occupations that these unions represent are significant: teachers, health care workers, communications workers, transit workers—that is, people vital to the functioning of a society, to its health, its electrical connectedness, its mobility or transportation and its perpetuation of knowledge and a civilized, coherent future. As organized groups of people in these areas of work are joining or at least endorsing the "Occupy Wall Street" groups in the financial nerve-center of the country and the world, their message is ever more easily spread. OWS in Oakland has already showed its muscle by closing down the city's ports or, more accurately and significantly, engaging the ports' stevedore union to do so. And, rather than intimidating the OWSers, being pepper-sprayed and beaten by militarized, rioting cops seems to increase their numbers and further empower them.

Michael Greenberg in an article in the *New York Review of Books* (Nov. 11, 2011) entitled "In Zucotti Park," makes the key point that the Occupy movement's "vague, open-ended character has been crucial to its success." This open-ended character allows for a universal identification— "99 percent." Not all the 99 percent exist on the same level of desperation, but certainly enough do to make this somewhat exaggerated yet authentic statistic a powerful rallying cry. At bottom, what it says is that a large part of America and the world is being grossly swindled by immensely powerful financial institutions and their governmental servants, and that this swindle has to end and be replaced by an egalitarian, compassionate society.

The horizontal dimension is central to the Occupy movement, a street-level embodiment of a society in embryo. The stress placed on *horizontal* rather than vertical or leader structure, and on retaining autonomy to avoid co-option, suggests not only a revolutionary character to this movement but one based on fundamental libertarian values like mutual aid, consensus-democracy, nonviolence and cooperation.

There was some talk among protesters, says Greenberg, of restoring the Glass-Steagal Act, but another OWS current of opinion urged that the established financial system itself was the cardinal problem and should be dissolved. If this ambition appears outlandish at first, consider Senator Bernie Sanders' statement that the Federal Reserve passed along sixteen *trillion* dollars to the major American (and even foreign) banks and corporations entirely secretly (Thom Hartmann radio program, November 2011). When one witnesses that kind of monstrous slight-of-hand by a private, not public, financial institution like the Fed, it is not only acceptable but *essential* that a tsunami of protest occurs to wash away such hideously plutocratic entities as the Federal Reserve and the dominant banking institutions.

Is such a revolutionary clean sweep likely? Who knows? But "everything is possible"—not only in Rousset's concentration-camp universe but in a later world in which the corporate and financial institutions have revealed a ferocity of avarice and contempt for society at large comparable to the most brutal tyrannies in history. The OWSers have fully awakened to this reality and are thus forming a cooperativist-anarchist-communalist movement that is creating its own powerfully autonomous reality. Not long ago Neocons in the Bush Administration were wont to claim that they *create* reality. The OWS movement, fluid as moving water, impressively flexible, hostile to co-option by politicians and to the serious proclivity of leadership to vertical power structures, inspired and energized by youth but also driven by individuals from many walks of society who have been left destitute by the wealthiest society in history, is not going to disappear overnight.

Very possibly, the OWS movement is here to stay and work creatively humane and egalitarian changes on an irreversibly corrupt society. But "stay" is a misleading word, because it is the very nature of this movement—and essential to its likelihood of perpetuation—to keep moving and changing. It will continue to evolve new modes of activism, argue with itself, suffer setbacks and schism, adjust while and through keeping faith with its core values of autonomy, consensus, classlessness. Thus, the OWS actions in November of 2011 to pursue social justice by mass protest against home evictions—at the home sites or at the locations of officials responsible for cutting taxes on the rich—exhibit a fluidity of moral action that, as Greenberg points out, prevents OWS from becoming a reification of idealized purpose, an immobilized ideal.

The Occupy/Arab Spring movement/revolution will never make up for the compounded 20th century societal horrors of Rousset's "everything is possible"—the world of concentration camps, nuclear bombs, slaughter of helpless peoples, war crimes, state torture and the ghastly rest. Nothing will. But it can embody a life-affirming "everything is possible" possibility by daring to show the powerful and rich in their empires of verticality and hierarchy that such demonic privilege and concentrated power will no longer be tolerated. Will it happen? Everything *is* possible. That is an unthinkable that we could feel and warmly welcome.

———————————

BIBLIOGRAPHY

Abbey, Edward. *The Monkey Wrench Gang*. New York: Harpers Perennial, 1975.

Aleeg, Henri. *La Question*. London: John Calder Publishers Ltd, 1958.

Arendt, Hannah. *The Origins of Totalitarianism*. Cleveland: World Publishing Co, 1951.

The U.S. Army. *Army Field Manual*. Date of Access: August 22, 2012. http://armypubs.army.mil/doctrine

Baskervill, Charles Read et. al. *Elizabethan and Stuart Plays*. New York: Henry Holt and Co., 1934.

Belton, Neil. *The Good Listener: Helen Bamber, A Life Against Cruelty*. New York: Pantheon Books, 1998. (Review, Ch. 11)

Bettelheim, Bruno. *The Informed Heart: Autonomy in a Mass Age*. Glencoe: Free Press, 1960.

Blum, William. *Rogue State*. Monroe: Common Courage Press, 2000. (Review, Ch. 7)

Bok, Sissela. *Secrets: On the Ethics of Concealment and Revelation*. New York: Vintage Books, 1983.

Bugliosi, Vincent. *The Prosecution of George W. Bush for Murder*. New York: Vanguard Press, 2008. (Review, Ch. 18)

Bush, George W. *Decision Points*. New York: Random House, 2010.

Caldicott, Helen. *Missile Envy: The Arms Race and Nuclear War*. New York: Bantam Books, 1986.

_____. *The New Nuclear Danger: George W. Bush's Military-Industrial Complex*. New York: New Press, 2002. (Review, Ch. 21)

Caro, Robert A. *The Years of Lyndon Johnson, v.3: Master Of The Senate*. New York: Vintage Books, 2003.

Carroll, James. *House of War: the Pentagon and the Disastrous Rise of American Power*. Boston: Houghton Mifflin, 2006.

Center for Defense Information. *The Defense Monitor*. Washington D.C.

Chomsky, Noam. *The New Military Humanism: Lessons from Kosovo*. Monroe: Common Courage Press, 1999.

Chomsky, Noam and Edward S. Herman. *The Washington Connection and Third World Fascism*. Boston: South End Press, 1979.

Central Intelligence Agency. *Kubark: Counterintelligence Interrogation Handbook*. 1963. Date of Access: August 22, 2012.
http://www.gwu.edu/~nsarchiv/NSAEBB/NSAEBB27/01-01.htm
_____. *Human Resources Exploitation Training Manual*. 1983. Date Of Access: August 22, 2012.
http://www.gwu.edu/~nsarchiv/NSAEBB/NSAEBB27/02-01.htm

Clark, Ramsey. *The Fire This Time: US War Crimes in the Gulf*. New York: Thunder Mouth Press, 1994.

Colley, Linda. *Captives: Britain, Empire, and the World, 1600-1850*. London: Cape, 2002.

Cusac, Anne-Marie. *Cruel and Unusual: The Culture of Punishment in America*. New Haven: Yale University Press, 2009.

Danner, Mark. *Torture and Truth: America, Abu Ghraib and the War on Terror*. New York: New York Review Books, 2004.

Des Pres, Terrence. *The Survivor: An Anatomy of Life in the Death Camps*. New York: Oxford University Press, 1976. (Review, Ch. 31)
_____. "The Writer In His World": A Symposium Sponsored by TriQuarterly Magazine. Boston: Atlantic Monthly Press, 1986.

Domhoff, G. William. *Who Rules America? Challenges to Corporate and Class Dominance*. Clearwater: Touchstone Books, 1967.

Duncan, Robert. *Ground Work: Before the War*. New York: New Directions, 1984.

Ehrenreich, Barbara. *Nickel and Dimed: On (Not) Getting By in America*. New York: Metropolitan Books, 2001.

Engelhardt, Tom. *The American Way of War: How Bush's War Became Obama's*. Chicago: Haymarket Books, 2010.

Fisk, Robert. *The Great War for Civilization: The Conquest of the Middle East*. New York: Vintage, 2005.

Foss, Christopher F. *Jane's Armour and Artillery 2009-2010*. Alexandria: Jane's Information Group, 2009.

Fussell, Paul. *Class*. New York: Ballantine Books, 1983.
_____. *Wartime: Understanding and Behavior in the Second World War*. New York: Oxford University Press, 1989.

Gareau, Frederich H. *State Terrorism and the United States: From Counterinsurgency to the War on Terrorism*. Atlanta: Clarity Press, 2004.

Gellhorn, Martha. *The Face of War*. New York: Knopf, 1986.

_____. *The View From the Ground*. New York: Atlantic Monthly Press, 1988.

Gibney, Alex, dir. *Taxi to the Dark Side*. Discovery Channel, 2007. Film.

Ginsberg, Allen. *Howl and Other Poems*. San Francisco: City Lights Books, 1956.

Glover, Jonathan. *Humanity: A Moral History of the Twentieth Century*. New Haven: Yale University Press, 2000. (Review, Ch. 15)

Green, Jonathan. *The Dictionary of Contemporary Slang*. New York: Stein and Day, 1984.

Greider, William. *Fortress America: The American Military and the Consequences of Peace*. New York: Public Affairs, 1999.

_____. "The Economic Collapse." *The Nation*. June 4, 2010.

Grey, Stephen. *Ghost Plane: The Untold Story of the CIA's Secret Rendition Program*. New York: St. Martin's Press, 2006.

Hedges, Chris. *Death of the Liberal Class*. New York: Nation's Books, 2010.

_____. *War Is a Force That Gives Us Meaning*. New York: Public Affairs, 2002. (Review, Ch. 14)

Heftel, Cecil. *End Legalized Bribery: An Ex-Congressman's Proposal to Clean Up Congress*. Santa Ana: Seven Locks Press, 1998.

Hicks, David B. "The Strange Fate of the American Boarding School." *The American Scholar* 65, no. 4. 1996.

Hersh, Seymour. *Against All Enemies: Gulf War Syndrome: the War Between America's Ailing Veterans and Their Government*. New York: Ballantine Publishing Group, 1998. (Review, Ch. 26)

Hitchens, Christopher. *The Trial of Henry Kissinger*. New York: Verso, 1998. (Review, Ch. 17)

"Human Rights Watch Report." *New York Review of Books* 52, no. 17. November 3, 2005.

Hook, Sidney. *Heresy Yes, Conspiracy No*. New York: J. Day Co., 1953.

Jackson, Paul. *Jane's All the World's Aircraft 1999-2000*. Alexandria: Jane's Information Group, 1999.

Jarecki, Eugene. *The American Way of War: Guided Missiles, Misguided Men, and a Republic in Peril*. New York: Free Press, 2008.

Johnson, Chalmers. *Blowback: The Costs and Consequences of American Empire*. Second Edition. New York: Henry Holt and Co., 2004.

_____. *The Sorrows of Empire: Militarism, Secrecy, and the End of the Republic*. New York: Henry Holt and Co., 2004. (Review, Ch. 27)

_____. *Nemesis: The Last Days of the American Republic*. New York: Henry Holt and Co., 2006.

Kafka, Franz. *The Castle*. Trans. Mark Harman. New York: Schoken Books Inc, 1998.

Kahn, Herman. *Thinking About the Unthinkable*. New York: Horizon Press, 1962.

Kinzer, Stephen. *All the Shah's Men: An American Coup and the Roots of Middle East Terror*. Hoboken: John Wiley and Sons, 2003. (Review, Ch. 4)

Klein, Naomi. *The Shock Doctrine: the Rise of Disaster Capitalism*. New York: Henry Holt and Co., 2007.

Kropotkin, Peter. *Mutual Aid: A Factor of Evolution*. Boston: Extending Horizons Books, 1955.

Lawrence, D. H. "Apropos of *Lady Chatterley's Lover*." New York: Bantam Books, 1968.

_____. *D H Lawrence and Italy*. New York: Viking Press, 1972.

_____. *Lady Chatterley's Lover*. New York: Bantam Books, 1968.

_____. *The Complete Poems of D. H. Lawrence*. New York: Viking Press, 1964.

_____. *Sons and Lovers*. New York: Viking Press, 1913.

_____. *Twilight in Italy*. New York: Viking Press, 1972.

_____. *Women in Love*. New York: Viking Press, 1960.

Loeffler, Jack. *Adventures With Ed: A Portrait of Abbey*. Albuquerque: University of New Mexico Press, 2002. (Review, Ch. 46)

Lundberg, Ferdinand. *The Rich and the Super-Rich*. New York: Bantam Books, 1969.

Mailer, Norman. *The Armies of the Night*. New York: Plume Books, 1968.

Mayer, Jane. "The Black Sites." *The New Yorker*. August 13, 2007.

_____. "Outsourcing Torture." *The New Yorker*. February 14, 2005.

McCarthy, Cormac. *The Road*. New York: Knopf, 2008.

McCoy, Alfred W. *A Question of Torture: CIA Interrogation from the Cold War to the War on Terror*. New York: Henry Holt and Co., 2006. (Review, Ch. 9)

Moore, Thomas. *Soul Mates*. New York: Harper Collins, 1994.

Nader, Ralph and William Taylor. *The Big Boys: Power and Position in American Business*. New York: Pantheon Books, 1986.

Nietzsche, Friedrich. *On the Genealogy of Morals*. Trans. Horace Samuel. New York: Boni and Liveright, 1913.

O'Brien, Tim. *If I Die in a Combat Zone, Box Me Up and Ship Me Home*. New York: Broadway Books, 1973.

Olshansky, Barbara. *Secret Trials and Executions: Military Tribunals and the Threat to Democracy*. New York: Seven Stories Press, 2002.

Ortiz, Dianna. *The Blindfold's Eyes: My Journey from Torture to Truth*. New York: Orbis Books, 2002. (Review, Ch. 12)

Orwell, George. *A Collection of Essays*. New York: Harcourt, Brace, Jovanovich, 1954.

Parenti, Christian. *Lockdown America: Police and Prisons in an Age of Crisis*. New York: Verso, 2000. (Review, Ch. 33)

Parenti, Michael. *Against Empire*. San Francisco: City Lights Books, 1995.

Paros, Lawrence. *The Erotic Tongue: A Sexual Lexicon*. New York: Henry Holdt and Co., 1988.

Partridge, Eric. *A Dictionary of Slang and Unconventional English*. Seventh Edition. New York: Routledge, 1970.

Pilger, John. *Freedom Next Time: Resisting the Empire*. New York: Nation Books, 2007.

_____. *The New Rulers of the World*. New York: Verso, 2003. (Review, Ch. 37)

Rejali, Darius. *Torture and Democracy*. Princeton: Princeton University Press, 2009.

Rexroth, Kenneth. *Bird in the Bush: Obvious Essays*. New York: New Directions, 1955.

_____. *The Dragon and the Unicorn*. Norfolk: New Directions, 1950.

Ritz, Dean, ed. *Defying Corporations, Defining Democracy: A Book of History & Strategies*. Toronto: Apex Press, 2001.

Robinson, Randall. *Quitting America: The Departure of a Black Man from His Native Land*. New York: Dutton, 2004. (Review, Ch. 34)

Rudovsky, David. *The Rights of Prisoners.* Carbondale: Southern Illinois University Press, 1988.

Scheer, Robert. *With Enough Shovels: Reagan, Bush, and Nuclear War.* New York: Vintage Press, 1982.

Schell, Jonathan. *The Fate of the Earth.* New York: Knopf, 1982.

Schulz, William F. "Cruel and Unusual Punishment." *New York Review of Books*, April 24, 1997.

Sinclair, Upton. *The Cry for Justice.* Philadelphia: John C. Winston Co., 1915.

Slater, Philip Elliot. *Earthwalk.* New York: Bantam, 1975.

Spick, Mike and Barry Wheeler. *Modern American Fighters and Attack Aircraft.* London: Salamander, 1992.

Taylor, Telford. *Nuremberg and Vietnam: an American Tragedy.* New York: Quadrangle Books, 1970.

Timerman, Jacobo. *Prisoner Without a Name, Cell Without a Number.* New York: Knopf, 1981.

Thomas, Lewis. *Lives of a Cell: Notes of a Biology Watcher.* New York: Bantam, 1974.

Traven, B. *The Night Visitor and Other Stories by B. Traven.* New York: Hill and Wang, 1966.

Trinquier, Roger. *Modern Warfare: A French View of Counterinsurgency.* New York: Praeger, 1961.

Whitehead, Alfred North. *Adventure of Ideas.* New York: New American Library, 1967.

Wolf, Naomi. *The End of America: Letters of Warning to a Young Patriot.* White River Junction: Chelsea Green Publishing Co., 2007. (Review, Ch. 20)

Zinn, Howard. "The Others." *The Nation.* February 11, 2002.

_____. *A People's History of the United States.* New York: Harper's Perennial Books, 1995.

_____. *The Zinn Reader.* New York: Seven Stories Press, 2004. (Review, Ch. 40)

ACKNOWLEDGMENTS

I wish to express my gratitude to Amador Publishers editor in-chief Zelda Gatuskin for accepting this manuscript and for her essential guidance towards making the collection into a book. Without her publishing acumen and wise advice and guidance, *Feeling the Unthinkable* might never have seen the light of day. I also wish to thank Ashley Jordan and Marilyn Brownstein, Ashley for pursuing all kinds of elusive details without which no book could be regarded as completed, and Marilyn for a quality of preliminary editing of the manuscripts which provided me an exemplar of good prose. I also want to thank my son Trajan for his crucial and generous assistance with the manuscript in matters electronic.

ABOUT THE PRESS

In 1986, Harry Willson and his wife, Adela Amador, founded Amador Publishers and dedicated their press to peace, equality, respect for all cultures and preservation of the biosphere. They quickly set about fulfilling that mission. In addition to publishing Harry's books, the press took on local authors of Southwest and literary fiction, including Michael H. Thomas, Ben Tarver, David L. Condit, Tim MacCurdy, Michelle Miller Allen, and Zelda Leah Gatuskin. Adela gained notoriety in her own right with her recipe books, New Mexico *cuentos*, and a 13-year stint as the author of the Southwest Flavor column in *New Mexico Magazine*.

After meeting Eva and Manfred Krutein through a cultural exchange program, Harry and Adela published four titles by the brilliant emigres and World War II survivors. They published the fiction works of acclaimed literary scholar Gene H. Bell-Villada, and the world's first anti-smoking novel by Arthur L. Hoffman. Harry's opposition to radioactive dumping in New Mexico led him to publish the anti-nuclear manifesto of physicist Charles L. Hyder, to support Dr. Hyder in his fast against the Waste Isolation Pilot Project in Carlsbad, New Mexico, and to personally provide testimony to the Department of Energy in opposition to the plant.

In 2006, Zelda Leah Gatuskin joined Harry and Adela as co-owner and managing editor of the press. In 2010 she succeeded Harry as editor-in-chief.

ABOUT THE AUTHOR

Donald Gutierrez was a member of the University of Notre Dame English Department faculty from 1968 to 1975, then joined the English Department at Western New Mexico University in Silver City. He retired from WNMU in 1994 and moved to Albuquerque, New Mexico with his wife Marlene Zander Gutierrez. He received a "New Mexico Eminent Scholar Award" in 1989.

Gutierrez has published six books of literary criticism, two of which focus on D. H. Lawrence and and one on Kenneth Rexroth. Since retirement, he has published over fifty essays and reviews, most of which concern social justice and American state terrorism abroad.

Donald Gutierrez at Notre Dame, 1974; photo by Ed Brower for *Scholastic*, Vol. 116, No. 6, November 22, 1974. (Article: The Reign of the "Brutos" in Chile. Caption: Prof. Donald Gutierrez Speaks Out on Chile.) Used with permission.

ABOUT THE ARTIST

Marlene Zander Gutierrez was born in 1932 of German-American parents. From a very early age she was strongly oriented towards creating art. Marlene's art education included the University of California Berkeley Art Department, the Pratt Graphic Workshop in New York City and the University of Notre Dame. Her art awards and solo and group exhibitions are, among many others, an Honors Award at the National Women's Art Exhibition (San Antonio), solo exhibition at the Adair Margo Gallery in El Paso and two group exhibitions each at the Art Museums of Santa Fe and Albuquerque. Despite a full-time involvement as a homemaker, wife and mother, Marlene turned out a large amount of significant and highly varied art including subtly symbolic collages and abstract expressionist work. Some of Marlene's categories of work—which include at least ten—are the Redemption of Matter (fourteen metal works of singular esthetic audacity), the Wound (of women) series, and the Inner Child series (twenty-four paintings of an adult sense of a child's unfettered creative imagination). Marlene created a considerable body of tough-spirited, numinous art with great delicacy of touch. She was a long-time member of the Albuquerque-based Society of Layerists in Multi-Media.

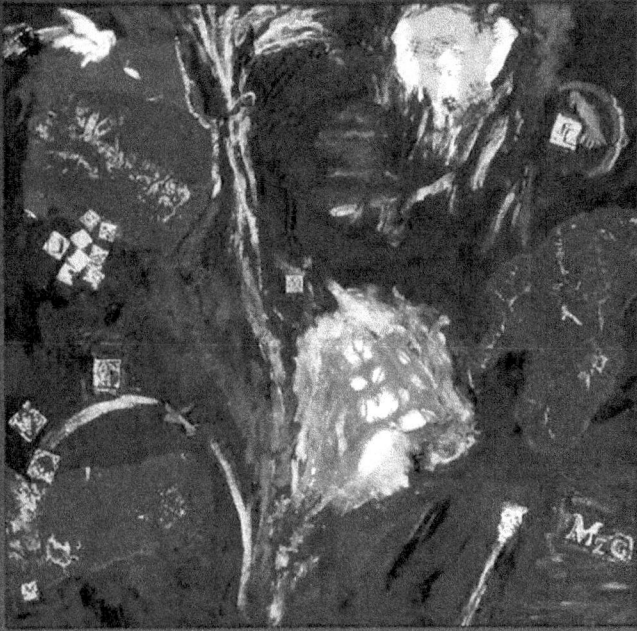

Cover Art:
"Illuminating the Dark Side" by Marlene Zander Gutierrez
Collage and acrylic, 2008, 24.5"x 40.5"